INTRODUCTION TO MICROSOFT GREAT PLAINS 8.0
FOCUS ON INTERNAL CONTROLS

TERRI E. BRUNSDON
THE UNIVERSITY OF AKRON

MARSHALL B. ROMNEY
BRIGHAM YOUNG UNIVERSITY

PAUL JOHN STEINBART
ARIZONA STATE UNIVERSITY

PEARSON
Prentice
Hall

UPPER SADDLE RIVER, NJ 07458

Cataloging data for this publication can be obtained from the Library of Congress.

Senior Acquisitions Editor: Wendy Craven
VP/Editorial Director: Jeff Shelstad
Product Development Manager: Pamela Hersperger
Project Manager: Kerri Tomasso
Media Product Development Manager: Nancy Welcher
Executive Marketing Manager: John Wannemacher
Senior Managing Editor (Production): Cynthia Regan
Production Editor: Denise Culhane
Production Manager: Arnold Vila
Manufacturing Buyer: Michelle Klein
Cover Design: Nancy Thompson
Cover Illustration/Photo: Photodisc
Printer/Binder: Bindright

Credits and acknowledgments borrowed from other sources and reproduced, with permission, in this textbook appear on appropriate page within text.

Microsoft® and Windows® are registered trademarks of the Microsoft Corporation in the U.S.A. and other countries. Screen shots and icons reprinted with permission from the Microsoft Corporation. This book is not sponsored or endorsed by or affiliated with the Microsoft Corporation.

Pearson Education LTD.
Pearson Education Singapore, Pte. Ltd
Pearson Education, Canada, Ltd
Pearson Education–Japan

Pearson Education Australia PTY, Limited
Pearson Education North Asia Ltd
Pearson Educación de Mexico, S.A. de C.V.
Pearson Education Malaysia, Pte. Ltd

10 9 8 7 6 5 4 3 2
ISBN 0-13-186064-X

PREFACE

INTRODUCTION TO MICROSOFT GREAT PLAINS 8.0: FOCUS ON INTERNAL CONTROLS enhances teaching of accounting information skills using Microsoft® Business Solutions, Great Plains® 8.0 software. The text includes the Great Plains software and sample database that provide students with "hands on" experience in capturing financial transactions, analyzing company performance, and instituting internal controls within a general ledger software environment. This text integrates Great Plains training with the guidelines recommended by the Committee of Sponsoring Organizations (COSO) Enterprise Risk Management model.[1] It is recommended that students use this text in conjunction with a text such as Marshall Romney and Paul Steinbart, *Accounting Information Systems* (10th ed., Prentice Hall 2006). The Great Plains Series covered are System Manager, Inventory Control, Sales, Purchasing, Payroll, and Financial.

INTRODUCTION TO GREAT PLAINS 8.0 expands student skills beyond capturing and recording transactions. Each chapter thoroughly explores issues surrounding business cycle activities, including instituting internal controls in a computerized accounting environment that monitor internal control compliance. The text approaches student learning from two levels. Level One focuses on using Great Plains to perform cycle activities and recognize Great Plains' internal control features. Level Two teaches students to implement Great Plains internal controls. Each chapter includes questions and tasks reinforcing skills learned at both levels.

To Instructors and Students

The software and company databases included with the text may be installed multiple times, accommodating use in a classroom lab or home environment. The company databases are portable, thus students can conveniently transport data between school and home. When planning to continue using company databases on the current machine, then databases do not have to be unloaded. However, when working in a school lab, you **must** unload data or the next user has access to this data. The data does not need to be removed from the lab's computer, as long as files are unloaded, the next user does not have access to another user's data.

For easy reference, Appendix A restates Chapter 1 instructions for backing up and restoring databases as well as resolving Great Plains Error messages. Appendix B provides detailed lists of the sample company's customer, vendor, employee, inventory, and chart of accounts. Appendix C contains procedures for correcting posting errors within each Series. Solutions for chapter exercises are located in Appendix D and an instructor's manual is available. Students are encouraged to experiment while learning Great Plains. Posting and processing errors occur frequently in a real world environment, thus emphasis is placed on implementing internal controls that timely detect and correct errors before impacting company performance and financial reporting.

---

[1] See Chapter 6, Marshall Romney and Paul Steinbart, *Accounting Information Systems* (10th ed., Prentice Hall 2006)

About the Authors

Terri Brunsdon is a Certified Public Accountant with a Masters in Taxation and is a member of the American Institute of Certified Public Accountants (AICPA). She has over twenty years experience practicing in public and industry accounting. Terri teaches full-time at The University of Akron, G.W. Daverio School of Accountancy and owns a consulting practice specializing in automated accounting solutions. Terri is an AICPA Certified Information Technology Professional (CITP) with a degree in computer programming and attends The University of Akron School of Law concentrating in Intellectual Property Law.

Marshall B. Romney, PhD, CPA, CFE, is the John and Nancy Hardy Professor of Accounting and Information Systems in the Marriott School of Management at Brigham Young University. Marshall has published 23 books, including the leading text on Accounting Information Systems. Marshall is a past president of the Information Systems section of the AAA and was a member of both the Information Technology Executive Committee and the IT Practices Subcommittee of the American Institute of Certified Public Accountants. He was an advisor to the National Commission on Fraudulent Financial Reporting. At BYU, Marshall is the Associate Director of the School of Accountancy and Information Systems and is the director of both the graduate and undergraduate Information Systems programs.

Paul John Steinbart is Professor of Information Systems at Arizona State University where he teaches courses on accounting information systems and computer security. He is co-author of the leading Accounting Information Systems textbook. Professor Steinbart's research has appeared in leading academic journals including *MIS Quarterly*, *The Accounting Review*, *Decision Sciences*, and the *Journal of Information Systems*.

Acknowledgments

Terri Brunsdon would like to express gratitude to Mike Slette and Janelle Daugherty with Microsoft Great Plains Business Solutions for spearheading development of the Great Plains Education Edition software. She also wants to thank Mary Hardin, Director of Technology for The University of Akron College of Business, for testing lab installation. Most importantly, deepest thanks go to her best friend, Bill Brunsdon, and sons, Jeremy and Billy, for offering love and inspiration while completing this text.

Chapter Signals

The textbook incorporates important symbols signaling chapter exercises, special issues, and additional ideas on approaching a task. The following table describes these symbols.

Symbol	Purpose
⚠	Students cautioned on potential errors or system warnings that may be encountered.
G P	Calls student attention to chapter exercise.
💡	Additional ideas or approaches on a chapter task.
📅	Student reminder to check Great Plains' system date or transaction date.
ⓘ	Supplementary information on the topic discussed.

TABLE OF CONTENTS

CHAPTER 1: GREAT PLAINS INSTALLATION AND INTERFACE 1

    Chapter Overview *1*
    Hardware and Operating System Requirements *2*
    Software and Database Installation *2*
    Exiting Great Plains *10*
    Backup and Restore the Dynamics and Company Databases *10*
    Returning to Great Plains *11*
    Company Background *11*
  LEVEL ONE 12
    Introduction to the Interface *12*
    Field Lookups and Hyperlinks *13*
    Toolbar Shortcut *16*
    Creating and Changing Master Records *17*
    Entering Transactions *19*
    Running Reports *23*
    Setting User Preferences *26*
  LEVEL TWO 27
    General Ledger Software and Company Objectives *27*
    Software Licensing and "Rights of Use" *28*
  LEVEL ONE QUESTIONS 31
  LEVEL TWO QUESTIONS 32

CHAPTER 2: THE S&S COMPANY DATABASE **33**

    Chapter Overview *33*
  LEVEL ONE 34
    The General Ledger Account Framework *34*
    General Ledger Account Types *38*
    General Ledger Trial Balance *41*
    Company Fiscal Periods *44*
    Payment Terms, Shipping Methods, and Bank Accounts *46*
    Smart List *48*
  LEVEL TWO 53
    The Database Management System (DBMS) and Great Plains *53*
    Series Integration *53*
    REA Data Model: Master and Transaction Tables *55*
  LEVEL ONE QUESTIONS 57
  LEVEL TWO QUESTIONS 58

CHAPTER 3: INTERNAL CONTROLS AND GREAT PLAINS SECURITY **59**

    Chapter Overview *59*
  LEVEL ONE 60
    Security Installed During Great Plains Installation *60*
    Posting Setup Controls *60*
    The Audit Trail *76*
    Activity Tracking Log *80*
  LEVEL TWO 82
    System Manager Security *82*
    Advanced Security: User Accounts and Permissions *83*
    Security Reporting *87*
  LEVEL ONE EXERCISES 88
  LEVEL TWO EXERCISES 89

CHAPTER 4: INVENTORY CONTROL SERIES..**90**

    Chapter Overview *90*

   LEVELS ONE AND TWO 91

    Inventory Setup..*91*

    Inventory Item Cards *95*

    Inventory Pricing...*97*

    Inventory Vendors *98*

    Inventory Adjustments *101*

    Physical Inventory Process *102*

    Inventory Inquiry and Reporting...*106*

   LEVEL ONE AND TWO QUESTIONS 110

CHAPTER 5: REVENUE CYCLE AND GREAT PLAINS SALES SERIES **111**

    Chapter Overview *111*

   LEVEL ONE 112

    Sales Series: Customer Master Records *115*

    Sales Series Transactions *120*

    Sales Department Activities *123*

    Warehouse and Shipping Activities *132*

    Accounts Receivable Activities *134*

    Sales Series: Basic Reporting *142*

    Receivables Sales Series Transactions..*147*

   LEVEL TWO 157

    Sales Series Setup and Internal Controls..*157*

    Customer Card Internal Controls *164*

    Sales Reporting as a Control Tool *165*

    Sales Series: Month-End and Year-End Closing Procedures...............................*165*

   LEVEL ONE QUESTIONS 167

   LEVEL TWO QUESTIONS 168

CHAPTER 6: EXPENDITURE CYCLE AND GREAT PLAINS PURCHASING SERIES...........................**169**

    Chapter Overview *169*

   LEVEL ONE 170

    Vendors...*172*

    Purchasing Series Transactions..*175*

    Purchasing and Departmental Activities *182*

    Receiving Department Activities *190*

    Accounts Payable Department Activities *194*

    Cashier Department Activities *209*

    Other Purchasing Series Transactions *211*

    Purchasing Series: Basic Reporting *213*

   LEVEL TWO 214

    Purchasing Series Setup and Internal Controls *214*

    Purchase Reporting As a Control Tool *217*

    Purchasing Series: Month-End and Year-End Closing Procedures......................*217*

   LEVEL ONE QUESTIONS 219

   LEVEL TWO QUESTIONS 220

CHAPTER 7: PAYROLL CYCLE AND GREAT PLAINS PAYROLL SERIES **221**

    Chapter Overview *221*

   LEVEL ONE 222

    Payroll Series Cards *224*

    Payroll Series Transactions *235*

    Cashier Department Activities *246*

    Accounts Payable Department Activities *248*

    Payroll Series: Basic Reporting...*248*

   LEVEL TWO 252

Setup of Pay Type, Tax, Deduction, and Benefit Codes 254
Payroll Posting Accounts 256
Payroll Series: Month-End and Year-End Closing Procedures 257
LEVEL ONE QUESTIONS 258
LEVEL TWO QUESTIONS 259

CHAPTER 8: FINANCIAL REPORTING AND GREAT PLAINS FINANCIAL SERIES 260
Chapter Overview 260
LEVEL ONE 261
Financial Cards 263
Financial Series Transactions 265
Review Activities 270
Report Activities 274
LEVEL TWO 275
Account Categories 275
Advanced Financials 276
Financial Series: Month-End and Year-End Closing Procedures 279
LEVEL ONE QUESTIONS 281
LEVEL TWO QUESTIONS 282

APPENDIX A: DATA BACKUP AND RESTORE PROCEDURES AND GREAT PLAINS ERRORS 283
Backup and Restore of Great Plains Dynamics and Company Databases 283
Great Plains Error Messages 284

APPENDIX B: COMPANY SPECIFICS 286
S&S, INC. CHART OF ACCOUNTS 286
S&S, INC. INVENTORY 291
S&S, INC. CUSTOMERS 292
S&S, INC. VENDORS 293
S&S, INC. EMPLOYEES 295

APPENDIX C: CORRECTING POSTING ERRORS 296
Common Errors 296
Error Correction Procedures 297

APPENDIX D: EXERCISE SOLUTIONS 302
Chapter 1 Exercises 302
Chapter 2 Exercises 305
Chapter 4 Exercises 308
Chapter 5 Exercises 310
Chapter 6 Exercises 325
Chapter 7 Exercises 331
Chapter 8 Exercises 334

CHAPTER 1: GREAT PLAINS INSTALLATION AND INTERFACE

CHAPTER OVERVIEW

The introductory chapter contains step-by-step instructions for installing Great Plains Standard 8.0 Education software as well as installing, backing up, and restoring the sample databases included with the textbook. The databases included are _S&S, Incorporated_ and a replica of this database named _S&S, Inc Project DB_. Providing two copies of the database allows you to use the first as a "sandbox" for practicing skills and chapter exercises and the second for completing tasks graded by professors.

After reading this chapter, you know:
- ➢ The minimum hardware and operating system requirements for software installation
- ➢ How to install Great Plains Standard 8.0 Education Edition software and the Series included during installation
- ➢ How to install, back up, and restore the company databases
- ➢ How to log into Great Plains, open a company database, navigate menus, record basic transactions, perform database inquiries, and prepare reports

Level One covers:
- ➢ Installing Great Plains software, loading databases, backing up databases, and restoring databases
- ➢ The Great Plains user interface used to enter and post transactions, perform inquiries, and print reports
- ➢ An introduction to Series integration

Level Two covers:
- ➢ Identifying and evaluating general ledger software intricacies related to a company's internal control environment and operating needs
- ➢ Adherence to software licensing and "rights of use" policies

HARDWARE AND OPERATING SYSTEM REQUIREMENTS

The minimum hardware and software requirements for installing Great Plains Standard 8.0 Education Edition are outlined in *T1:1*.

Hardware:	210 MB Hard Drive
	128 MB Ram
	Pentium III 350 MHz (or equivalent)
	SVGA (900x600) with 16-bit video driver
	DVD or CD-Rom Drive
Operating Systems:	Windows 2000 Server with SP 3 or SP 4
	Windows XP Professional with SP 1a or SP 2
	Windows XP Tablet PC Edition
	Windows 2000 Professional or Server Editions with SP 3 or SP 4
	Windows 2003 Standard Edition with SP 1

T1:1 Hardware and Operating System Requirements

SOFTWARE AND DATABASE INSTALLATION

This textbook contains a single user license for Great Plains. There are three stages to installation before using this software. The first stage installs Great Plains, the second installs company data files, and the final prepares Great Plains for use.

Stage 1: Install Software
Insert the CD labeled <u>Great Plains Standard 8.0 English Education</u> into your computer's drive. The CD automatically initiates the installation process illustrated in *F1:1*. Click Next.

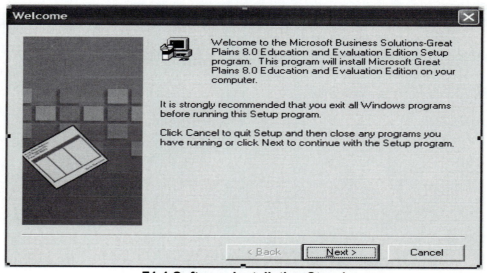

F1:1 Software Installation Step 1

⚠ Alternative procedure for software installation

Occasionally the CD does not automatically initiate installation. When this occurs, click on Window's Start menu and select <u>Run</u>. Click the Browse button to locate the file named <u>Setup.exe</u> on the installation CD. Highlight the file and then OK to begin installation.

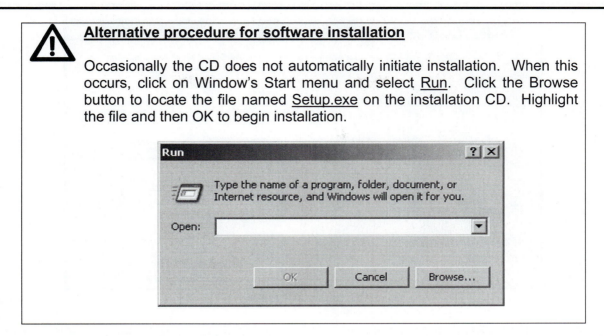

After clicking Next, the Software License Agreement window appears (*F1:2*). Read the agreement before clicking <u>I Accept</u>. Acceptance confirms your promise to use the software in accordance with this agreement. Software licensing is discussed in Level Two.

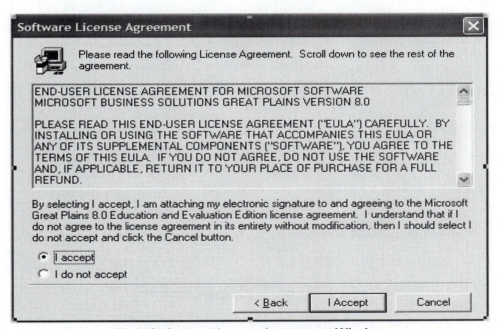

F1:2 Software License Agreement Window

The next window (*F1:3*) that appears requests the entry of a password for the *sa* user account. It is recommended you also use *sa* as the password. If you choose to use a different password and later forget this password, the software must be removed and reinstalled to establish a new password. Great Plains passwords are case sensitive, meaning the software differentiates between upper and lower case letters. Please be careful when creating this password and click Next when finished.

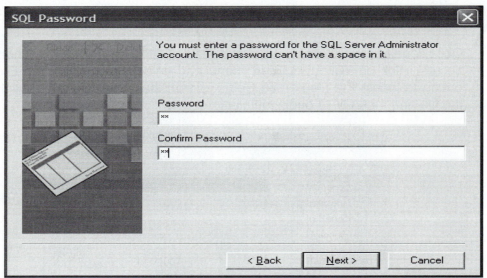

F1:3 sa User Password

The next window (**F1:4**) confirms the directory used to install Great Plains. Note that the location is *C:\Program Files\Microsoft Business Solutions\Great Plains-Education*. Click the Install button.

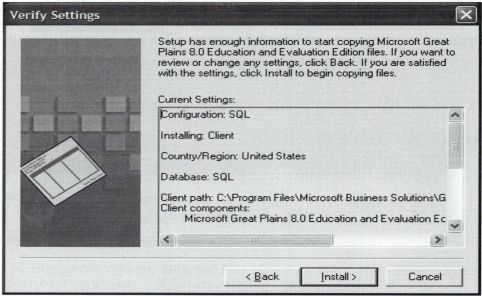

F1:4 Great Plains Software Directory

The software updates you on the progress of installation (***F1:5***). Do not interrupt installation, otherwise you will have to delete partially installed files and restart.

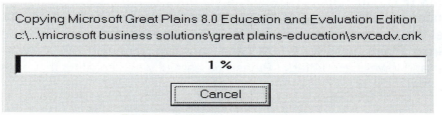

F1:5 Install Progress Indicator

During installation, the Great Plains interface and database management (DBMS) system are copied to your computer (*F1:6*). The DBMS will be discussed in Chapter 2, Level Two.

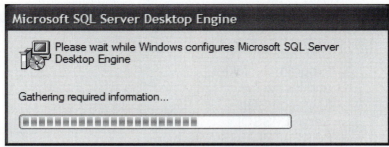

F1:6 DBMS Configuration

When Great Plains notifies that installation is complete (*F1:7*), click Finish and move on to copying the company database files to your computer.

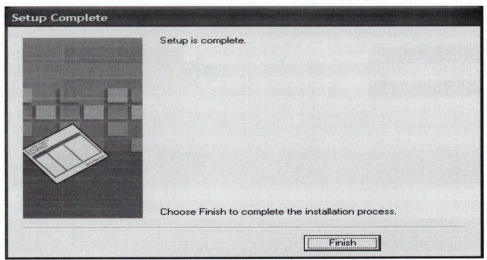

F1:7 Great Plains Successfully Installed

Stage 2: Copy Company Database Files

The database files are located on the CD included with your text labeled *GP Data Files*. Insert this CD and then right click on Window's Start button and select Explore. Locate the C drive folder created during software installation called *Program Files\Microsoft SQL Server\MSSQL $GREATPLAINS* (*F1:8*). Copy the six data files located on the CD to this folder on your computer's C drive (*F1:9*).

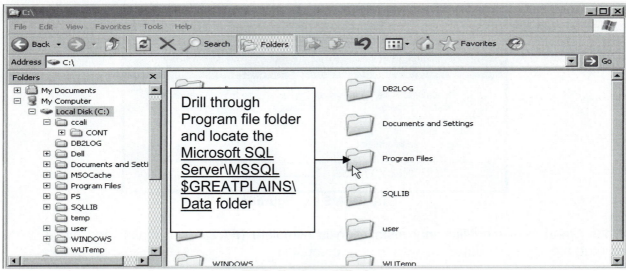

F1:8 Explorer Window

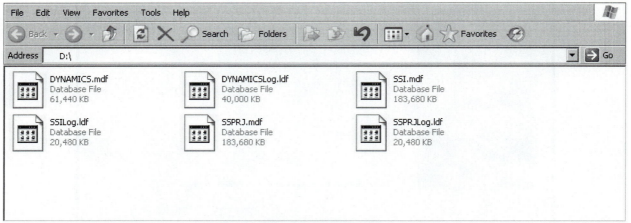

F1:9 CD Data Files

Stage 3: Launch Great Plains

Return to Window's Start menu and open Great Plains using the *All Programs>>Microsoft Business Solutions>>Great Plains-Education* menu. This path is used every time you open Great Plains. The message in *F1:10* appears the first time you open the software after installation. Click Yes to install the additional code required to run Great Plains.

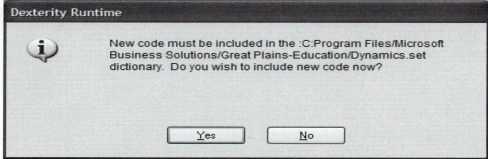

F1:10 Message to Include New Code after Install

After including new code, Great Plains opens the login window (**F1:11**). Enter _sa_ as the User ID and then the password created during installation. The next screen (*F1:12*) appears, prompting you to attach the company databases. Click Yes, then locate the folder containing the copied database files.

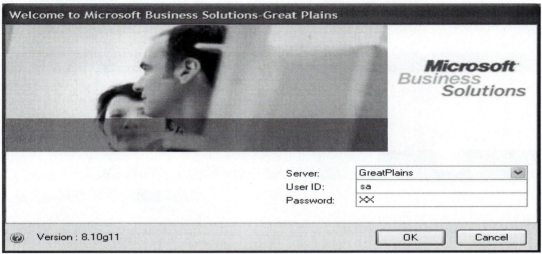

F1:11 Great Plains Login

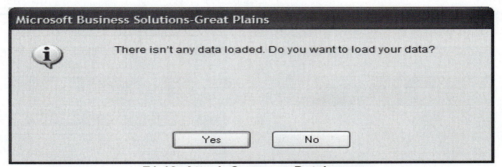

F1:12 Attach Company Databases

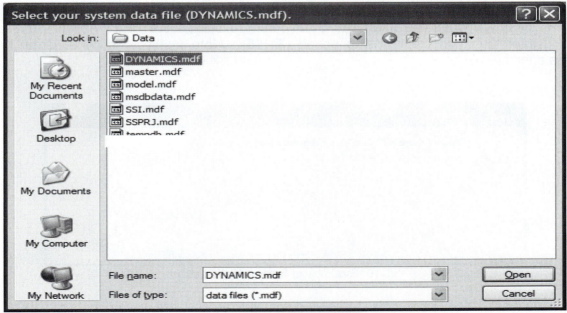

F1:13 DYNAMICS.mdf File

Highlight the *DYNAMICS.mdf* file and click Open (**F1:13**). Great Plains initializes the company databases for use and then displays the company selection screen (**F1:14**). Click on the dropdown list to show *S&S, Inc Project DB* and *S&S, Incorporated* as the databases. As previously discussed, the first database may be used for completing projects and assignments and the second as a "sandbox" for practicing Great Plains skills. Select *S&S, Incorporated*, then click OK to enter the Great Plains environment (**F1:15**).

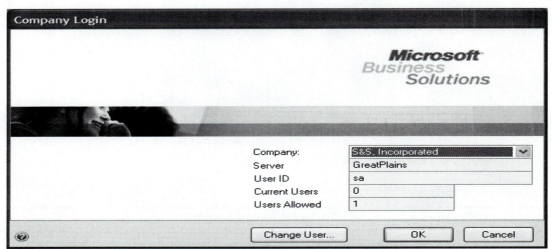

F1:14 Company Database Selection

F1:15 Great Plains Environment

The first time you open the interface, Great Plains initializes the Fixed Assets Series and displays information on the licensing period (**F1:16**). Note that your copy of Great Plains expires after 120 days.

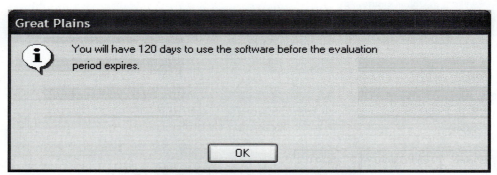

F1:16 Evaluation Period Notification

Congratulations! You have now completed installation and are ready to begin using the software.

Your copy of Great Plains comes with the Series outlined in *T1:2*. In addition, you also have the Human Resources and Fixed Asset Series, which are not covered in this text.

Series	GP Menu References	Traditional Journal/Ledger References	Series Tasks
System Manager	System		♦ Required for all Series to manage overall software behavior such as user IDs, passwords, series security, audit trails, etc. ♦ Establishes company defaults such as name, address, fiscal periods, etc.
Financial	Financial and Company	General Ledger, General Journal, and Chart of Accounts	♦ Create and maintain the chart of accounts ♦ Enter adjusting, accrual, deferral, and correcting journal entries ♦ Produce trial balance, financial statements, worksheets, and other financial analysis reports
Receivables Management, Invoicing, and Sales Order Processing	Sales	Accounts Receivable Ledgers, Sales Journal, and Cash Receipts Journal	♦ Create and maintain customers ♦ Enter sales orders, order shipments, invoices, cash receipts, merchandise returns, debit memos, and finance charges ♦ Produce customer statements, accounts receivable aging, and other sales analysis reports
Payables Management and Purchase Order Processing	Purchasing	Accounts Payable Ledger, Purchases Journal, and Cash Disbursements Journal	♦ Create and maintain vendors ♦ Enter purchase orders, receipts against purchase orders, vendor invoices, cash disbursements, returns, and credit memos ♦ Produce accounts payable aging, cash requirement report, and other purchasing analysis reports
Inventory Control	Inventory	Inventory Ledgers	♦ Create and maintain inventory items ♦ Establish inventory valuation method ♦ Enter inventory adjustments ♦ Produce inventory analysis reports
Payroll	Payroll	Payroll Journals	♦ Create and maintain employees ♦ Enter payroll data and produce paychecks ♦ Produce tax liability and other payroll analysis reports

T1:2 Great Plains Series Covered in the Text

It makes sense to think of each Series as fitting within the functional areas of a company's business operation. Often textbooks refer to these areas as accounting cycles. Each standalone Series (other than System Manager) contains all the subsidiary ledgers and journals used by a particular cycle. The table also outlines the Great Plains menus used for accessing each Series, the traditional accounting journals and ledgers incorporated into that Series, and the tasks performed within each Series. Great Plains sells additional Series and add-ins not covered in this text.

You are not required to download security patches or updates for the Education software. However, you should make security a priority whenever using a computer. Continual monitoring for software patches and upgrades is critical.

EXITING GREAT PLAINS

Select the *File>>Exit* commands from Great Plains' menu. The prompt in ***F1:17*** asks you to unload the databases. Databases are unloaded for portability between school and home. If you plan to continue using the company databases on the current machine, then select No. However, when working in a school lab, you <u>MUST</u> unload the databases or the next user has access to your data.

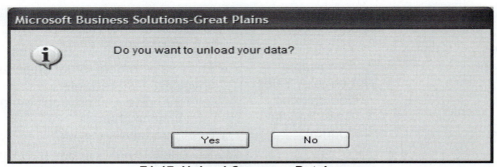

F1:17 Unload Company Databases

After unloading, the databases are ready for copying to a removable storage disk for relocation to a different computer. When relocating data, all six files illustrated in ***F1:9*** must be copied. (Note: You do not have to remove data files from a lab computer. As long as files are unloaded, the next user does not have access to your data files). When data files are unloaded, Great Plains prompts you to reattach as previously illustrated in **F1:12**. As the next topic illustrates, the procedures for detaching and reattaching databases are different from those used to backup and restore databases.

BACKUP AND RESTORE THE DYNAMICS AND COMPANY DATABASES

After using Great Plains, you should perform a backup of the databases by selecting the Great Plains menu *File>>Backup*. Great Plains prompts for a system password and this password is *sa*. (Note: This password is separate from the password created during installation and used to login to Great Plains.) ***F1:18*** displays the company and system databases available for backup. You should backup the company database used during a session as well as the system database.

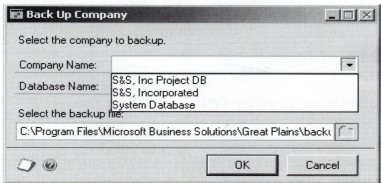

F1:18 Database Backup Window

Choose a database and then click OK to create a backup file in the pathname shown. You can click the folder icon to select a different path and to rename the backup file; however, remember this location and filename for future use. By default, each time a backup is performed, Great Plains names the backup file using the company name and the date of the backup.

To restore the backup, return to the *File* menu and select the *Restore* command. The restore window looks the same as the window used to backup data files. Highlighting a company database activates the folder icon for browsing and selecting the backup file to restore. The restore process takes time, therefore be patient and do not close any windows.

IF YOU HAVE NOT PERFORMED A BACKUP, backup files do not exist and, therefore, cannot be restored. Consequently, you must return to the original CD and recopy the original data files. Unfortunately, any changes to data files will be lost.

RETURNING TO GREAT PLAINS

Again, Great Plains is located under Programs on the Window's Start menu. Each time you open the software, Great Plains prompts for the user's login account (User ID) and password. In addition, when company database were previously detached, Great Plains prompts to reattach the files.

 Note: In the event your last session ended improperly (i.e. the hardware system crashed or the software irregularly closed), Great Plains prompts to delete the previous login. See Appendix A to resolve this issue.

COMPANY BACKGROUND

Before beginning the tasks in this text, become familiar with the sample company. S&S operates a mid-sized distribution company in Northeast Ohio. The company operates on a calendar year basis and the current open accounting period is March of 2007. The company's inventory includes small electronics, televisions, cameras, and audio equipment. S&S' chart of accounts, customers, vendors, inventory items, and employees are located in Appendix B. Take a few minutes to review this information before continuing.

LEVEL ONE

INTRODUCTION TO THE INTERFACE

Before practicing the examples, emphasis must be placed on changing Great Plains' system date each time you enter the software and/or begin recording transactions. The system date is located on the menu bar (*F1:19*). Double clicking the displayed date opens a window to change the date. All examples in this textbook occur in March of 2007. Be careful to change the system date before beginning an example as well as each time you log into Great Plains.

IMPORTANCE OF THE SYSTEM DATE:

Warning: Transactions may be posted in the wrong accounting period.

Great Plains uses the system date as a default for transactions, inquiries, and some of the reports. Great Plains initially selects this date from the computer's system date. Since you will be working on the financial records for March 2007, overriding the initial date ensures working in the correct accounting period. In addition, when performing particular exercises and problems in the text, you will want to change to the date matching the task. Always remain conscious of the date before performing any task. Whenever you see the calendar symbol to the right, this signals you to observe the date.

The Great Plains interface screen appears in *F1:19*, illustrating the location of menu commands and shortcut toolbars. An overview of Great Plains' menus is provided in *T1:3*. The Edit, Windows, and Help menus are omitted from this table since these commands function similarly to other Microsoft Office products. Toolbar shortcuts are discussed later in the chapter.

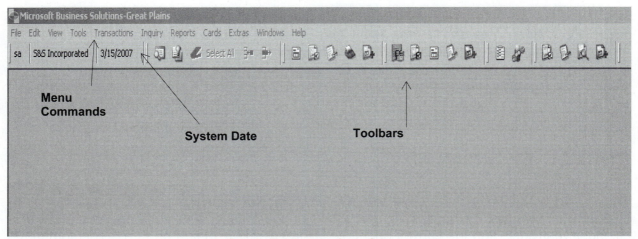

F1:19 Basic Interface Screen

Menu Item	Submenu	Description
File	1) User and Company	1) Change user or company
	2) User Date	2) Change default date used during transaction entry
	3) Maintenance	3) Routines to repair data files
	4) Backup	4) Backup data files
	5) Restore	5) Restore data files from a backup copy
		Print Setup and Exit are self-explanatory. The Process Monitor controls distributed printing for networks and is not covered in this text.
View	Submenus correspond to installed Series	Turns on/off or customizes menu bars. Also used to open/close other shortcuts and the Smart List.
Tools	1) Setup	1) Setup and configure Series features such as security, default forms, user preferences, and audit trail codes
	2) Utilities	2) Data file maintenance utilities for removing transaction history and reconciling out of balance conditions
	3) Routines	3) Used to perform posting, year-end, month-end and other user routine checklists
Transactions	Submenus correspond to installed Series	Access to Series' transaction entry menus used for processing day-to-day transactions
Inquiry	Submenus correspond to installed Series	Access to read-only views of data, permitting lookups to supporting transactions
Reports	Sub-Menus correspond to installed Series	Prints reports
Cards	Sub-Menus correspond to installed Series	Create master records such as customers, vendors, general ledger accounts, inventory, and employees.

T1:3 Menu Commands

FIELD LOOKUPS AND HYPERLINKS

During data entry or inquiry, users frequently need quick access to account data and details. Hyperlinks and lookups provide quick access to other menus that open inquiries, cards, and transaction details. Lookups open windows accessible through the Inquiry or Cards menus. Hyperlinks provide quick links to specific transactions. For instance, S&S' accountant, Ashton, needs to locate details on a transaction posted to the cash account on January 8, 2007. He clicks the menu items *Inquiry>>Financial>>Detail* to open the window illustrated in **F1:20**.

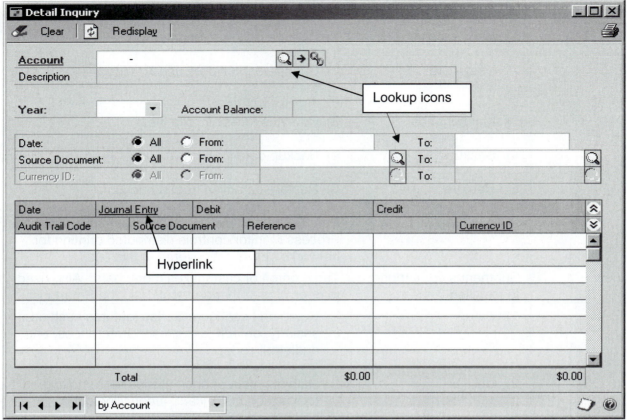

F1:20 Detail Inquiry Window

After opening, Ashton cannot remember the cash general ledger account number, so he clicks the Lookup icon located beside the Account field and the window in *F1:21* opens.

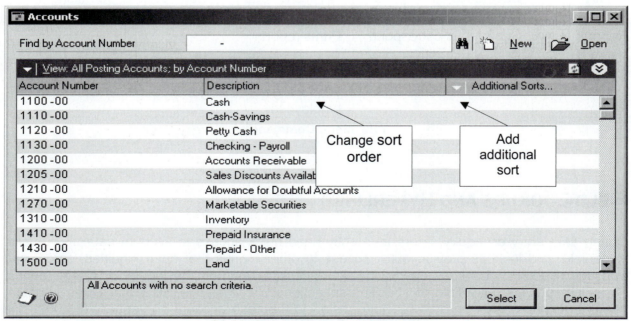

F1:21 Accounts Lookup Window

This window sorts data by account number. When the account does not appear towards the top, Ashton changes the sort order by clicking the Description heading or by using the dropdown menu that adds additional sorts. In addition, Ashton uses the binocular icon to search for the account, the New button to add accounts, and the Open button to modify existing accounts.

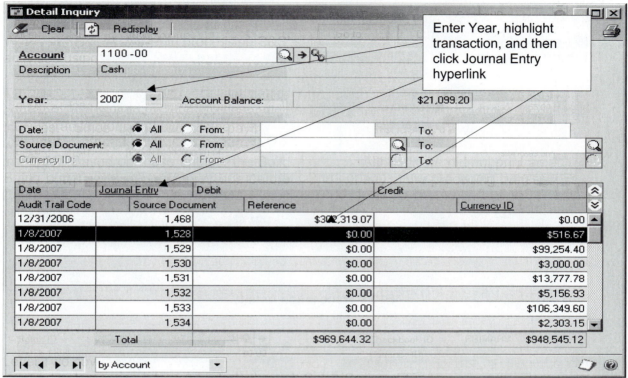

F1:22 Cash Account Transactions

Highlight account 1100-00 Cash and click Select. The Detail Inquiry window now displays transactions for the this account. Highlight the transaction illustrated (*F1:22)* and click the Journal Entry hyperlink to view details on this transaction. Ashton could also drill down to the transaction's source document by clicking the Source Document hyperlink (*F1:23).*

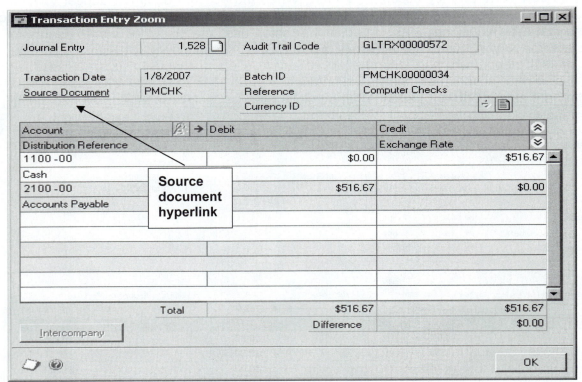

F1:23 Transaction Details

Ashton asks you to inquire into a transaction recorded on January 25, 2007 for $138,412.50 that posted to the sales account for the East. He would like to know the customer billed, the invoice number, and the inventory items sold.

After locating this information, you could also experiment with looking up the same transaction using the *Inquiry>>Sales>>Transaction by Customer* or *Transaction by Document* menu.

Practice using other Inquiry menus and see that Great Plains facilitates inquiries by knowing the general ledger account number, the customer name, or the specific invoice number.

E1:1 Practice Lookups and Hyperlinks

TOOLBAR SHORTCUT

Shortcuts are useful to create quick links to often-used menu commands. Shortcuts are setoff into groups by separator bars. *F1:24* shows the shortcut groups currently displayed. These icons open menus for the Sales, Purchasing, Payroll, and General Ledger Series.

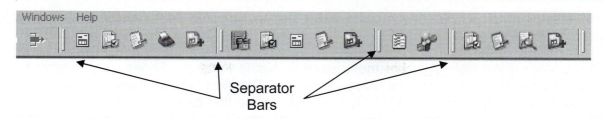

Separator
Bars

F1:24 Shortcuts

Feel free to customize shortcuts for use in performing tasks. You customize the toolbar by clicking the *View>>Toolbars>>Customize* menu. Highlight the toolbar to add, delete, or rearrange shortcut items (*F1:25*).

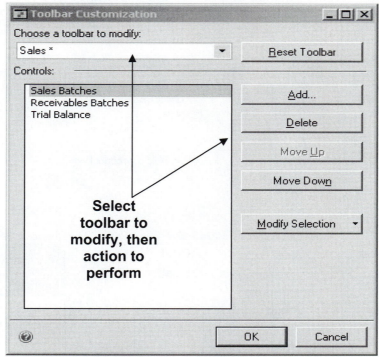

F1:25 Toolbar Customization Window

Click OK to close the Toolbar Customization window and practice using shortcuts. Hold your mouse over the shortcut icons until the Sales Transaction Entry shortcut is located (second icon on the Sales Group). Click the icon to open the Sales Transaction Entry window. The menu commands to perform this same task are *Transaction>>Sales>Sales Transaction Entry*. You now see the benefits of establishing shortcuts. Close the transaction window by using the x icon.

CREATING AND CHANGING MASTER RECORDS

Master records are created before recording transactions. In Great Plains, these records are created using the Cards menus. In relational database terms, the customer, vendor, inventory, employee, and general ledger accounts are called master records.[1] Transaction records are

---
[1] See Chapter 2 for more information on master records.

linked to master records. For instance, a sales transaction links to a customer's card, a purchase transaction links to a vendor's card, and so on.

Open the Cards>>Financial>>Account menu used to create Financial Series master records. These records are also called general ledger accounts. The Account Maintenance window for general ledger accounts is shown in *F1:26*, now look up the first cash account. This account contains a basic description and an alias name that speeds transaction entry and lookups (remember the additional sort options available in the lookup window). Notice that this account also contains options for selecting the Posting Type and Typical Balance. These options determine the account's appearance on financial statements as well as whether the account's balance is increased by a debit or credit. In addition, the Category field is used to group accounts on financial statements. For instance, this account appears under the Cash category of the Balance Sheet. These settings emphasize the importance of possessing knowledge of accounting when creating general ledger accounts.

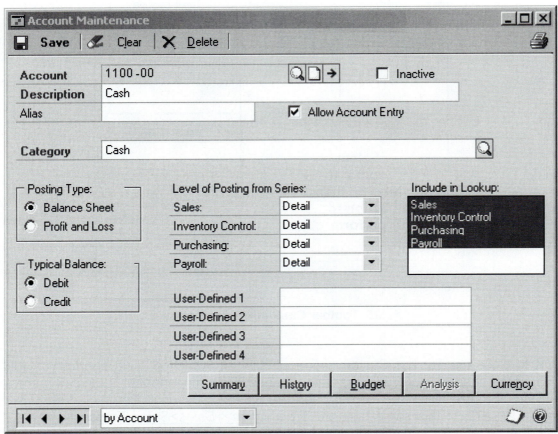

F1:26 Account Maintenance Window

The Allow Account Entry option determines whether transactions can post to an account. The Include in Lookup option permits lookups to account information within other Series.   Finally, the Level of Posting from Series option determines the level of transaction detail stored for transactions. When the level is set to Detail, then all information is available for inquiries and reporting.

Also notice the buttons for Summary and History. These buttons open windows that view current or historical transactions in the account. A word of caution, it is extremely dangerous to perform data inquiries using the Account Maintenance window because this window also permits record additions, changes, and deletions. Although Great Plains denies deletions of master records with transaction history, accounts can still exist for which deletion is not denied. Thus, <u>Card</u> menu access should be restricted to individuals authorized to create master records and <u>Inquiry</u> menus should be used to view transactions. [2]

Now that we have looked at general ledger accounts, use the *Cards>>Sales>>Customer* menu to open a Sales Series master record. These records are also called customer accounts. Pull up Zears' customer account and review the fields (*F1:27*). Customer card

 Typing ZEA in the Customer field before launching the lookup takes the user to customer names beginning with ZEA. This feature works for all lookups.

fields are fully explained in Chapter 5. For now, notice the scroll buttons located at the bottom left of the window that allows sequential movement through customer records. In addition, you can change the lookup's sort properties by clicking the sort dropdown menu located beside the scroll buttons. Before moving on to the next topic, take the time to explore master records in other Series.

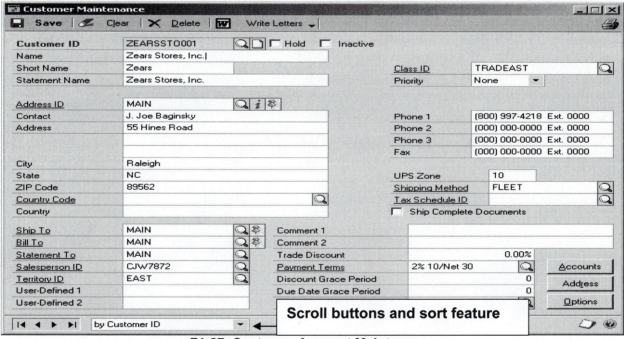

F1:27 Customer Account Maintenance

ENTERING TRANSACTIONS

With knowledge that transactions link to cards, we learn to record transactions. Transactions post the day-to-day activities of a company, thus, many users need access to transaction menus. We'll start by discussing whether transactions should be posted individually or by batch.

---

[2] Authorization is discussed in Chapter 3.

Transactions are entered individually when you need to immediately post. For instance, on March 15, 2007, accounts receivable clerk, James Richmond, needs to immediately post a sale

Great Plains automatically increments an auto-filled document number when the software posts, deletes, or voids transactions. Therefore, the user should disregard differences between illustrated document numbers and actual numbers displayed during transaction entry.

to Better Buy so shipping can begin customer delivery. James opens the Sales Transaction Entry window (**F1:28**) by clicking on the toolbar shortcut. He changes the transaction type to Invoice, tabs to the Customer ID field, and looks up Better Buy. Notice as you tab past the Document No. field that Great Plains auto-fills its value. This is a document control feature discussed in Chapter 5.

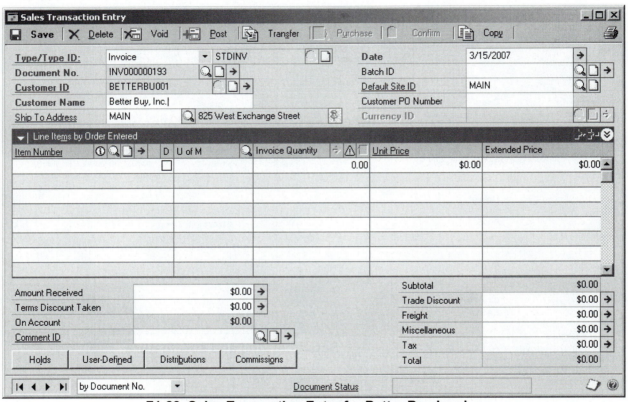

F1:28 Sales Transaction Entry for Better Buy Invoice

James then tabs to the inventory line item area and enters Better Buy's order for 40 MP3 players (**F1:29**) by clicking the Item Number lookup and selecting AUDSNCDMP3. He expands the entry's details by clicking the Detail Expansion button and verifies that the quantity is in stock and the Qty Fulfilled indicates 40 (see **F1:30**). After entering this data, James attempts to save the transaction by clicking the Save button and the informational message in **F1:31** appears. Since James did not enter the transaction to a batch, his choice at this point is to either post, delete, or void the transaction. James clicks the Post button, printing posting reports to the screen. Posting reports are control reports that show the transaction's effect on inventory, customer, and general ledger accounts. Subsequent chapters discuss transaction posting and control reporting in detail. For now, close the reports and return to the main screen.

You entered the wrong customer and now Great Plains does not provide access to change the customer's ID. This occurs because the transaction is already linked to the customer's record. Delete or void the order and then reenter using the correct Customer ID. The same holds true when you enter the wrong item number. This time you delete the row, not the entire transaction, and reenter the correct item number. To delete the row, use the add/delete row buttons located beside the Details Expansion button or use the menu commands *Edit>>Delete Row*.

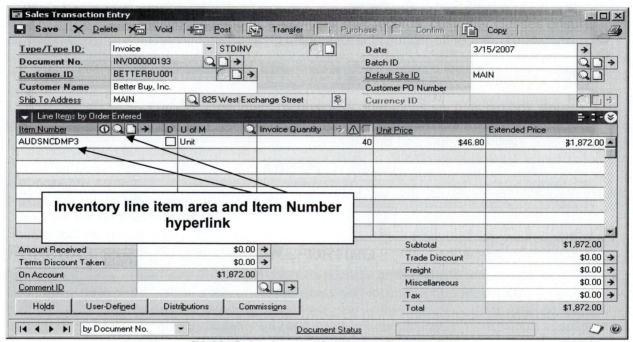

F1:29 Sales Invoice Inventory Selection

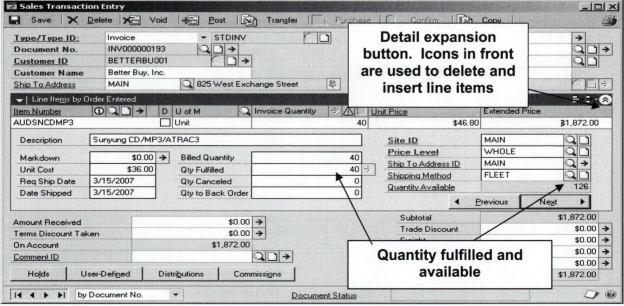

F1:30 Sales Invoice Inventory Details

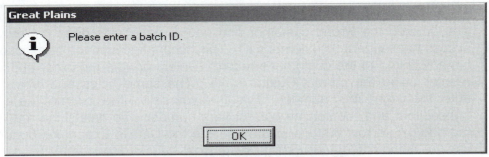

F1:31 Sales Transaction Save Error Message

Transaction entry is inefficient for processing large numbers of transactions because each entry transaction requires a separate post.   Furthermore, several internal control features are bypassed when transactions post outside batches. Finally, certain transaction types, such as sales orders, are not permitted to post; therefore, must be saved to batches. All of the aforementioned features are discussed in depth in Chapters 3 and 5. For now, turn to the batch concept.

Batches are folders that store transactions for posting at a later time. Click on the _Transactions_ _>>Sales>Sales Batches_ menu and create the batch folder illustrated in **F1:32**. The Batch ID is chosen by the user to uniquely identify transactions stored in the batch. The Origin identifies transaction posting types. Verify the batch date is correct and then click the Transactions button. Enter a sales order to customer, Book Buy Earnest, for 50 digital camcorders as illustrated in **F1:33**. Notice the ID from the batch folder appears in the transaction's Batch ID

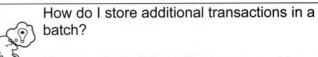

How do I store additional transactions in a batch?

It's easy, just click on the menu used to create the batch and look up the Batch ID. Next, click the Transactions button, enter the new transaction, and save.

field.   Since this transaction window was opened from the Batch window, the ID was automatically assigned.   Click Save to store the transaction for later posting, close the transaction entry window using the x icon, and return to the now empty Batch window.

To reopen this transaction, look up the Batch ID and click the Transactions button. In the transaction window, look up the sales order or use the scroll buttons to move to the transaction. Now close the transaction window and the batch window and return to the main screen.

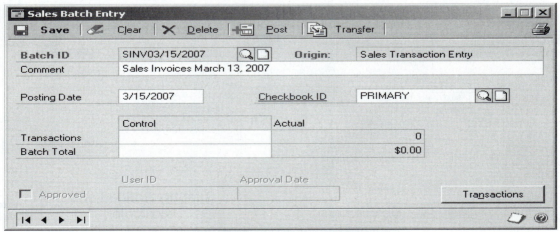

F1:32 Sales Batch Entry Window

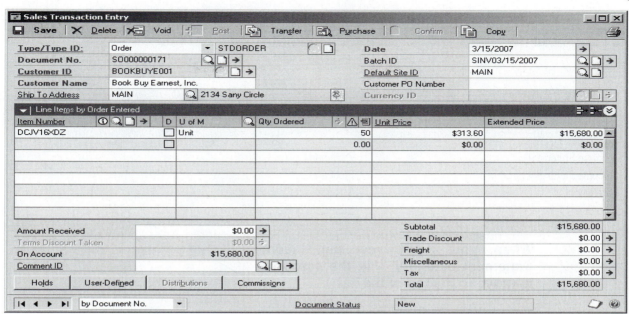

F1:33 Sales Order Entry

DATES…DATES…What's all these dates?

By now, you know that dates appear on batches and transactions. These dates do not have to be the same, however, both impact accounting data.

What does the batch date do?

Under Posting setup, the accountant determines whether the batch or transaction date determines the period used to post transactions to general ledger accounts. We discuss Posting setup in Chapter 3. Until then, know that Ashton configured the option to use the batch date unless a transaction posts individually.

What does the date on the transaction do?

The master accounts for other Series always use the date on the transaction. For the Sales Series, the transaction date posts an invoice to a customer's card using the invoice date. This date then determines the invoice's due date, discount date, and days outstanding.

RUNNING REPORTS

Reports are at the heart of analyzing financial performance. Great Plains offers many options for reporting data and all reporting originates under the Reports menu. In subsequent chapters, we discuss reports in greater depth. For now, let's try to run a few of the basics.   We'll start with financial statements. These reports are accessed from the *Reports>>Financial>>Financial Statements* menu. Look up the list of financial report categories (*F1:34*), highlight the Income Statement category, and then click Select.

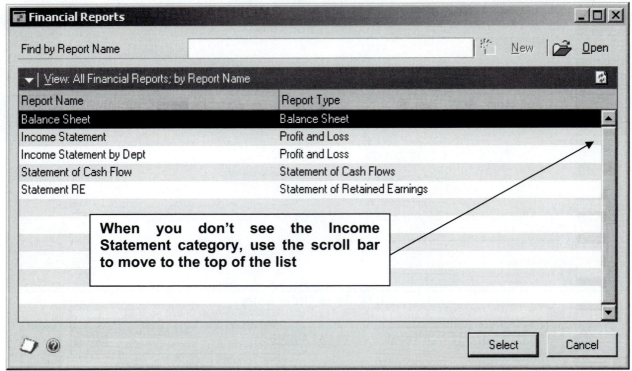

F1:34 Look Up to Report Categories

You find one report under this category named <u>Company Inc Stmt</u> (*F1:35*). Highlight this report and click Modify.

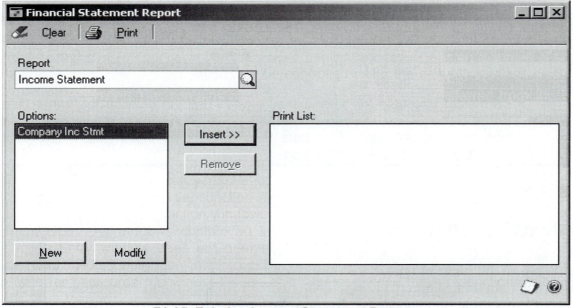

F1:35 Existing Income Statement Reports

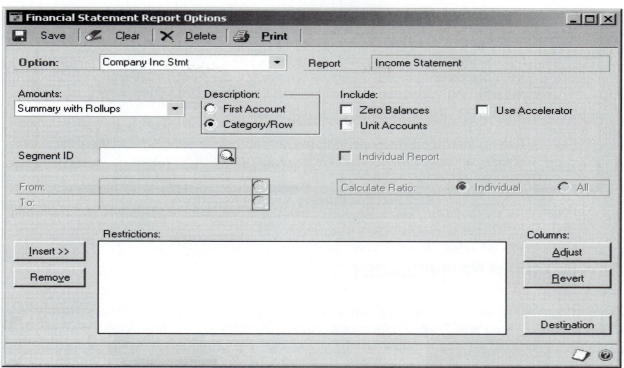

F1:36 Window to Modify Income Statement Options

This window (**F1:36**) provides few options for modifying the income statement. For instance, there is no option to enter the report's date (more on this later). This report is printed by clicking the Print button. However, before printing, verify that the report will print to the screen by clicking the Destination button. You can always send the report to a printer after printing to the screen. The Destination button also lets you save a report to Excel.

Now click the Print button and notice that the report shows results as of March 31, 2007. How did the report select this time period? Financial statements use the system date to determine the reporting period. Since the date is currently set to March of 2007, the report is as of this month. Change the system date to February 25, 2007 and rerun the report. It now displays results as of the end of February. While financial statements use the system date, other Great Plains' reports include an option for entering dates.

 If your system date shows a time period before 2006, an error appears on the report stating:

"The user date falls within a fiscal year that hasn't been set up."

This is because S&S did not use the software before 2006 and the report uses Great Plains system date to select the reporting period. Make sure the system date is set to March of 2007.

Test a few of the report's options by changing current settings and clicking Print. When finished, use the x icon to close this window and choose to discard your changes. When you want to print a report without modifying, highlight the report's name, click the Insert button to place the report in the Print List, and then click Print. In addition, you can insert multiple reports from different categories and print reports simultaneously. All Series report windows work similarly but offer different reporting categories.

Try printing multiple financial statements. First, insert the income statement report just viewed to the Print List section, then insert a report from the balance sheet category. Now click the Print button and view the reports. As you close one report, the other appears. Also, at the top of each report is the option to send it to the printer.

Setting the report destination to the screen before sending it to the printer is an economical way of reviewing output before using paper.

E1:2 Practice Printing Multiple Reports

SETTING USER PREFERENCES

Preferences allow users to customize screen display and printer options for local installations of Great Plains. Open the User Preferences window by clicking on the *Tools>>Setup>>User Preferences* menu. In this window (**F1:37**), you can set reminders, display properties, key movement actions, default printer options, and more. Take time to explore the features and make changes, if desired. When finished, click OK to save your changes or Cancel to discard.

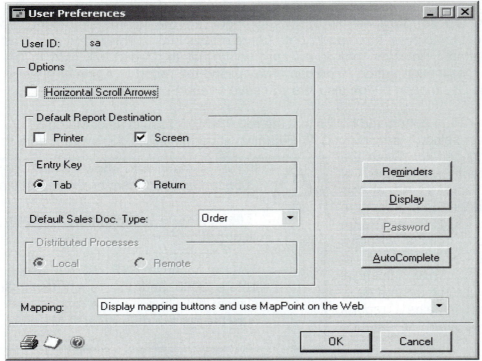

F1:37 User Preferences Window

LEVEL TWO

GENERAL LEDGER SOFTWARE AND COMPANY OBJECTIVES

With all the information presented thus far, we have failed to address the complexities involved in selecting an appropriate accounting package in the first place. It is important to understand that most mid-market general ledger software is sold in a modular fashion; recall the table presented in Level One. While smaller packages may include features similar to Great Plains, these packages are sold bundled with all features. The smaller packages referred to have familiar names such as Microsoft Small Business Accounting® and Peachtree®. These packages are very suitable and affordable for small businesses. In addition, they are often simpler to use and provide features meeting most small business accounting needs, including inventory, payroll, and low-level job costing. However, while these "commercial-off-the-shelf" (COTS) packages are easier to use, this ease comes with restrictions and limitations. For instance, customizing user permissions is limited, audit trail reporting less sophisticated, and reporting less customizable.

Mid-market software costs more but offers significantly more features and greater flexibility. These packages are not sold through retail outlets. Instead, they are purchased through business partners (sometimes called VARs or resellers.) In addition, the modular structure of these packages gives customers greater flexibility in designing their accounting systems. This modular design also provides scalability by allowing a company to add additional features as business grows or strategies change.   Furthermore, these packages run over top of a sophisticated database management system that accommodates customizing internal controls and expanding data analysis capabilities. Keep in mind that these packages also require increased hardware specs to install and deliver desired system performance.

To illustrate, let us assume you are a regional accounting firm providing audit, consulting, and tax services to area firms. Your client base is comprised primarily of small to mid-size firms with annual sales ranging from $100,000 to $3,000,000.   One of your clients has recently experienced rapid growth and desires a computerized accounting solution. The owner seeks your assistance in selecting a general ledger package. The client currently provides management consulting services to customers in a tri-state area and would like to eventually expand into selling related products. The company's payroll is outsourced to a third party. It employs 50 people in a tri-state area, and staffs 5 people in the accounting department. It is a privately held LLC, thus no SEC reporting requirements. However, it does have loan covenants with area banks requiring submission of monthly financial reports within two weeks after month-end.

The client has already prepared a feasibility study and developed a budget for the project. The budget for general ledger software ranges from $20,000 to $30,000. In addition, the project team put together a report outlining proposed purchases of hardware and operating software. Your client's biggest obstacle is selecting accounting software to fit current needs and future expansion plans. After meeting with several software resellers and looking at different products available at area retail stores, the client has narrowed the choice between Peachtree and Great Plains. While both packages fall within their budget, the difference in price is measurable. However, you caution your client to evaluate the purchase on more factors than price. They should also weigh scalability features, reporting options, and internal controls. You also advise your client that the inherent sophistication of larger packages brings an increased user learning curve and inquire about the budget for training.

After further discussion, you determine the client wants to use remote locations in other states. The customer wants these offices to perform sales order entry and sales reporting, but all other accounting and reporting will remain at the corporate office. In addition, you discover your client wants a system that provides strong accounting controls and allows flexibility in assigning user security. Finally, you note that the client will sell inventory in the future, requiring multiple sales tax tables for the tri-state region. Once you and the client have finished this discussion, the decision to purchase Great Plains results from the client's need to have strong internal controls, flexible financial reporting, and multi-state sales tax reporting.

While this is an oversimplification of the process, it provides insight into the issues involved in evaluating accounting software. It is important that customers have an opportunity to work with software candidates and test features prior to making any decision. Oftentimes accountants play an important role in assisting companies with this process.

SOFTWARE LICENSING AND "RIGHTS OF USE"

Accountants are often responsible for assessing company threats and instituting policies that minimize threats. In the software area, companies are continually exposed to two specific threats. First, employees may install software without the company owning a license. Second, employees may be using software outside the vendor's "rights of use" policy. Both threats expose companies to legal action, often resulting in monetary loss that compensates the software company for theft of intellectual property. Violators may also face criminal sanctions for their actions.

Before we begin, let's clear up a frequent misnomer about software. Software purchasers often believe that they own the software purchased, thus are free to resell, copy, use, or distribute as needed. However, if you thought of the software industry's business model, you would understand why these companies cannot sell ownership and remain viable. To assist in understanding this model, we contrast it to an automobile manufacturer's business model. Just as automobile manufacturers make investments in raw materials, labor, and other resources to produce a car, software companies make similar investments. Raw materials used to produce a car are easily visualized, taking the form of steel, rubber, and other tangible items. In contrast, software's raw materials are intangible, taking the form of intellectual contributions by especially talented employees. Hence, software is referred to as intellectual property; however, this term also extends to products produced by the music and movie industries.

Let's return to our comparison. Both the automobile and intellectual property industries rely on product sales to sustain operations and to further investments in research and development that enhance products. However, unlike the automobile industry, software, music, and movie industry sales are threatened because their products are easily reproduced and freely shared and the original purchaser retains the benefits of purchasing. Could you imagine manufacturing your car or giving your car to someone else? Of course not, but these are the realities faced by intellectual property manufacturers. To mitigate revenue threats, the intellectual property industry protect profits by licensing products instead of selling ownership. Thus, the buyer of software, music, or movies purchases a license to use and agrees to use the product within the sellers "rights of use" contract.

For instance, a license for Great Plains legally grants the purchaser the right to use and install the software on any machine located at the purchasing site and to create as many different company databases needed to run the licensing company's operations. This is referred to as the "rights of use" policy. However, this right does not permit the company to lease, rent, or give the software to others. In addition, Great Plains' standard "rights of use policy" does not give the licensing company a right to use an unlicensed Series or to use the product for commercial purposes such as maintaining unrelated company financial records for compensation. Nor does the licensing company own the right to install the product on a Web server for use by other companies. While it is possible to use Great Plains in these fashions, the licensing company must contract for a different "rights of use" policy.

In addition to "rights of use," a licensing company contracts to access the software in accordance with the license agreement. Not all companies license products the same. Some software is licensed on a per-user basis, whereas others are licensed on a per-seat basis. The methodology employed depends on the software model. Larger packages, like Great Plains, are client/server models. This means that the "brain" of the software, the server piece, is installed on a computer functioning as a central server. The software's client piece is then installed on each terminal requiring access to the central server. Thus, the server holds the main processing software, along with the Great Plains data, while client machines simply process and retrieve existing data.

Generally, a company using client/server software buys licenses to access the software on a per-user basis. Per-user refers to the number of concurrent users permitted to access the server's software. With client/server software, the server piece controls the number of concurrent users. For instance, your copy of Great Plains licenses one concurrent user. Thus, when logging in to Great Plains, the number "1" displays in the total number of authorized users field. In addition, you installed both client and server software on your machine, thus it functions as both client and server. However, suppose a company installs Great Plains' client piece on ten client computers, but only five users need simultaneous access to Great Plains. In this hypothetical, the company would purchase a five-user license for Great Plains. Remember, Great Plains permits unlimited client installations on machines located at the purchasing company's site, but grants concurrent access to the server based on the number of licenses purchased. Thus, while the company may have ten locations for using Great Plains, a five-user license fulfills its concurrent user needs. When concurrent access requirements grow, the company purchases additional user licenses.

Let's contrast this to software sold on a per-seat basis. Software such as Microsoft Office sells in this fashion. Per-seat licensing requires a separate license for each computer installation; think of this as each seat that sits in front of a computer containing the software requires a license. Thus, in our previous hypothetical, the company would purchase ten licenses to install the software on ten computers. (Companies can purchase bulk licensing without purchasing separate copies of the software.) Consequently, unlike client/server licensing controls, per-seat software installations pose greater difficulties in mitigating threat posed by installing unlicensed software. Therefore, companies should institute preventative controls by configuring a computer's operating system to deny users the right to install software.

Regardless of whether software is licensed on a per-seat or per-user basis, it is important that companies track software licenses and ensure products are used within the "rights of use" agreement. Installing pirated software (unlicensed software) is a serious legal offense subjecting companies, **and you**, to the threat of significant financial losses, criminal sanctions, and public scrutiny. Just remember the next time you are offered an unlicensed piece of software, a free movie, or a free music download, or witness any of these so-called "free"

LEVEL ONE QUESTIONS

Menu Navigation Questions

1. List the menu path that opens the window used to create vendor master records.

2. You need a summary general ledger trial balance report. List the menu path and the name of the existing report that prints this report.   After locating, print the report and describe what information this report contains.

3. You would like to turn on the Purchasing toolbar. List the menu path to accomplish this.

4. An employee's address has changed. List the menu path used to update the address.

5. You need to enter a purchase order. What menu path allows you to complete the task?

Drill Down and Lookup Questions

6. Ashton has requested that you inquire into the total sales for 2007 for Fillard's, Inc.

    a. What menu path opens the window containing this information?

    b. What are the total sales for fiscal year 2007? (Hint: Change to Summary View, enter the date range, and then click Calculate.)

7. One of your suppliers, Canyon Cam, wants to know if S&S submitted payment for its invoice INV23453 sent in February of this year. What is your response? (Hint: After you locate the document, click on the Details Expansion button illustrated earlier in the chapter.)

LEVEL TWO QUESTIONS

1. Your client decides to purchase Great Plains. Since this software is sold in Series, recommend the Series your client should initially purchase. List any questions you would ask the client that may impact your recommendation.

2. Your client seeks information on Great Plains licensing. The company owns 25 laptops and workstations. Three workstations are in the shipping department, which operates two full-time shifts. There are ten full-time salespeople needing Great Plains on their laptops. Six full-time accounting clerks will use Great Plains. The clerks work in two shifts with three to a shift. Finally, the controller needs Great Plains on his workstation. What optimal number of licenses would you recommend your client to purchase? Will this permit your client to install the client software on all workstations? Explain.

CHAPTER 2: THE S&S COMPANY DATABASE

CHAPTER OVERVIEW

The topics in Chapter 1 and information in Appendix B provided a brief overview of the S&S company database. This chapter contains in-depth information on the company's data file settings.

After reading this Chapter, you will be familiar with:
- ➢ S&S' chart of accounts and departments
- ➢ General ledger account types such as posting, fixed allocation, variable allocation, and unit
- ➢ Printing the chart of accounts, summary trial balance, and detailed trial balance reports
- ➢ Opening and closing accounting periods
- ➢ Series integration and the relational database model used by Great Plains

Level One covers:
- ➢ The general ledger account framework forming the basis for S&S' chart of accounts
- ➢ The departments used by S&S and account segments that identifying departments
- ➢ Creating general ledger accounts and understanding account types
- ➢ Creating company reports for the chart of accounts and trial balance
- ➢ Creating, opening, and closing fiscal periods
- ➢ Creating payment terms, shipping methods, and bank accounts
- ➢ Using the Smart List to export data to Excel

Level Two covers:
- ➢ The database management system's role in Great Plains
- ➢ Series integration
- ➢ Relational database concepts such as master and transaction tables

THE GENERAL LEDGER ACCOUNT FRAMEWORK

Please review the chart of accounts (COA) table located in Appendix B before reading this topic. This table lists existing general ledger accounts used by S&S. General ledger account numbers are governed by the account framework established when Great Plains is installed. This framework sets the maximum account length and maximum account segments that apply to company databases. You were not required to supply this information; however, normally these maximums are entered during installation. The Account Format Setup window displays information on S&S' account framework (*F2:1*). This window is opened by clicking on the *Tools>>Setup>> Company>>Account Format* menu.

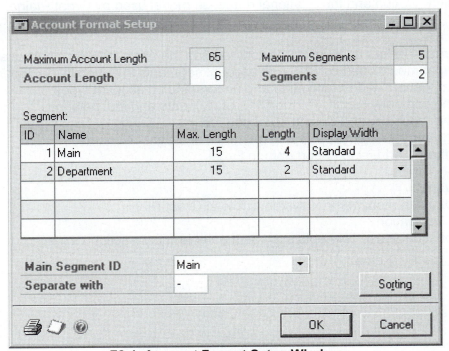

F2:1 Account Format Setup Window

The window shows that S&S could have created a maximum account length of 65 characters with a maximum of 5 segments. Thus, given these maximums, the characters can be separated (segmented) into 5 maximum segments of 15 each (i.e., 65 divided by 5). However, the maximum affects only the outer boundaries for company databases. S&S' actual general ledger account length is 6 characters. The first 4 represent the main segment and the remaining two represent the department segment.

Click OK to close the Account Format Setup window and then click the *Tools>>Setup>> Financial >>Segment* menu. Look up the Department Segment ID (you may have to scroll up in the lookup window) and then look at descriptions for departments by clicking on the lookup icon for the Number field. *F2:2* shows the names S&S has assigned to departments and the segment number used to identify the department. For instance, the number 01 in the department segment assigns the general ledger account to the East department. Segment 00 does not have a name because general ledger accounts with this segment are not used for departmental reporting. Segment 05 is also not assigned a name because general ledger accounts with this segment are used as allocation accounts, discussed later in the chapter.

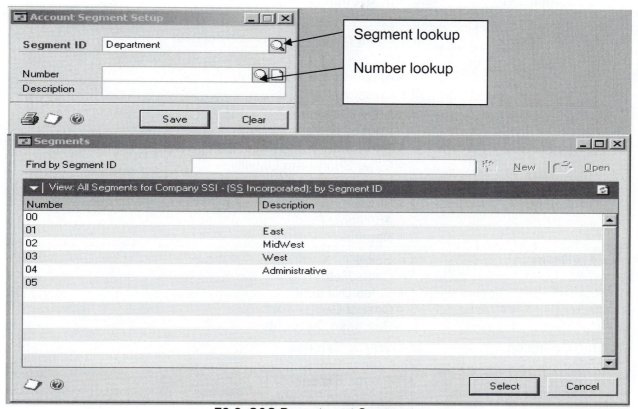

F2:2 S&S Department Segments

In addition to department segments, Ashton established policies to use when creating numbers for the main segment. These policies require the first digit to classify an account as asset, liability, equity, revenue, or expense. The second digit breaks these classifications into groups such as cash, receivables, inventory, or short-term and long-term liabilities. The remaining two digits sequentially number multiple accounts within a group. For instance, general ledger account 4400-01 represents:

Tables *T2:1* and *T2:2* list descriptions on S&S' general ledger account and department numbers.

Main Segment First Digit Classification	Main Segment Second Digit Account Grouping
0 = Unit Account	An account containing nonfinancial data
1 = Asset	1 = Cash 2 = Accounts Receivable 3 = Inventory 4 = Prepaid Assets 5 = Fixed Assets
2 = Liability	1 = Short-term Trade Payables and Debt 2 / 3 = Other Short-term Liabilities 4 = Long-term Liabilities
3 = Equity	0 = Stock 1 = Additional Paid-in-capital 3 = Retained Earnings
4 = Revenue	1 = Sales 3 = Sales Return 4 = Sales Discount 5 = Cost of Goods Sold 6 = Purchase Discounts
5 = Operating Expense	1 = Wages/Salaries 2 = Commissions 3 = Payroll Expenses 4 = Employee Benefits 5–8 = Other Operating Expenses
6 = Not assigned	
7 = Other Income	0 = All Other Income
8 = Other Expense	0 = All Other Expenses
9 = Taxes	0 = Income Tax Accounts

T2:1 Account Classifications and Groupings

Segment Two Numbers	Department
01	East
02	Mid-West
03	West
04	Administrative
05	Allocation Accounts

T2:2 Account Departments

Did you notice the 9999-00 Suspense account on the chart of accounts (COA)? The suspense account is posted to when one of the general ledger posting accounts affected by a transaction is unknown at the time of recording. Instead of delaying transaction posting, the amount related to the unknown account is posted to the Suspense account.

For instance, at the time of recording a payable invoice you are unsure if the purchase represents a fixed asset or an office expense. Instead of waiting to post the invoice, the expense amount in question is debited to the suspense account. The suspense amount is later reclassified to the proper account.

Suspense accounts must be reviewed monthly for reclassifications.

With knowledge on general ledger account numbers, review a general ledger account's settings. Remember the path from Chapter 1 was *Cards>>Financial>>Account*. Look up the salaries account for the East department (**F2:3**). As mentioned in Chapter 1, the account card contains

 Because you know S&S' account structure, rapidly locate the Salaries Expense account by typing a 5 in the Account field before clicking the Lookup icon.

options that determine financial statement grouping and report appearance. For instance, the salaries account prints on the income statement under the Salaries Expense heading. In addition, the Typical Balance instructs Great Plains to increase the account's balance for debit postings and decrease the balance for credit postings.

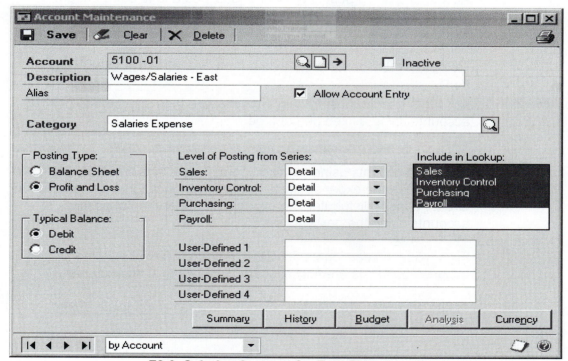

F2:3 Salaries Account for East Department

We revisit the Account Maintenance window to emphasize one other point. This window creates accounts assigned to Posting type. Account types are the subject of the next topic.

S&S is building an addition to its current location and needs a new account to record construction costs. Create this account and save the record.

Drill down to redisplay the new account. Compare your account to the one illustrated in Appendix D. When finished, click the Delete button to remove the new account.

E2:1 Create and Delete a General Ledger Posting Account

GENERAL LEDGER ACCOUNT TYPES

Posting accounts are used to post financial transactions. Great Plains has additional account types that serve different purposes. *T2:3* explains these account types and their uses.

Account Type	Description
Posting	Accounts used to post financial transactions and to store budget projections. These are the only accounts that appear on financial statements. These accounts are created using the *Cards>>Financial>>Account* menu.
Fixed Allocation	Accounts used to post transactions that are then allocated to posting accounts using a fixed percentage. For instance, insurance expense can be allocated to four departmental expense accounts using the fixed percentages of 20%, 20%, 20%, and 40%. When the expense posts to the fixed allocation expense account, Great Plains redistributes the expense to departmental posting accounts using the percentages. Fixed allocation accounts do not appear on financial statements because balances are fully allocated to other posting accounts. These accounts are created using the *Cards>>Financial>>Fixed Allocation* menu.

Variable Allocation	Accounts that work the same as fixed allocation accounts, except postings are allocated using factors that change over time. These factors are based on balances in breakdown accounts.
	Breakdown accounts can be posting accounts, such as sales and expense accounts, or can be unit accounts that store the number of employees per department or office square footage. When transactions post to a variable allocation account, posting is spread to the departmental accounts using the percentages calculated by Great Plains. The percentages are determined by dividing a balance in one breakdown account by the total balances in all breakdown accounts.
	For instance, S&S tracks revenue and expense by sales department. The wage expense for warehouse workers is distributed to three departmental wage expense accounts based upon the monthly revenue for each sales department. Great Plains calculates the percentage used to allocate these wages by dividing each department's revenue by total revenue.
	Again, like fixed allocation accounts, variable allocation accounts do not appear on financial statements.
	These accounts are created from the *Cards>>Financial>>Variable Allocation* menu.
Unit Accounts	Unit accounts are similar to posting accounts. Both accept transaction entry and store historical and budget information. However, quantities are posted to these accounts instead of financial transactions. In addition, these accounts do not appear on financial statements.
	Unit accounts are useful for comparing financial and nonfinancial information. You can use them to create calculations on customized reports, for instance, to show sales per employee. Unit accounts also serve as breakdown accounts for variable allocations, for instance, to allocate rent expense based on each department's square footage. Unit accounts do not appear on financial statements.
	These accounts are created from the *Cards>>Financial>>Unit Account* menu.

T2:3 Account Type Descriptions

Open the fixed allocation account for utilities. List the posting accounts receiving expense allocations and the percentage allocated.

Open the variable allocation account for wages/salaries of truckers and warehouse employees. What breakdown accounts are used to allocate transactions? What are the account names receiving the distributed expense?

E2:2 Variable and Fixed Allocation Accounts

Before leaving this section, print a chart of accounts (COA). Click on the *Reports>>Financial>>Account* menu to open the window illustrated in *F2:4*. Click on the report dropdown list to see reports available in this window. We find these reports are based on account type. Select Posting and find a report named COA. Insert the report to the Print List area and then click Print. Compare your first page results to those in *F2:5*.

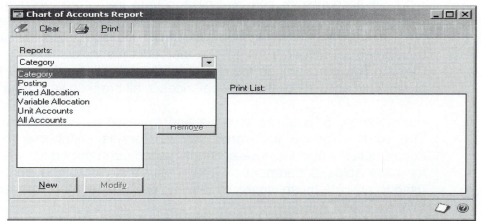

F2:4 COA Report Window

```
System:      3/25/2005   11:58:10 AM              S&S Incorporated                      Page:    1
Us                                            POSTING ACCOUNTS LIST                   User ID: sa
                                                 General Ledger

Ranges:                  From:                              To:
  Account                First                              Last
  Account Description    First                              Last
  Category               First                              Last

Sorted By: Main                                       Include:

Account                  Description                              Alias              Account Entry
  -------------------------------------------------------------------------------------------------
  Category                            Active  Account Type        Posting Type       Typical Balance
  -------------------------------------------------------------------------------------------------
    User-Defined 1            User-Defined 2          User-Defined 3      User-Defined 4
  -------------------------------------------------------------------------------------------------
1100-00                  Cash                                                        Yes
  Cash                               Yes    Posting Account      Balance Sheet       Debit
1110-00                  Cash-Savings                                                Yes
  Cash                               Yes    Posting Account      Balance Sheet       Debit
1120-00                  Petty Cash                                                  Yes
  Cash                               Yes    Posting Account      Balance Sheet       Debit
1130-00                  Checking - Payroll                                          Yes
  Cash                               Yes    Posting Account      Balance Sheet       Debit
1200-00                  Accounts Receivable                                         Yes
  Accounts Receivable                Yes    Posting Account      Balance Sheet       Debit
1205-00                  Sales Discounts Available                                   Yes
  Accounts Receivable                Yes    Posting Account      Balance Sheet       Debit
1210-00                  Allowance for Doubtful Accounts                             Yes
  Accounts Receivable                Yes    Posting Account      Balance Sheet       Credit
1270-00                  Marketable Securities                                       Yes
  Short-Term Investments             Yes    Posting Account      Balance Sheet       Debit
1310-00                  Inventory                                                   Yes
  Inventory                          Yes    Posting Account      Balance Sheet       Debit
1410-00                  Prepaid Insurance                                           Yes
  Prepaid Expenses                   Yes    Posting Account      Balance Sheet       Debit
1430-00                  Prepaid - Other                                             Yes
  Prepaid Expenses                   Yes    Posting Account      Balance Sheet       Debit
```

F2:5: Page 1 of COA Report

Ashton has not created a report for fixed allocation accounts. He asks you to create this report. If you do not remember report creation, refer to the topic in Chapter 1. Print the report to the screen and compare your results to those in Appendix D.

Take the time to create and review reports for other account types.

E2:3 Generate COA Report

GENERAL LEDGER TRIAL BALANCE

While a COA report lists company general ledger accounts (posting accounts), a trial balance lists beginning and ending balances, debits, credits, and net changes for these accounts. Before the advent of computers, the trial balance was an essential tool to test whether a company's general ledger accounts were in balance. That is:

Assets = Liabilities + Equity + Net Income (Loss)

When manually posting accounting information, it was easy to make transposition errors, to enter a debit as credit, or to add and subtract incorrectly. Computers have replaced the tedious balancing process by posting internally. Thus, a company's trial balance should not be out of balance unless Great Plains was interrupted during posting. Interruptions may occur because of hardware failure, electrical outages, or improper system shutdown. These events may corrupt data files and a backup may be the only solution that restores a database's integrity. Data backup and restore procedures were covered in Chapter 1 and are repeated in Appendix A. These procedures are important, so please take time to read this information.

To print a trial balance, click on the *Reports>>Financial>>Trial Balance* menu. Like COA reports, trial balance reports are grouped into categories (*F2:6*) that supply different reporting options. Select the summary category and then the existing trial balance report. Click the Modify button to open the window illustrated in *F2:7*. This illustration explains options for the report. Print the report, comparing your results to those in *F2:8*. Review this information and notice that the report is "in balance" when the ending balance is zero.

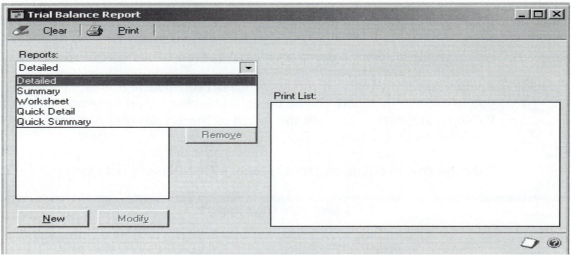

F2:6 Trial Balance Report Window

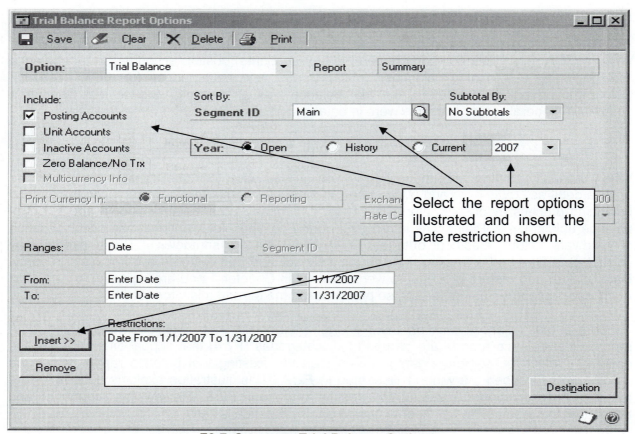

F2:7 Summary Trial Balance Options

If you get an error message stating . . .

"The user date falls within a fiscal year that hasn't been set up."

. . . make sure your system date falls within fiscal year 2007, then reprint the report.

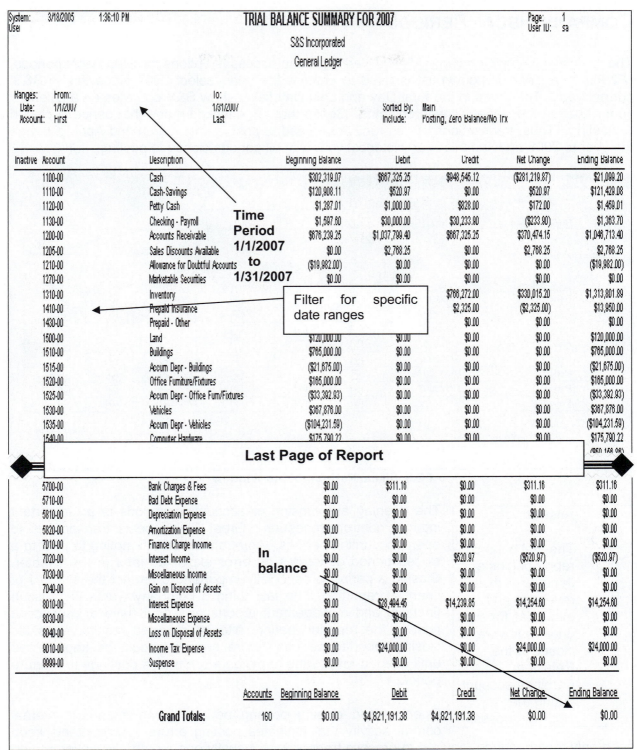

F2:8 Trial Balance Summary Report

Why do revenue and expense accounts have a zero beginning balance?

Read on to find the answer.

COMPANY FISCAL PERIODS

The *Tools>>Setup>>Company>>Fiscal Periods* menu accesses options for S&S' fiscal periods, (**F2:9**). The Year dropdown list is used to change the year, select 2007 since this is S&S' current year. The dates in the First Day and Last Day fields show S&S operates on a calendar year. Look at the Series Closed columns. Series that are checked mean that period is closed to posting. Thus, transactions are currently permitted to post in only March and April. Change the year to 2006 and find this is an historical year with all periods closed to posting.

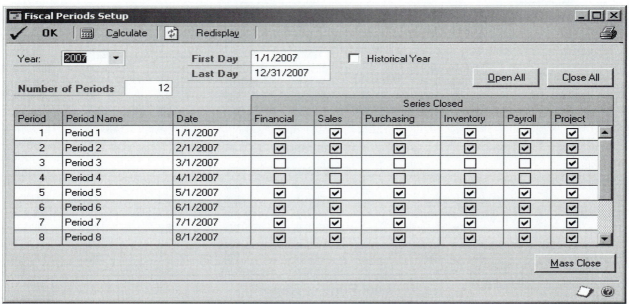

F2:9 Fiscal Periods Setup Window

Answer:

The trial balance report begins at January 1, thus revenues and expenses for the prior year were closed to the Retained Earnings account during the closing process.

The opening and closing of accounting periods is an important internal control procedure. Great Plains posts transactions to open accounting periods. Any transaction attempting to post to a closed period generates an error explained later in the chapter. Closing a period is especially important to protect the integrity of financial reporting. The last thing a company wants is to issue financial and management reports and then have a transaction post to the reported period, altering reported results. Besides closing reported periods, future periods should be kept closed until needed for posting to mitigate erroneous postings to a future period.

Opening and closing posting periods is an important internal control activity that mitigates posting errors. Accountants keep open only those periods required to process transactions, usually one month. However, during the beginning of a month, two periods remain open for a few days because companies routinely process transactions for the previous and current months during this time.

To control the length of time two periods remain open, accountants set cutoff dates for processing prior month transactions. On the cutoff date, the accountant closes the previous month and remaining transactions affecting the closed period are entered as journal entries using the Financial Series. We will practice journal entries in Chapter 8.

Great Plains generates warning and error messages when attempting to post to a closed period. First, Great Plains warns the user during transaction entry that the date falls within a closed period (see *F2:10*). This warning appears regardless of whether the date is entered on a batch or a transaction.

 How do I set up a new fiscal year?

You may have noticed that S&S has only two fiscal periods, the closed year of 2006 and the open year of 2007. To create 2008, type this year in the Year field, then click the Calculate button.

F2:10 Closed Period Warning

When the user disregards the closed period warning and attempts to post a single transaction, then the error message in *F2:11* appears.

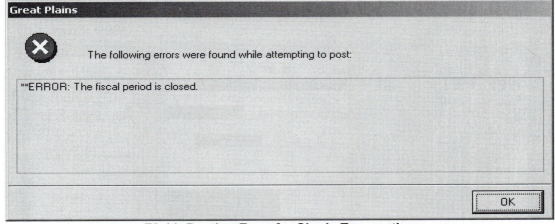

F2:11 Posting Error for Single Transaction

When warning is ignored on a batch and the user posts, the posting report displays the error message shown in *F2:12*. Procedures for reposting batches with errors are explained in Appendix A.

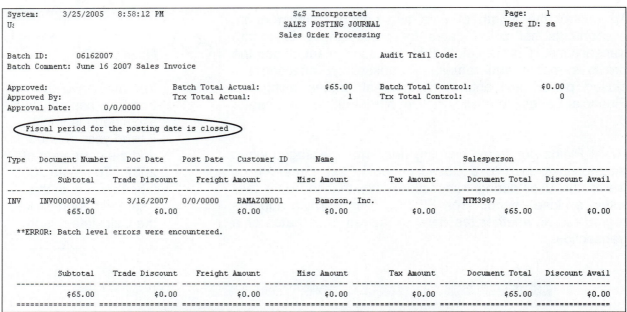

```
System:     3/25/2005   8:58:12 PM            S&S Incorporated              Page:     1
U:                                           SALES POSTING JOURNAL          User ID: sa
                                             Sales Order Processing

Batch ID:     06162007                                      Audit Trail Code:
Batch Comment: June 16 2007 Sales Invoice

Approved:                       Batch Total Actual:        $65.00   Batch Total Control:        $0.00
Approved By:                    Trx Total Actual:               1   Trx Total Control:              0
Approval Date:      0/0/0000

   ( Fiscal period for the posting date is closed )


Type  Document Number   Doc Date   Post Date   Customer ID    Name                    Salesperson
------------------------------------------------------------------------------------------------------
        Subtotal    Trade Discount   Freight Amount    Misc Amount    Tax Amount   Document Total  Discount Avail

INV   INV000000194      3/16/2007  0/0/0000    BAMAZON001     Bamozon, Inc.           MTM3987
        $65.00          $0.00            $0.00           $0.00          $0.00        $65.00          $0.00

  **ERROR: Batch level errors were encountered.



        Subtotal    Trade Discount   Freight Amount    Misc Amount    Tax Amount   Document Total  Discount Avail
      ---------------  ---------------  ---------------  ------------  -----------  --------------  -------------
        $65.00          $0.00            $0.00           $0.00          $0.00        $65.00          $0.00
      ===============  ===============  ===============  ============  ===========  ==============  =============
```

F2:12 Posting Error Report for Batch Transaction

PAYMENT TERMS, SHIPPING METHODS, AND BANK ACCOUNTS

There are three remaining company setup items to discuss. First, S&S' payment terms are accessed from the *Tools>>Setup>>Company>>Payment Terms* menu. These terms apply to both customer and vendor transactions. For example, the 2% 10/Net 30 term offers customers a 2% discount when payments are received within ten days of the invoice's date. In addition, employees use this term for vendor transactions offering S&S similar payment terms. Review *F2:13*, noting that care must be exercised when selecting the items used to calculate the discount.

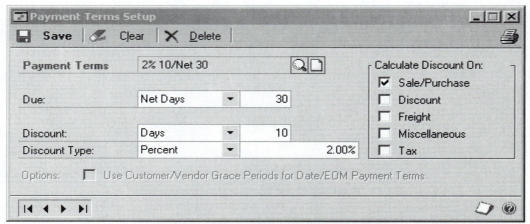

F2:13 Payment Terms Setup Window

S&S' shipping methods are accessed from the *Tools>>Setup>>Company>>Shipping Methods* menu (see *F2:14*). Again, these methods apply to both customer and vendor transactions. However, these methods are for informational purposes. Great Plains does not automatically compute shipping charges. Thus, charges are entered during transaction entry. S&S' employees truck most customer orders and the FLEET Shipping Method identifies company delivery.

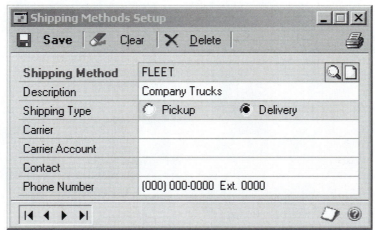

F2:14 Shipping Method Setup Window

Finally, S&S created bank records to store information on banking relationships. Bank accounts are accessed from the *Tools>>Setup>>Company>>Bank Accounts* menu. S&S maintains two bank accounts with First National Bank. The first account is used for all cash transactions other than payroll. The second account processes payroll transactions. The Bank Maintenance window (*F2:15*) stores only general information about bank accounts.

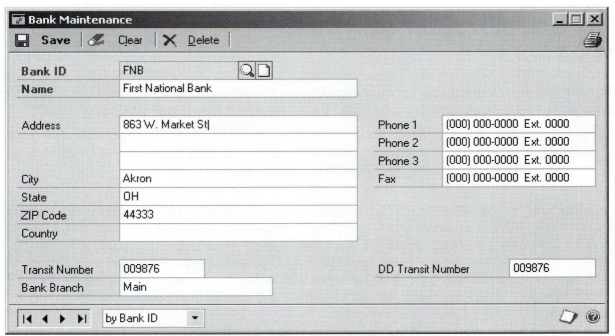

F2:15 Bank Maintenance Window

The *Cards>>Financial>>Checkbook* menu creates bank account records used during reconciliation. Click on this menu to open the Checkbook Maintenance window (*F2:16*) and look up the PRIMARY checking account. This card links transactions posted to the 1100-00 general ledger account to the bank reconciliation feature of Great Plains.

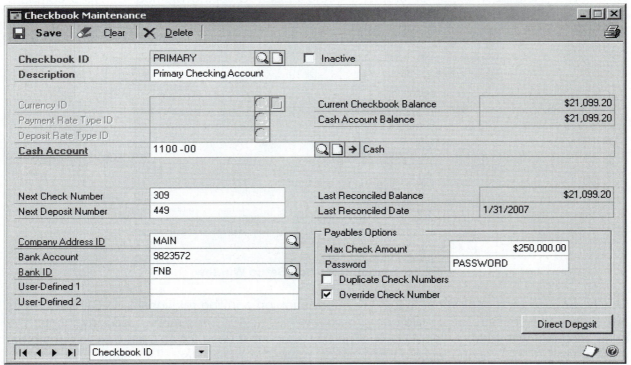

F2:16 Checkbook Maintenance Record

SMART LIST

The Smart List is a great tool for querying data and exporting data to Excel. The Smart List often generates the quickest view into data. It is also a great way to get data out of Great Plains for additional analysis. To open the Smart List, look on the toolbar for the light bulb icon.

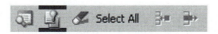

Click the icon to open the Smart List window shown in *F2:18*. The left side of this window displays categories of available views into Great Plains data. Click the plus sign to expand the Account Summary category. Highlight the Trial Balance view and data appears on the right. The right side operates like an Excel spreadsheet. Columns can be expanded and data sorted by clicking on column headings. You can also add or delete columns by clicking the Columns button at the top. In addition, you can click the Search button to filter the view.

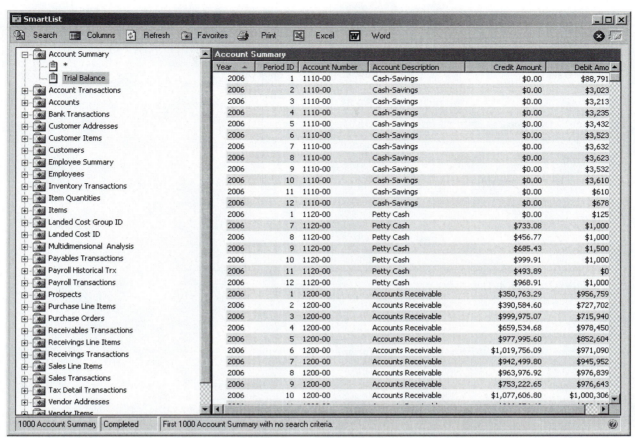

F2:17 Smart List Window

Let's illustrate the usefulness of this tool. You are having problems reconciling the Accounts Receivable account for January 2007. You want to create a view listing all entries to the Accounts Receivable general ledger account for January. After creating the view, you will export the results to Excel.

First, we create an initial view into general ledger account transactions by expanding the Account Transactions category in the left window and then selecting the Current Financial Journals view.

Next, we modify this view to obtain the desired data. Click on Search and set the view's options for the data range and account number shown in *F2:18*. You could also add or delete columns of data by clicking the Columns button at the bottom of the Search window to open the window shown in *F2:19*. Since we don't need to change the data columns, close this window without modifying the columns. Click OK to close this window.

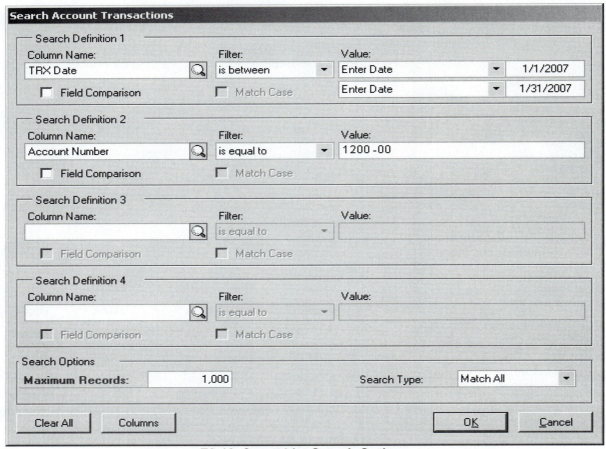

F2:18 Smart List Search Options

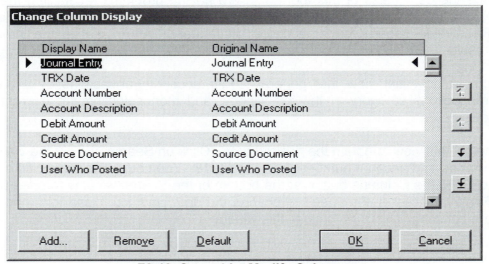

F2:19 Smart List Modify Columns

Sort the view by transaction date by clicking on Trx Date column heading. You might want to use this view again so save it to the Account Transactions category by clicking Favorites and completing the Favorites window as shown in *F2:20*. When finished, click the Add button and your new view exists under the Account Transactions category (*F2:21*). Since we saved the view as visible to the System, anyone using Great Plains may access this view.

F2:20 Smart List Add to Favorites

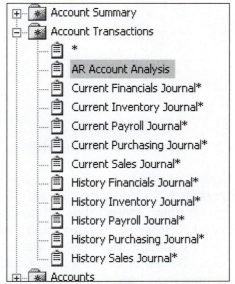

F2:21 Smart List Favorite Added

Finally, let's export the data by clicking the Excel button. (Note: You must have Excel on your computer to use this feature.) Excel opens and the data appears in a new workbook, ready for data manipulation and analysis, (see **F2:21**).

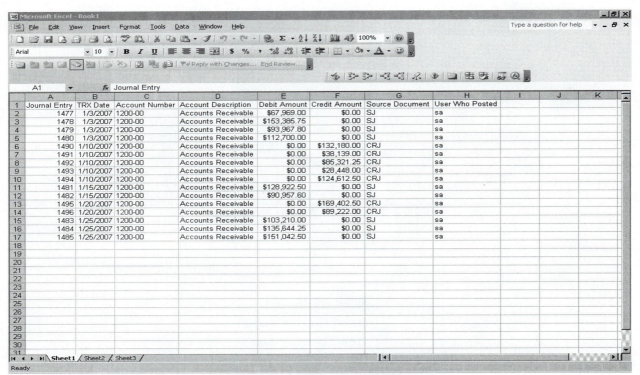

F2:22 Exported Excel Spreadsheet

In Excel, you can reconcile accounts receivable. First, sort entries by source document, searching for source codes not created by the Sales Series. Transactions affecting accounts receivable should originate through this Series, thus a source document originating from another Series indicates an erroneous posting. In our results, we find only SJ (Sales Journal) and CRJ (Cash Receipts Journal), which are both Sales Series source documents. We will discuss source documents for each Series in Chapter 3. In addition, you will have a greater appreciation for this exercise after reading Chapter 5.

THE DATABASE MANAGEMENT SYSTEM (DBMS) AND GREAT PLAINS

In Chapter 1, we also installed the Great Plains DBMS (database management system) when installing the software. Great Plains runs on either Microsoft's SQL or its streamlined MSDE version. While both versions operate identically, MSDE requires less hard drive space since it comes without the SQL database interface tools and supports fewer users. For smaller companies, the MSDE version offers a more affordable option without sacrificing functionality. In fact, you copy of the software uses the MSDE version.

For Great Plains, the DBMS is the engine that manages table creation, data manipulation, data queries, data forms, and reporting. During Great Plains installation, a template containing all the required data tables, forms, queries, and reports was installed to the Dynamics directory on the server. Thereafter, when users create new company databases, Great Plains draws from this template to establish the required database components. You might think of this process as similar to creating a database by using an Access database wizard.

Students studying database concepts know the basic requirements of a relational database. Primary and foreign keys are the fields used to create table relationships and enforce entity and referential integrity. Furthermore, students studying data modeling concepts recognize that tables are classified as master, transaction, and linking tables (used to establish many-to-many relationships). Because the DBMS creates all the tables used by Great Plains, table relationships are immediately present in newly created company databases.

While we are not delving into specific tables used by Great Plains or specific table relationships, we need to understand that data manipulation may affect one or more tables depending upon the relationship. In addition, transaction windows may supply data to one or more tables and reports may pull data from one or more tables; therefore, restricting access to tables may generate unexpected errors. This information is important when setting user access privileges in Chapter 3.

SERIES INTEGRATION

Besides table relationships, another aspect of Great Plains is Series integration. Each Series maintains its own set of related Master and Transaction tables. Additionally, a particular Series interacts with related tables in other Series. Chapter 1 illustrated a table explaining Series covered in this text. Series integration makes it possible to post data through one Series that automatically records data in another Series. *F2:23* illustrates Series integration. This figure shows that the System Manager functions as the "brain" and manages system-wide settings for security, audit trails, and activity tracking.

System Manager

F2:23 Series Integration

The following is an example illustrating series integration for a transaction originating in the Sales Series.

Sales Order Processing

Step One: A salesperson or order entry clerk enters a customer sales order for inventory. During order entry, the customer, inventory items, and salesperson are linked to the order. The order is saved for further processing, which "flags" the inventory items as unavailable to other orders.[1] At this point, the order is not posted because an economic exchange has not occurred. An order is merely a commitment of company resources. The economic exchange occurs in Step Three.

Step Two: The warehouse fills and ships the order to the customer. An employee in the shipping department sets a field on the order that flags the transaction as ready for invoicing.

---

[1] The behavior of inventory commitments depends upon setup options instituted under the Inventory Control Series. Great Plains provides different options for handling inventory commitments. This example applies to the setup used by S&S.

Invoicing

Step Three: An accounts receivable clerk transfers the order to a customer invoice and posts. At this point, the economic exchange occurs and the financial transaction is recognized when the transaction posts.[2] The post process created an invoice transaction record linked to the customer's master record stored in the Sales Series, created a transaction record linked to the inventory item's master record stored in the Inventory Control Series, and created transaction records linked for each general ledger master record stored in the Financial Series affected by the transaction.

Receivables Management

Step Four: The customer remits payment for the invoice. The accounts receivable clerk posts the payment and applies it to the outstanding invoice record. The post process creates additional transaction records linked to the customer's master record in the Sales Series and for each general ledger master record in the Financial Series affected by the transaction.

Database integration means that posting errors created in one Series must be corrected in the originating Series. For instance, placing a sales order for the wrong inventory item cannot be corrected by making an entry in the Inventory Control or the Financial Series. The order must be corrected at the origination point, the Sales Series. Appendix C provides an extensive discussion on correcting posting mistakes for each Series.

REA DATA MODEL: MASTER AND TRANSACTION TABLES

In the previous topic, we discussed transaction records linked to master records. Another way to explain this is to state that transaction records were created in the Sales Series' transaction tables and linked to records in master tables of the Sales, Inventory, and Financial Series. Recognizing the different table types is pertinent to discussing Great Plains security in Chapter 3. To determine the types of tables affected by posting, refer to the REA data model of the revenue cycle[3] shown in *F2:24*.

The squares on the left represent resources, the middle squares represent events, and the left squares refer to agents taking part in the event. Each square represents a table.   Resources and agents are master tables and events are transaction tables. In addition, the labeled lines represent linking tables, which are also transaction tables. Master tables are the permanent files of a company.   These files require minimal data maintenance and are linked to daily transaction processing. Adding to or deleting records from these tables is an authorization function as defined by internal controls. On the other hand, transaction tables store the records generated by day-to-day posting activities.

---

[2] The rational for this recognition is found in the Accounting Conceptual Framework. The revenue recognition principal states that revenue is recognized when earned or deemed to have been earned. In our example, revenue is earned when legal title transfers (when inventory ships assuming FOB shipping point.) Thus, posting an invoice triggers recognition in the financials because this occurs after shipping. This is an important point for auditors testing period-end cut off transactions.

[3] Data model from Marshall Romney and Paul Steinbart, *Accounting Information Systems* (10th ed., Prentice Hall 2006), p. 590.

Employees performing the recording function, as defined by internal controls, create transaction records.[4] Keep these concepts in mind when reading Chapter 3.

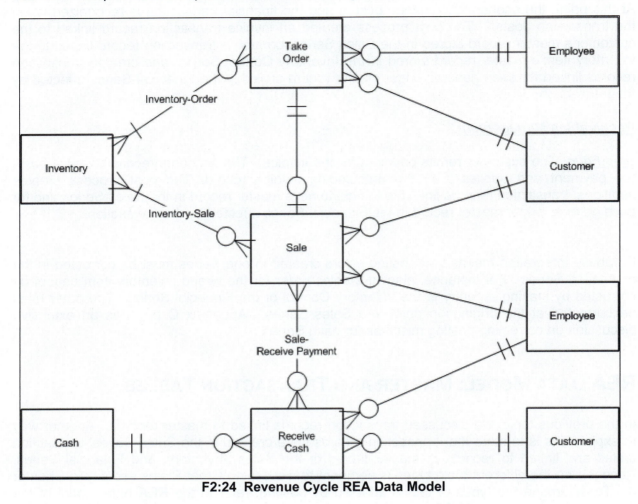

F2:24 Revenue Cycle REA Data Model

---

[4] For more understanding on data modeling, refer to Chapter 16 in Marshall Romney and Paul Steinbart, *Accounting Information Systems* (10th ed., Prentice Hall 2006).

LEVEL ONE QUESTIONS

1. Ashton needs to allocate company insurance to the three sales departments. Currently all insurance expense is recorded in the 5620-04 Insurance Expense–Administration account. He asks you to create the departmental expense accounts for insurance and to establish an allocation account for spreading costs 25% across the board.

2. Because S&S maintains departmental segments in the COA, the owners want an income statement for January 2007 by department. They ask you to generate these reports.

3. Ashton is performing a month-end closing as of February 2007. He needs you to review the details of transactions recorded to the general ledger for February. Prepare the report that assists you with this task.

4. Create an Excel spreadsheet to analyze customer sales growth by region, compare February 2007 growth over February 2006.

LEVEL TWO QUESTIONS

1. Open a vendor card. Have you accessed a master or transaction table? Please explain.

2. The vendor card contains numerous data fields. List the field name storing the vendor record's primary key and any foreign key fields on the vendor card. Explain why the vendor record uses this data file structure.

3. Click the Accounts button on the vendor card. These accounts are integrated to which Series?

4. Open a Sales Transaction Entry window, select the invoice document type, and then review the data entry fields.

    a. Besides the Sales Series, list other Series integrated to this invoice transaction. (Remember to expand the detail section of the invoice.)

    b. Will this invoice record be stored in a master or transaction table?

    c. Use database terminology to describe the Customer ID field on the invoice record.

5. Perform the same steps in Question 4 for a purchase order.

CHAPTER 3: INTERNAL CONTROLS AND GREAT PLAINS SECURITY

CHAPTER OVERVIEW

This chapter focuses on the internal control features of Great Plains that are configured in the System Manager Series such as system access, Series posting setup, and reporting controls. These controls are independent of additional controls that are set within each Series. Security settings in the System Manager function as pervasive controls, meaning the controls govern all aspects of Great Plains. We will explore other Series' controls in subsequent chapters.

As we discuss internal controls throughout this text, it is important to understand the COSO Enterprise Risk Management (ERM) framework. This framework guides decisions on setting Great Plains' controls to comply with segregation of duties,[1] independent checks on performance, and authorization policies. In light of recent developments in accounting oversight, particularly the Sarbanes-Oxley Act of 2002 (SOX), accountants must understand implementation and evaluation of internal controls in a software environment to comply with Section 404 of SOX. For additional information on the ERM framework, SOX, and internal controls, see Chapters 6 and 7 of Marshall Romney and Paul Steinbart, _Accounting Information Systems_ (10th ed., Prentice Hall 2006).

Although our discussion applies to Great Plains, many general ledger software packages provide security. The Great Plains topics covered in this chapter are usually performed by system administrators and accountants with responsibility for internal controls and security. In particular, we will discuss selecting software access permissions using advanced security and other internal control features offered through activity tracking, posting setup, and the audit trail. These features are invaluable in implementing a company's internal control policies and objectives.

Level One covers:
  ➢ Security implemented during Great Plains installation
  ➢ Posting setup internal control features
  ➢ The audit trail and activity tracking

Level Two covers:
  ➢ System administration and security
  ➢ Advanced security and security reporting

---

[1] Segregation of duties separates employee responsibilities into the functional areas of authorization, recording, and custody. Each employee should hold responsibilities under only one of these functional areas.

SECURITY INSTALLED DURING GREAT PLAINS INSTALLATION

During Great Plains installation, the _sa_ User ID was created and you assigned this account a password. This User ID is an acronym for system administrator. By default, the _sa_ account is an owner of the database management system, granted full control over Great Plains' administration. For instance, the _sa_ account can create or delete company databases and perform database maintenance tasks such as data integrity checks, backups, and restores. Therefore, it is important to protect this account's password. In real world settings, this password should be changed frequently. However, for simplicity, you will always use the _sa_ password created at the time of installation.

In addition, Great Plains incorporates a separate password restricting access to Great Plains security accessed under the _Tools>>Setup>>System_ menu. This password was also initialized to the _sa_'s password during installation. However, this password functions independently from login passwords because responsibility for System Manager security is often delegated to accountants not having login access through the _sa_ account.[2] Thus, the System Manager password should be different from the _sa_ account and the menu used to change this password is _Tools>>Setup>>System>> System Password_. For simplicity, do not change the password and continue using the _sa_ account's password whenever Great Plains prompts for authorization to access System Manager security. This chapter focuses on implementing System Manager security; therefore, you will often be prompted to enter this password when accessing the menus shown in **F3:1**.

User
User Classes
User Access
Company

Security
SmartList Security
Advanced Security
System Password
Activity Tracking
User Activity

F3:1 System Manager Menus

POSTING SETUP CONTROLS

Before discussing security, we look at the menu items that control Great Plains' posting and audit trail documentation under the _Tools>>Setup>>Posting_ menu (**F3:2**). Posting controls exist for each Series and are accessed using the _Posting_ menu. Posting setup determines how Great Plains posts transactions and prints control reports after posting. Click on this menu to open the Posting Setup window and change the Series and Origin fields to the items shown in **F3:3**.

Posting
Posting Accounts
Source Document
Audit Trail Codes
Payroll Accounts

F3:2 Posting Setup Menus

---

[2] For an in-depth discussion on the COBIT Framework, refer to Marshall Romney and Paul Steinbart, _Accounting Information Systems_ (10th ed., Prentice Hall, 2006), p. 195.

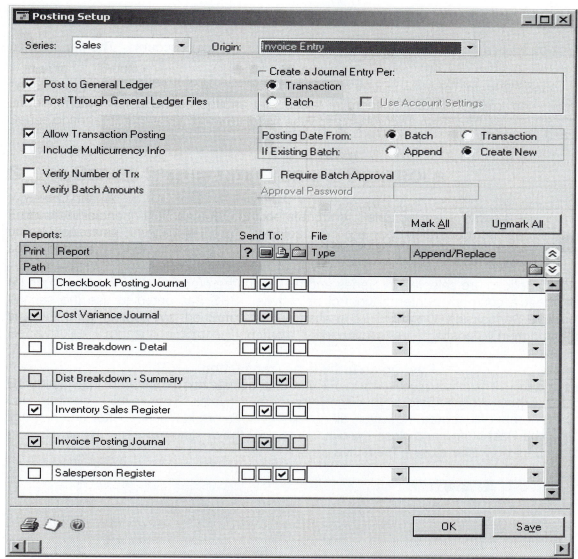

F3:3 Posting Setup for Sales Series Invoices

The window now displays S&S' settings that control Sales Series invoice posting and invoice posting reports. The dropdown menu for the Series field reveals posting and report options exist for each Series. In addition, the dropdown menu for the Origin field shows Series settings are based upon the posting activity.

F3:3 tells us that Ashton configured S&S' Sales Series invoices to:
1) Post directly to general ledger accounts when batch posting is performed
2) Permit individual transactions to post, not requiring all transactions post in a batch, and batches do not require control totals or batch approval before posting
3) When transactions are posted in batches, entries to general ledger accounts are made on the batch date, new batches are created when suspended batches are present, and each transaction in a batch posts in detail
4) Print the posting reports selected in the Reports section

The following explains the internal control implications of these options, in order of appearance.

1) *Post to General Ledger and Post Through General Ledger Files Options*

Great Plains offers two methods to finalize posting to general ledger accounts. The first method is implemented by selecting the Post to General Ledger option. With this option, transactions post in the originating Series but not in the Financial Series. Therefore, transactions are not finalized until a second post records these entries to the general ledger accounts. (Remember, general ledger accounts reside in the Financial Series.) Suspended transactions are then reviewed and posted by selecting the *Tools>>Routines>>Master Posting* menu. This method is often used when a company opts to have all postings to general ledger accounts controlled by the accounting department.

The second method is implemented by selecting the Post to General Ledger and the Post Through General Ledger Files options. With this method, transactions posted in batches immediately finalize to general ledger accounts. However, transactions posted individually continue to be suspended, requiring a second post.

These posting options are selected by Series and by Origin; therefore, posting treatment can be tailored to meet a company's internal control objectives. S&S has opted to use the second method for all Series and Origins. Let's illustrate this method by posting an individual transaction and then by posting a transaction using a batch.

Posting an Individual Transaction

Enter the invoice transaction illustrated in *F3:4*. This transaction is entered individually by selecting the *Transactions>>Sales>>Invoice Entry* menu. (Note: Your invoice number may vary from the number illustrated; however, all remaining fields are identical.) After entering this invoice, click the Post button and close the window to print the posting reports.   (Note: Posting reports often print only after closing the active window.)

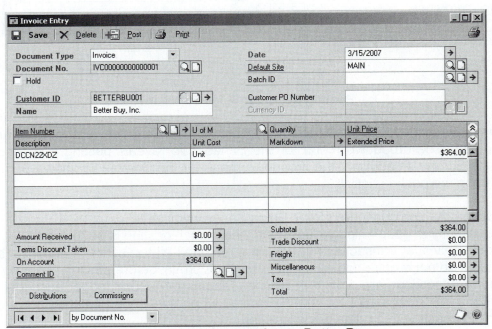

F3:4 Invoice Transaction to Better Buy

The Invoice Posting Journal prints, listing the general ledger accounts affected by posting. However, do not be fooled by the appearance of these accounts. We find later that this invoice has not finalized to general ledger accounts. Close this report and the Inventory Register prints. (Note: When several posting reports are printed to the screen, one report must be closed before the next appears.) Review the information on this report and then close the report. The reports that printed after posting are determined by S&S' internal control procedures and documentation requirements. We discuss selecting the posting reports that print later in the chapter.

Posting a Transaction Using a Batch

Before checking on the status of the last posting, post the same invoice using a batch. First, create the batch by selecting the *Transactions>>Sales>>Invoicing Batches* menu. Assign the Batch ID of <u>INVBETTERBUY</u> (see *F3:5*) and then click the Transactions Button. Enter the previous transaction shown in *F3:4* and click the Save button. Close the transaction window, returning to the batch window. Look up the <u>INVBETTERBUY</u> batch and click the Post button. Review the posting reports. This time the last report that printed is the General Posting Journal. The presence of this report signals the transaction finalized in general ledger accounts.

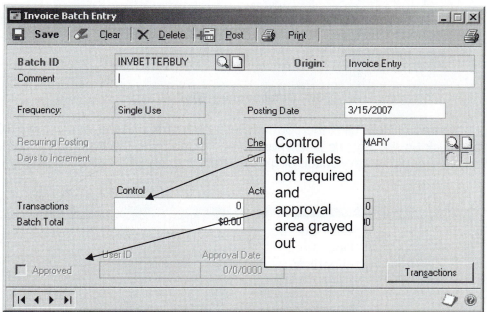

F3:5 Invoice Batch Entry Window

Let's confirm that the individually posted invoice remains suspended while the batched transaction posted to the general ledger. First, review entries posted to the accounts receivable general ledger account by selecting the *Inquiry>>Financial>>Detail* menu. Look up account 1200-00 and filter for March 15th transactions. You find only one debit transaction for $356.72 (see *F3:6*). (Note: The original invoice totaled $364.00; however, the amount posted to accounts receivable is $356.72. This difference occurs because 2% of the invoice is a potential customer discount that posted to the discount available account. Chapter 5 discusses the Sales Series option that tracks potential discounts.)

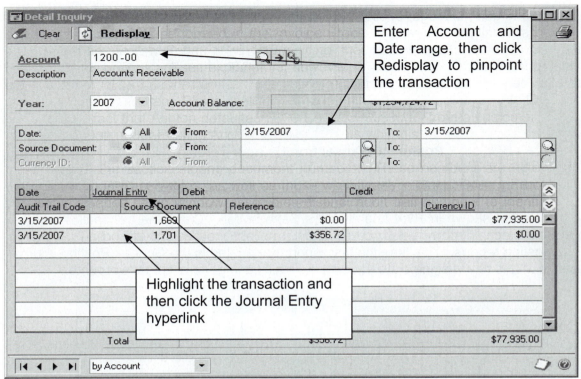

F3:6 Detail Inquiry Window

Now highlight the transaction, click the Journal Entry hyperlink and the window in *F3:7* appears. In this window, click on the Source Document hyperlink and find the transaction contains Batch ID information, verifying this transaction originated from the INVBETTERBUY batch (*F3:8*).

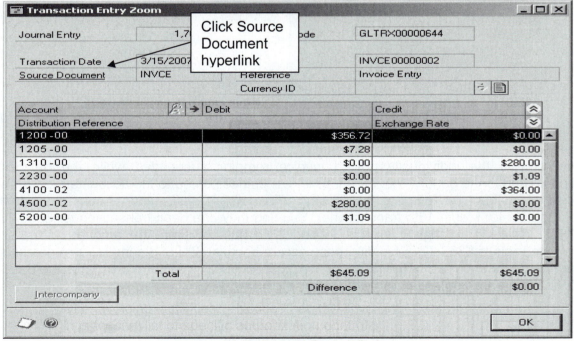

F3:7 Journal Entry Window

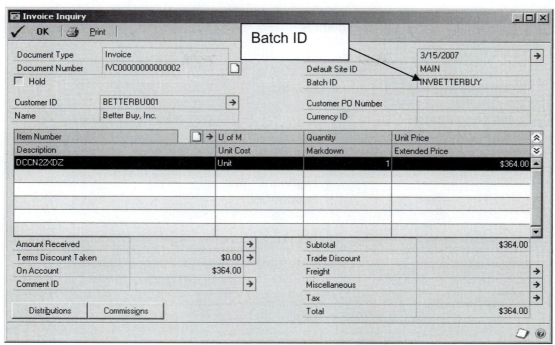

F3:8 Source Document Window

So where is the individual transaction? Remember, method two finalizes only transactions posted in batches and individual postings remain suspended. Click on the *Tools>> Routines>>Master Posting* menu to open the Master Posting window shown in *F3:9*. This window lists suspended and pending items for all Series. (Note: Pending items are saved batches that have not been posted.) Change the Series filter to Financial and find several pending items and one suspended item with the Batch ID beginning with INVCE. (Note: This is the audit trail code for posted sales invoices. Audit trail codes are discussed later in the chapter.)

Highlight this transaction and click the Batch ID hyperlink. The Go To window opens, select General Ledger Batch Entry and click Go To. This opens the window used to enter Financial Series batches (*F3:10*). Look up the INVCE batch and then click the Transactions button. Open the transaction in this batch by following the instructions shown in *F3:11*. Click on the Expand Details icon to see additional information on this transaction.

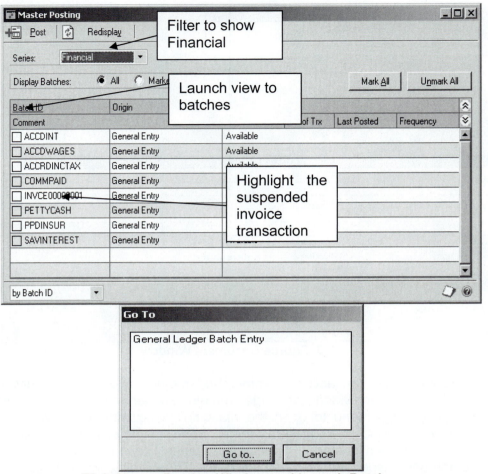

F3:9 Master Posting Window and Launch Batches

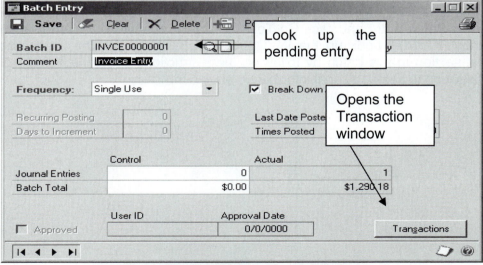

F3:10 Financial Series Batch Window

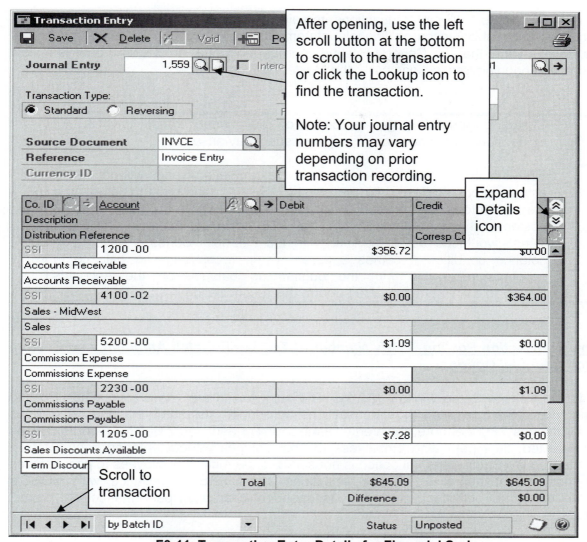

F3:11 Transaction Entry Details for Financial Series

Since this entry is not posted, general ledger accounts can be changed. However, changes made here will not be reflected in the Series used to originate the transaction. (Note: See the warning that follows.)

There is another menu for viewing Financial Series suspended transactions. Click on the *Transactions>>Financial>>Series Post* menu to open the Master Posting window already filtered for items in the Financial Series. From here, the steps used to locate information remain the same. (Note: Each Series contains a menu item for opening the Master Posting window filtered to show only transactions pending in that Series.)

Close the transaction and batch windows, returning to the Master Posting window. Finalize this transaction by checking the box in front of the INVCE entry and clicking Post. The General Posting Journal now prints, confirming the transaction posted to the general ledger. To verify this, return to the accounts receivable inquiry instructions previously used to locate the batch posting and now find both transactions present.

This confirms that individually posted transactions do not affect general ledger accounts until posted a second time. When transactions remain suspended, account balances are not adjusted, thus account balances on financial statements are incorrect. To avoid this kind of mistake, always verify that the General Posting Journal prints after posting and always review suspended and pending transactions using the Master Posting window.

> Changing general ledger accounts on suspended transactions is not recommended because data integrity issues may arise.
>
> First, inquires on posting details within the originating Series will not reflect actual accounts affected by the posting. Second, and most importantly, a transaction could be accidentally deleted in the Financial Series, thus never posted to the general ledger. If this occurred in our example, the Sales Series would be out of balance with the Financial Series. This out-of-balance condition becomes apparent when reconciling the balance in accounts receivable with the outstanding balance on the Accounts Receivable Aging report. We perform this reconciliation in Chapter 5.

2) *Allow Transaction Posting, Verify Number of Trx, Verify Batch Amounts, and Require Batch Approval Options*

Return to the Posting Setup window (*F3:3*). The selection of the Allow Transaction Posting option permits S&S employees to post transactions individually, instead of requiring transactions to post in batches. Furthermore, the Verify Number of Trx and Verify Batch Amounts options are not selected, thus permitting employees to post batches without entering control totals. Finally, the Require Batch Approval option is not selected, permitting employees to post batches without independent approval. These selections affect S&S' compliance with COSO's recommended control activities,[3] particularly independent checks on performance that protect data integrity.

Deny Individual Transaction Posting

We first look at data entry controls that require all transactions to post in batches. Return to the *Tools>>Setup>>Posting>>Posting* menu and change the Series and Origin to those shown in *F3:12*. Uncheck the Allow Transaction Posting option and save. Keep the Posting Setup window open so we can change other options.

---

[3] For an in-depth discussion on COSO's ERM Framework, refer to Marshall Romney and Paul Steinbart, *Accounting Information Systems* (10th ed., Prentice Hall 2006) p. 195.

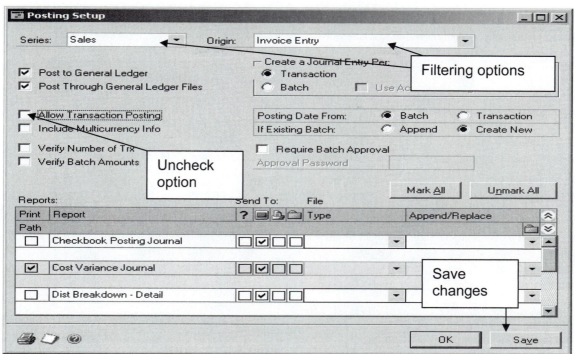

F3:12 Posting Option Denying Individual Transactions

Click on the *Transactions>>Sales>>Invoice Entry* menu and enter the transaction previously illustrated in **F3:4**. Click the Post button and you receive the message shown in **F3:13**.   This message appears because posting setup now denies posting individual transactions. Click OK and Great Plains returns you to the transaction window.

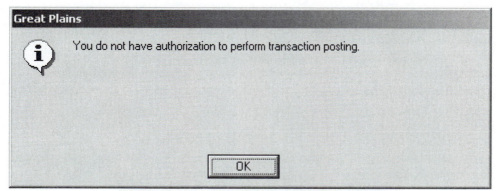

F3:13 Transaction Posting Not Permitted

Saving or deleting this transaction is now your only option. Save the transaction by typing BATCHCONTROL in the Batch ID field. The batch window opens for you to create this batch. Enter a comment and set the Posting Date to 3/16/2007. (Note: This is different than the transaction's date.) Save the batch and transaction, then close both windows.

Require Batch Approval and Control Totals

Return to the Posting Setup window and set the options as shown **F3:14**. Also, set the approval password. Save the changes.

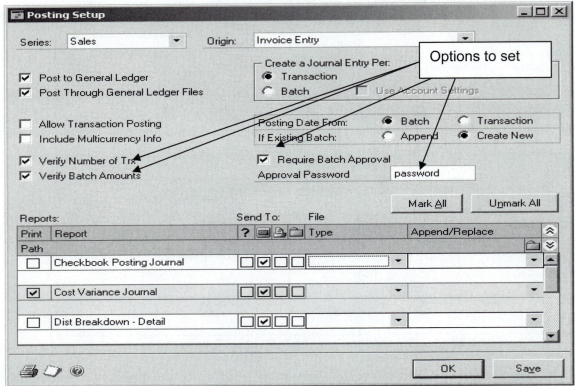

F3:14 Posting Options Requiring Control Totals and Authorization

Return to the *Transactions>>Sales>>Invoicing Batches* menu and look up the *BATCHCONTROL* batch. Click the Post button and the message in *F3:15* appears because approval is now required to post. Click OK.

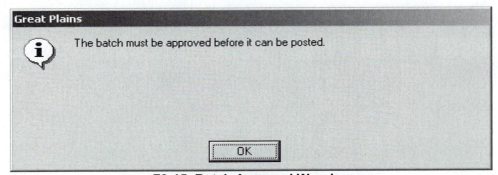

F3:15 Batch Approval Warning

Return to the Batch window, select the Approved option, and enter the password when Great Plains prompts. After accepting this password, Great Plains clears the transaction for posting. Click the Post button again and receive a second message (see *F3:16*) stating batch totals are required. Click OK to return to the Batch window.

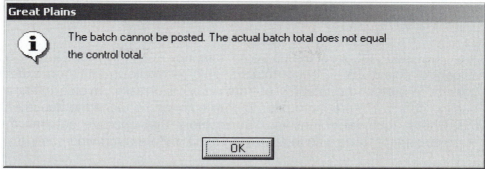

F3:16 Batch Totals Required

Deselect the Approved option to reset the batch. Enter the control totals that correspond to the total number of transactions and the total amount of transactions saved in the batch (see **F3:17**). Again, select Approved and enter the password. Post the entry.

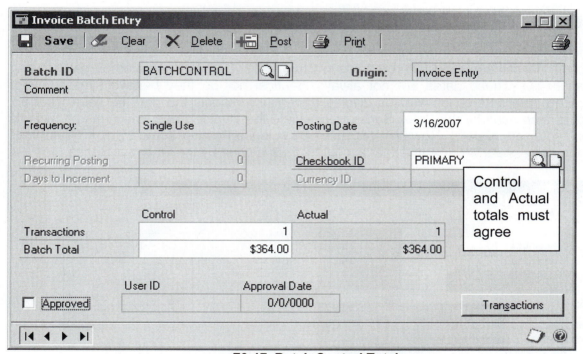

F3:17 Batch Control Totals

You have just experienced Great Plains' batch control features that implement control totals and independent checks on performance. In addition, to implement these controls for all transactions, you must combine batch controls with the first control that forced all transactions to post in batches.

Before leaving this discussion, we want to turn off options to simplify future examples. Return to the Posting Setup window and select Allow Transaction Posting and deselect Require Batch Approval, Verify Number of Trx, and Verify Batch Amounts. Save the changes.

So why not wait until all transactions are entered in the batch and complete the batch control fields?

We just illustrated that Great Plains permit this; however, this procedure fails to serve control objectives. Control totals should reconcile to totals on external documents to protect the integrity of data entry. Normally, invoice totals and transaction counts are prepared prior to data entry and attached to documents. This is where approval comes in. Supervisors that approve batches then compare document totals with totals on the batch before approving posting.

This illustrates that internal control procedures rely on both software controls and procedural controls.

3) _Create a Journal Entry Per, Posting Date From, and If Existing Batch Options_

Open the Posting Setup window for sales invoices (*F3:18*). We first discuss the Posting Date From option. Recall the discussion on dates in Chapter 1? Dates are entered on batches and on transactions. These dates are not always identical nor do they behave similarly. For instance, the date entered on a sales invoice transaction reflects the day the sale occurred. This date is then used by the Sales Series to calculate the invoice's age, which also affects its due date and discount date. However, the date option in the Posting Setup window determines the day the entry posts to general ledger accounts, thus is used by the Financial Series.

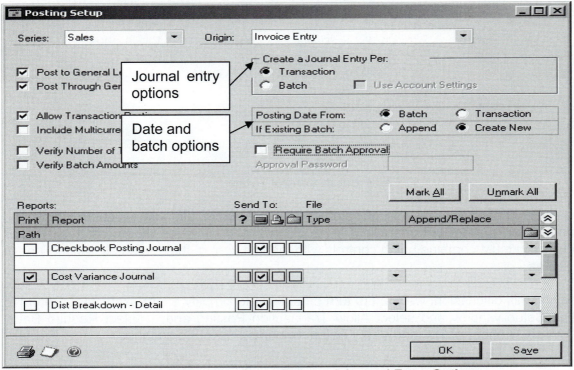

F3:18 Posting Setup Date and Journal Entry Options

S&S uses the Posting Date From the Batch option, thus transactions post to general ledger accounts on the batch date instead of the transaction date. (Note: You can verify this by looking up the accounts receivable entry the batch previously posted. You will find an entry to the account the batch date (3/16/2007) instead of the transaction date (3/15/2007).

The posting date option impacts S&S posting procedures, especially around month-end and year-end. For instance, if a data entry clerk created a batch dated 10/31/2007, but entered transactions for both October and November, all transactions will post to the general ledger as of 10/31/2007. The company now has November transactions on October financial statements, impacting financial reporting and decision making. When erroneous postings are material, financial statements must be restated and financial markets react poorly to this because it shows a lack of internal controls, raising other investor concerns. In addition, management reports are erroneous, impacting company decisions. These issues do not infer Great Plains should not be configured to post using the Batch date. Rather, they emphasize the importance of documenting and complying with internal control procedures and training employees on these procedures.

The If Existing Batch Append option also affects general ledger entries when suspended batches are not timely posted. With Append and the Posting Date From Batch options selected, transactions posted individually will append to suspended batches until batches are finalized. When suspended batches contain October postings and November transactions are then posted, these transactions append to the October batch. Consequently, timing errors occur suspended batches are finalized. S&S uses the Create New option for all Series and Origins, therefore suspended transactions are placed into separate batches.

The Create a Journal Entry Per Transaction option means each transaction in a batch posts a separate entry to the general ledger rather than entering a single entry for the batch. To illustrate, use the *Reports>>Financial>Trial Balance>>Detailed* menu to access the detailed trial balance report. Highlight the Detailed TB report and click Modify. Insert the report options illustrated in *F3:19*.

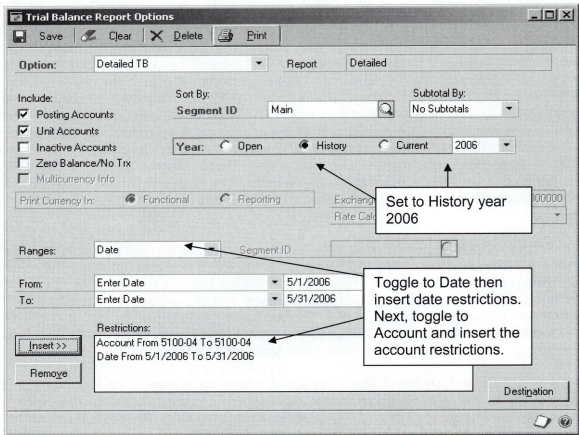

F3:19 Historical Detail Trial Balance

These filters print payroll expense accounts because Ashton originally set the Payroll Series option to Create a Journal Entry Per Transaction. After recording payroll expense for May 15th, he discovered that employee paycheck information posted in detail to the general ledger, compromising the confidentiality of payroll information. To correct the breach, Aston changed the Payroll Series option to Create a Journal Entry Per Batch. Print the report and review the output (*F3:20*), noting the difference in information provided for entries before and after May 15th.

F3:20 General Ledger Pay Details

One final point, the Create Journal Entry Per Transaction requires more disk space than selecting Batch. However, the ability to view transactions in detail often outweighs additional disk space requirements. Thus, when disk space is not of concern, the Transaction feature is the better option.

4) *Reports Options*

The bottom section of the Posting Setup window (*F3:21*) selects control reports that print after posting, as well as printers that receive output. These options provide flexibility in customizing output. For instance, payroll reports and checks can be sent to a printer with controlled access over output and accounts payable checks can be sent to a different printer containing check stock. In addition, companies can customize control report printing to meet internal control objectives. Open the Posting Setup window and review the reports selected for Sales Series Invoice Entry. There are four control reports selected to print after posting.

Take the time review options for other Series and Origins. Be sure to look at report options. Posting reports are invaluable internal control tools used in subsequent chapters.

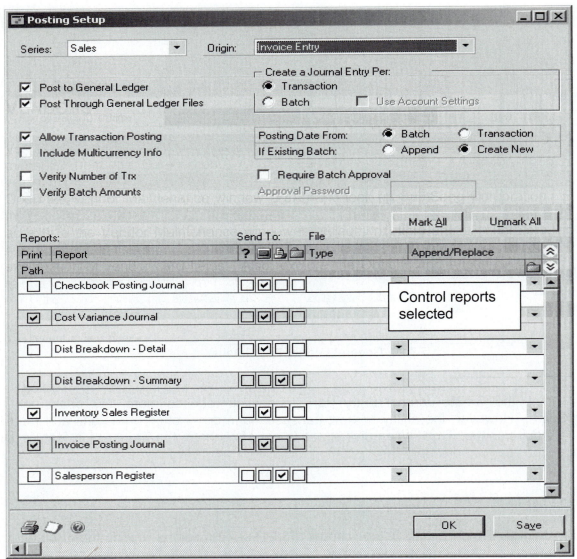

F3:21 Sales Series Invoice Entry Control Reports

THE AUDIT TRAIL

Audit trails are an important component of internal controls. The audit trail documents the source of general ledger postings. Accountants and auditors use the audit trail to trace transactions from the point of origin to the general ledger and vice versa. In Great Plains, the audit trail functions automatically, but can be customized to a limited extent.

Source document codes are the first component of Great Plains' audit trail. These codes identify the transaction's point of origin. For example, did a transaction originate in the Sales or the Purchasing Series? Great Plains supplies source document codes and permits some customization. Source document codes are stored in the window shown in *F3:22*. This window is opened by using the *Tools>> Setup>>Posting>>Source Document* menu. Each Series uses its own set of codes (*F3:23*) to associate transactions with that Series.

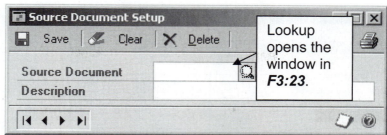

F3:22 Source Document Setup Window

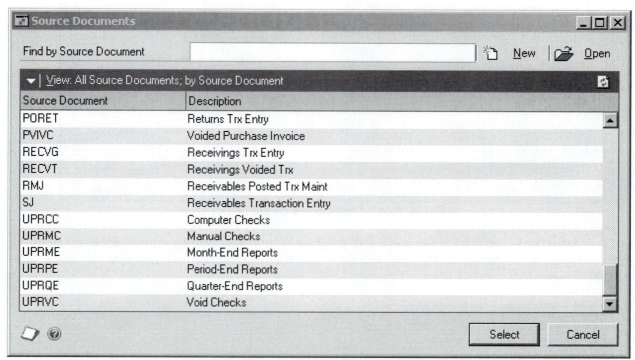

F3:23 Lookup to Source Document Codes

Scroll through source codes in the lookup window and locate the SJ code. SJ is the source document code assigned to transactions posted in the Receivables Transaction Entry window of the Sales Series.

Click on the *Tools>>Setup>>Posting>>Audit Trail Codes* menu, opening the Audit Trail Codes Setup window, and change to display Sales (*F3:24*). Locate the SJ code in the Source Document column. This code appears three times because SJ identifies documents posted as receivables sales, sales transactions, and voided sales transactions. Now look at the Prefix column. This is where the audit trail for SJ codes are distinguished. For instance, sales transactions are assigned the SLSTE prefix, along with a document number. Thus, the next time a sales transaction posts, the audit trail for this transaction will be SLSTE75.

(Note: Document numbers increment each time a transaction posts, therefore your numbers may differ from those illustrated.)

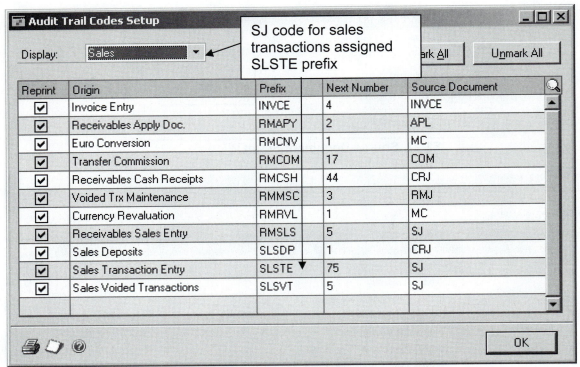

F3:24 Audit Trail Codes Setup Window

Let's review the audit trail. Click on the *Inquiry>>Financial>>Detail* menu, look up account 1200-00 (Accounts Receivable), and highlight the first transaction for January 15, 2007 (see *F3:25*).

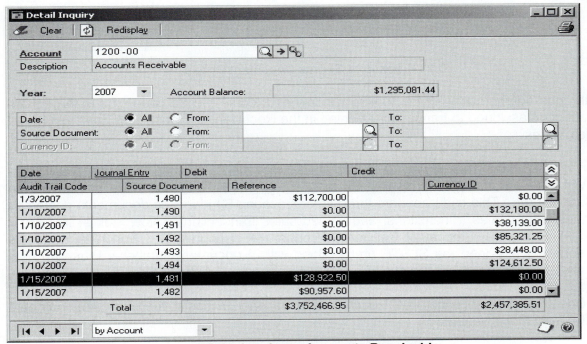

F3:25 Inquiry to Accounts Receivable

Now click the Journal Entry hyperlink and review the information in *F3:26*.

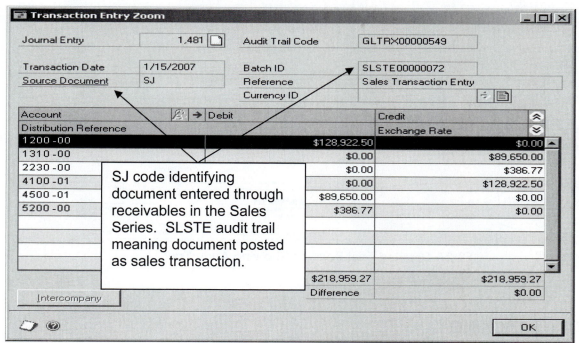

F3:26 Journal Entry Audit Trail Codes

Notice that the inquiry window also shows the audit trail assigned by the Financial Series. This trail was GLTRX00000549 with the Journal Entry number of 1,481. Besides appearing in inquiries, this transaction's audit trail appears on the general ledger detailed trial balance report (*F3:27*).

Become familiar with Great Plains audit trail codes so you can easily identify a transaction's source. Use the *File>>Print* command while in the Audit Trail window to print a list of these codes.

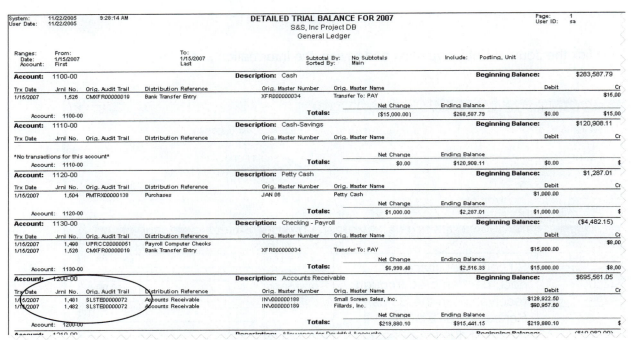

F3:27 Detailed Trial Balance Showing Audit Trail

ACTIVITY TRACKING LOG

Activity tracking logs user activities when activated under the *Tools>>Setup>>System>>Activity Tracking* menu. Open this window and review *T3:1*, explaining activities available for tracking.

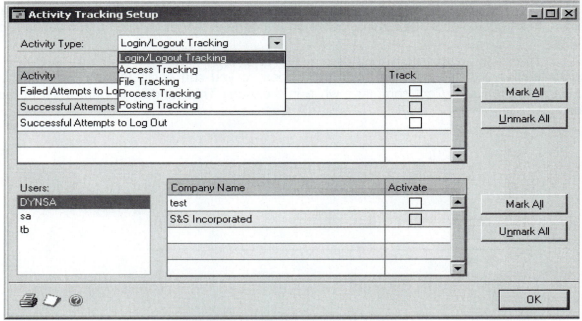

F3:28 Activity Tracking Window

Category	Activity Tracked	Description
Access	Successful and failed attempts to open a table, window, or print a report	When Great Plains security is active, this category tracks successful and denied attempts.
Login/Logout	Successful login/logouts and failed logins	Reports login and logout activities.
File Tracking	Additions/deletions/ modifications to master, setup and transaction tables.	Reports on user Save, Delete, and OK button selections.
Process	Table maintenance, routines, and utilities processes	Reports on table maintenance routines such as rebuilding files, checking links, clearing data, and shrinking file sizes.
Posting	Posting activities	Reports transaction postings by Series.

T3:1 Activity Tracking Categories

Activities are tracked by highlighting the user's ID and then selecting an activity for tracking. After activating, reports are prepared using the *Reports>>System>>General* menu. Since tracking consumes additional hard drive space, companies seldom activate successful attempts to log in or out of Great Plains.

Reports on user activities are printed from the *Tools>>Utilities>>System Menu>>Activity Details* menu. You can also clear activity histories using this window (see **F3:29**). You can print reports for all users or by specific user or date range. The options at the bottom of the window specify whether you are printing a report or removing tracking history.

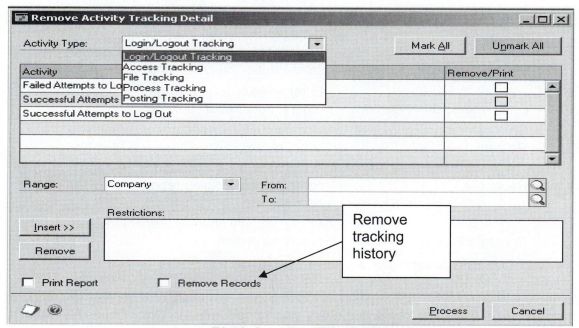

F3:29 Security Activity Reporting

SYSTEM MANAGER SECURITY

The System Manager Series controls Great Plains security. System Manager security is implemented by creating user IDs and granting users permission to access company databases and to perform activities in the database. For some companies, security is implemented by the controller or chief accountant. For other organizations, chief information officers (CIOs) implement and internal audit departments review security. Since accountants play a vital role in developing and monitoring company security, it is important for you to understand software security.

Prior to implementing, an Access Control Matrix is developed for use in creating user IDs, and granting user permissions to authorize master records, to post transactions, and to produce reports. The _sa_ account then implements Great Plains security using the control matrix. Great Plains security serves internal control objectives by enforcing segregation of duties. *T3:2* is provided to aide in understanding segregation of duties from a Great Plains perspective.

Category	Great Plains Activity	Examples
Authorization	Create or delete master records	Add customer, delete vendor, create general ledger account, etc.
	Implement security	Create/delete users and assign permissions
	Approve Transactions	Approve batches, perform write-offs, enter a discount, etc.
	Field controls	Establish customer credit limits, payment terms, override pricing, permit sales exceeding credit limit, etc.
Recording	Enter and post transactions	Enter sales orders, change purchase orders, post transaction, etc.
	Change non-critical master file data	Update customer addresses, employee address, etc.
	Reconcile	Prepare bank reconciliations, perform comparisons of aging reports to control account, etc.
Custody	Print information	Print company checks, preprinted purchase orders, etc

T3:2 Great Plains Activities Segregated into Duties

This table is not all-inclusive. In addition, reporting and inquiries will appear under both authorization and recording. The key is that every activity performed in Great Plains fits within a segregation of duties category. Chapter 6 of Romney and Steinbart's _Accounting Information_

Systems discusses segregation of duties.[4] You should also review Chapters 10 through 14 for information on internal control concerns by accounting cycle.

The next topic illustrates using System Manager security to control user access and user permissions. The Financial, Sales, Purchasing, Inventory Control, and Payroll Series provide additional controls that are discussed in subsequent chapters.

ADVANCED SECURITY: USER ACCOUNTS AND PERMISSIONS

The System Manager provides an advanced security tool to assist in creating users and defining user permissions. This tool is opened from the *Tools>>Setup>>System>>Advanced Security* menu. (Remember, the password to access System Manager menus is *sa*.) The Advanced Security window, illustrated in *F3:30*, contains two sections. The left section lists Great Plains activities by category and the right section shows company databases and user login accounts. The plus symbol expands activity categories to show specific activities for the category.

CAUTION: Exercises performed in this topic must be completed prior to porting the database to a new computer. Unfortunately, user IDs are not copied with database files. Consequently, user IDs existing in the Advanced Security window (other than *sa*) are for illustrative purposes only. These IDs are not recognized as valid login accounts.

Highlight the *sa* account on the right and expand the Posting Permissions category on the left. You now see a list of posting activities by installed Series. Expand the Sales Series to view a list of posting activities within this Series. To grant user permission to an activity, highlight the user's ID and check the activity. For instance, to permit April Levine to post sales transactions, except commission transfers, highlight her account on the right, check the box in front of the Sales folder, and then uncheck the Transfer Commission envelope.

The System menu provides other ways of creating users and configuring security, however, you must use either the individual menu paths or the advanced security tool. Our discussion is limited to the security tool since it provides a more efficient method for assigning permissions.

Expand the activities under the by Menu category. Controlling access to Great Plains menus is another method used to set permissions. When users cannot open a menu, the user also cannot access any menu items. Sometimes this is the quickest way to customize permissions.

---

[4] Marshall Romney and Paul Steinbart, *Accounting Information Systems* (10th ed., Prentice Hall 2006).

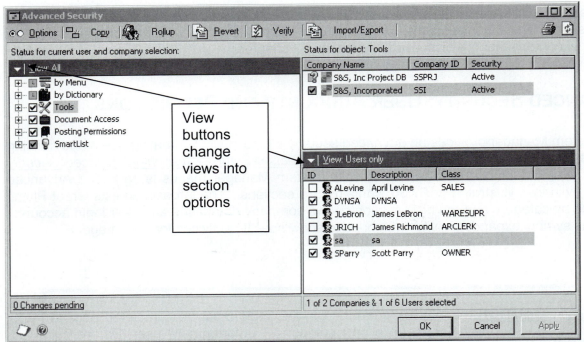

F3:30 Advanced Security Window

While Great Plains permits implementing security by user ID, this method is inefficient for large numbers of users. A more efficient method is assigning permissions to classes of users. This is performed by creating a class, setting permissions for the class, and then assigning users to the class. For instance, S&S has several sales clerks with permission to post sales transactions and to perform sales inquiries. These permissions can be granted by creating a sales clerk class, assigning permissions to the class, and then assigning these sales clerks' IDs to the class. Let's implement this example.

First, use a couple of shortcuts to open the window that creates classes. Highlight JRich (or any user) on the right and double-click to open the User Setup window. Next, click Clear to reset the User Setup window and then click the Class ID hyperlink that opens the User Class Setup window. In the User Class Setup window, type <u>SALESCLERK</u> into the Class ID field and supply the description shown in *F3:31*. Since class permissions will be assigned using the Advanced Security window, click Save and close the User Class Setup window. This returns you to the User Setup window.

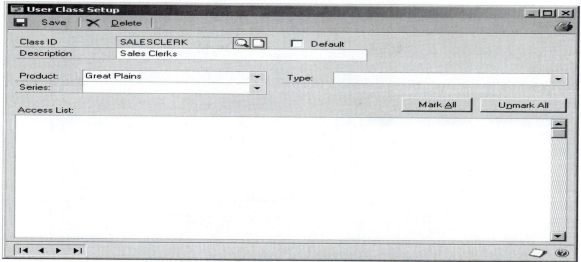

F3:31 User Class Setup Window

In the User Setup window, create the new user shown in *F3:32* and choose a password. Be sure to assign Susan to the <u>SALESCLERK</u> class. Click Save when finished and close this window.

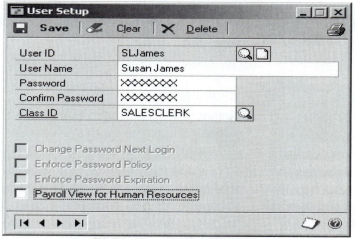

F3:32 User Setup Window

You are now back to the Advanced Security window and ready to set permissions for the new class. To see the new class, change the View to either Classes or All. Now, all that remains to grant Susan permission to post sales and view sales transactions is selecting these activities on the left. We will not complete this portion of the example because this task is reserved for an end of chapter exercise. Just remember, when setting permissions, the <u>SALESCLERK</u> class must be highlighted before selecting the activity.

Granting Susan permission to perform activities does not complete her security. She must also be granted access to a company to perform these activities. To grant company access, double-click one of the company names appearing on the right, opening the window shown in **F3:33**. Highlight Susan's ID on the left and then check the Access box for the company. Click OK to return to the Advanced Security window.

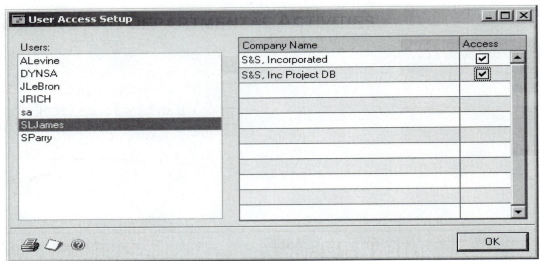

F3:33 Company Access Permission

Before leaving Advanced Security, expand the Smart List category. Without restricting access to these activities, users are permitted to view restricted data. For instance, despite restricting access to payroll menus, failure to deny payroll in the Smart List permits users to still view payroll data. Be careful to test a user's ID before turning it over for login. While Advanced Security makes setting user permissions fairly simple, there is still some degree of expertise required. *T3:3* explains permissions set within Advanced Security. Click OK when finished with reviewing the advanced security window.

Type	Purpose	Explanation
Toolbar	Control menu access	Activities correspond to menu items. Denying access to a menu means users will not be able to perform any activities on the menu.
Dictionary	Control access to forms, reports, and tables used by each Series	Forms are the windows used to enter, modify, and deleting transactions. Great Plains recommends not restricting access to tables because this may affect reporting and create conflicts when entering data.[5]
Tools	Control permission to modify forms, reports, and data	Includes report writer used to customize forms and reports and the data import utility.
Document Access	Control permission to modify document templates	Document templates provide the layout of forms and reports.
Posting Permissions	Control transaction posting	Restricts access to posting, but not the ability to enter transactions.
Smart List	Control views into transactional data	Despite other restrictions, data can still be viewed without restriction Smart List access.

T3:3 Permission Category Features

---

[5] Chapter 2, Level Two explains why restricting table security may produce errors during data entry.

The final step to activating security is activated the Security option in the window accessed using the *Tools>>Setup>>Company>>Company* menu. For S&S, this feature is already activated. However, left unchecked, Great Plains reminds you to activate security upon exiting Advanced Security.

SECURITY REPORTING

Security reporting is accessed using the *Reports>>System* menu. Reports are classified into user, general, and group categories. These categories are explained in *T3:4*.

Categories	Purpose
User	Reports user permissions, class assignments, and company access permissions.
General	Reports system-wide settings and current activity.
Groups	Group the above reports for printing multiple reports simultaneously.

T3:4 Security Reporting Categories

These reports are printed to document security and reviewed for compliance with internal controls objectives.

LEVEL ONE EXERCISES

1. Using Posting Setup, name the control reports Ashton selected to print after period ending the Payroll Series.

2. You are training a new accounts payable clerk. Describe batch processing to the clerk and explain the company's month-end procedures for posting vendor invoices when the Posting Date From option for the Purchasing Series is set to Batch.

3. Ashton asks you to explain the difference between the Post to General Ledger and the Post Through General Ledger options under Posting Setup.

4. The only information you have on a transaction comes from the following detail trial balance.

Trx Date	Jrnl No.	Orig. Audit Trail	Distribution Reference	Orig. Master Number	Orig. Master Name	Debit
5/16/2006	666	PMCHK00000012	Accounts Payable	983	Office Rex, Inc.	$2,303.15

a. What can you tell Ashton about the transaction by just looking at the report?

b. Can you provide addition information after using Great Plains to research the transaction? Please explain.

LEVEL TWO EXERCISES

1. Develop an Access Control Matrix for the User Class called <u>APCLERKS</u>. Open the Advanced Security window and refer to *T3:2* to develop your recommendations. Also, refer to the permission categories on the left side of the Advanced Security window when listing <u>APCLERKS</u> permissions.

AP Clerks Access Control Matrix for Great Plains		
Category	**Sub Categories**	**Item**
By Menu		
View		
Tools		
Transactions		
Inquiry		
Reports		
By Dictionary		Great Plains recommends full access
Tools		
Document Access		
Posting Permissions		
Smart List		

2. Use your Access Control Matrix from above and the Advanced Security window to implement security for the <u>APCLERKS</u> class. Remember to first create the class and then set permissions. Print a security report showing these permissions.

3. You need to add Betsy Lane as a user. Create <u>BLANE</u> as the User ID and assign a password. In addition, place Betsy in the <u>APCLERKS</u> class.

4. Discuss the advantages of assigning permissions to user classes instead of individual users.

5. When you created the <u>APCLERKS</u> class, did you grant permission to enter purchasing transactions and to print checks? Justify your answer by referring to segregation of duties.

6. Login with the User ID, <u>BLANE</u> and test her security. Explain what you learned from this exercise.

CHAPTER 4: INVENTORY CONTROL SERIES

CHAPTER OVERVIEW

Our journey has progressed through the traditional path of implementing a computerized accounting system. First, we installed the software and then became familiar with the Great Plains interface. We learned to create company master records such as general ledger accounts and customers. We gathered knowledge on Series integration and transaction posting. Finally, we implemented Great Plains security and worked with posting setup controls. We now focus on inventory sold to customers.

As discussed in Chapter 1, S&S is a distributor of small electronics. Therefore, the company's business activities revolve around inventory. Accordingly, our task is to learn the Inventory Control Series. Ashton has created inventory master records and recorded current stock levels. Once again, the table of inventory items is located in Appendix B. In addition, remember that S&S sells to customers located throughout the United States and owns a fleet of delivery trucks for shipping customer orders.

This chapter covers:
- ➢ Inventory setup, including valuation, pricing methods, unit of measure schedules, and inventory classes
- ➢ Maintaining inventory items, price lists, and associating preferred vendors to inventory items
- ➢ Recording inventory adjustments and physical counts
- ➢ Performing inventory inquiries and printing reports

Since inventory is the basis of S&S' business model, this chapter is directed towards both Level One and Level Two readers.

INVENTORY SETUP

Before using the Inventory Control Series, we become familiar with Series setup. Click on the path *Tools>>Setup>>Inventory>>Inventory Control* and open the Inventory Control Setup window. **F4:1** serves as the backdrop for discussing inventory controls. The following describes the options that are not self-explanatory.

User Category creates optional fields on inventory items, such as special handling procedures for items containing hazardous materials or requiring refrigeration. Next Document Number initializes document control numbers assigned to inventory adjustment, transfer, variance, and production transactions. Recall that document control numbers are part of the audit trail discussed in Chapter 3. Default Decimal Places set inventory item quantity and currency defaults. Override options determine whether users can override default entries to fields during transaction entry. Finally, the Enable Multiple Bins option lets companies track items by bins.

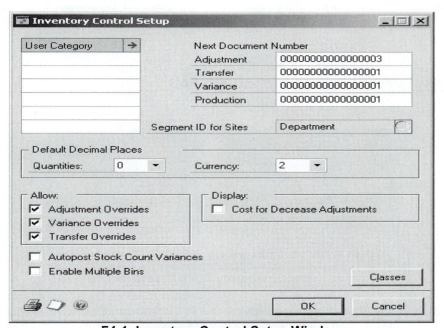

F4:1 Inventory Control Setup Window

S&S uses a simple inventory structure. Inventory purchases are nontaxable since S&S is a wholesaler and items are stored in one warehouse. The <u>Main</u> ID identifies this location and was created using the *Cards>>Inventory>>Site* menu (see **F4:2**). At this stage, S&S does not use bins or serial numbers to track inventory, however, Great Plains is scalable and these features can be activated at any time in the future.

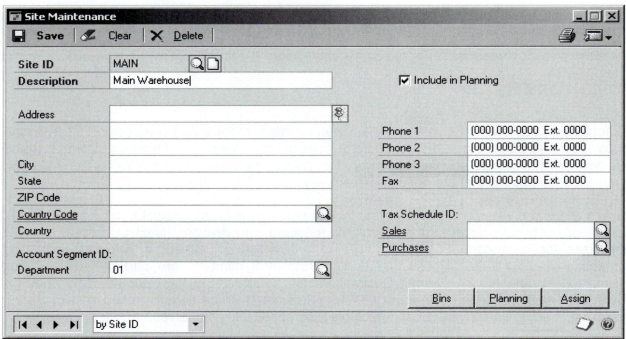

F4:2 Inventory Site Maintenance Window

S&S uses one price level, assigned the ID of WHOLE. Price levels are located under the *Tools>>Setup>>Inventory>>Price Level* menu, see **F4:3**.

F4:3 Inventory Price Levels

S&S is a bulk distributor, thus purchases inventory in large quantities. Consequently, S&S has several units of measure (UOM) schedules. These schedules are located under the *Tools>>Setup>>Inventory>>Unit of Measure Schedule* menu. Open the Unit of Measure Schedule Setup window (**F4:4**) and review existing schedules. We will see the interplay of schedules when performing tasks in the Purchasing Series chapter.

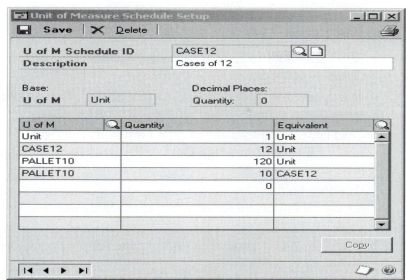

F4:4 Unit of Measure Schedule Setup Window

In addition, Ashton created item classes that group inventory items sharing similar attributes. The Item Class Setup window is accessed from the *Tools>>Setup>> Inventory>>Item Class* menu. (You can also open this window using the Classes button on the Inventory Control Setup window in *F4:1.*)

Item classes speed data entry for new items and help ensure data consistency among similar items.   Furthermore, item classes assist in analyzing inventory sales and purchasing data. Classes work by auto-filling several fields on new inventory records.   Our discussion works with the CARAUD class. Pull up this class and review *T4:1* for descriptions on class fields.

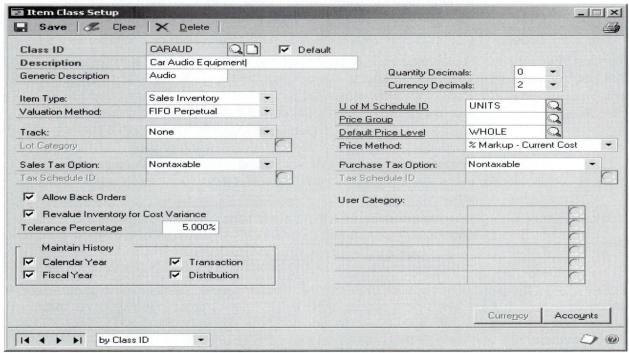

F4:5 CARAUD Inventory Class

Item Class Field	Description
ClassID	Primary key that uniquely identify the class.
Description	Class description.
Item Type	The type of inventory linked to the class. The dropdown list reveals other types such as discontinued, kit, and services.
Valuation Method	Traditional inventory valuation methods recognized by GAAP such as LIFO, FIFO, and Average Cost. S&S uses FIFO Perpetual for all inventory.
Track	Optional field for tracking items by serial or lot numbers. For instance, it may be important to track cell phones by serial number or baby food by lot number.
Sales Tax Option	Items are either taxable or nontaxable. As previously discussed, S&S' inventory is nontaxable.
U of M Schedule ID	Links an item to the UOM schedule discussed previously.
Price Group and Default Price Level	Links an item to S&S' price level table. S&S offers customers a single price level of WHOLE; however, many companies offer a variety of customer pricing options such as volume discounts or specials. For these companies, price groups are also assigned to items.
Price Method	Determines an item's sales price. The Inventory Control Series tracks item costs from purchases made in the Purchasing Series. However, price method calculates the item's sales price. S&S uses the %Markup-Current Cost method to determine sales prices. With this method, Great Plains refers to the item's price list and obtains a mark-up percentage. This percentage is then applied against the items cost to determine the sales price. Consequently, an item's sales price changes with increases and decreases in inventory costs.
Allow Back Orders	Option that permits back orders on sales of out of stock items.
Revalue Inventory for Cost Variance with Tolerance Percentage	Revalues inventory cost when the purchase variance exceeds the tolerance percentage. For instance, the CARAUD class tells Great Plains that a purchase variance on items for the class posts to the inventory asset account (instead of the purchase variance expense account) when the purchase price exceeds 5% an item's current cost. Thus, Great Plains revalues the item's inventory cost. In Chapter 6, we demonstrate the effect of this setting on inventory sales pricing, especially where weak internal controls fail to protect vendor invoice entry.
Maintain History	Options to retain historical transactions. Selecting options lets S&S print historical reporting.

T4:1 Item Class Field Descriptions

Before closing the class window, click the Accounts button. Great Plains looks to general ledger accounts shown in *F4:6* when posting transactions. In later chapters, you discover that other Series also contains default accounts. In addition, the *Tools>> Setup>>Posting>>Posting Accounts* menu opens a window that also stores default accounts.

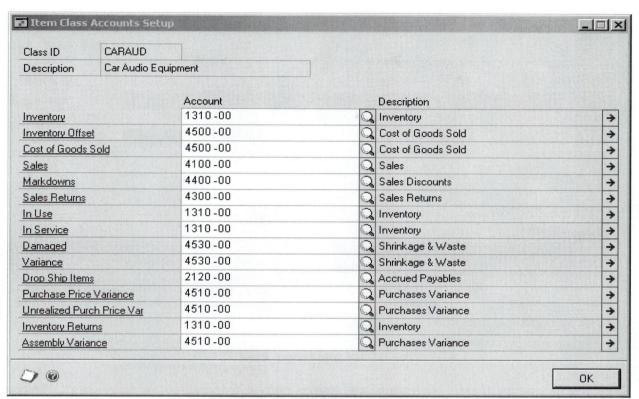

F4:6 Item Class Accounts

In Chapter 6, we differentiate the various locations storing general ledger default accounts. For now, understand that Great Plains cannot post a transaction without being supplied a general ledger account and Ashton instructed Great Plains to post sales transactions using customer card defaults instead of inventory card defaults. Therefore, default accounts appearing on inventory items are used when posting transactions originating in the Inventory Control Series.

INVENTORY ITEM CARDS

With Inventory Control under our belt, let's look at inventory master records. The _Cards>> Inventory>>Item_ menu opens the Item Maintenance window for these records. Pull up the first item, AUDJV50WMP3 (see **F4:7**). Many of the fields are already familiar from the previous topic. Notice this card's class is CARAUD; therefore, several field values defaulted from the class record. However, values in a field can be changed for the item without affecting the class.

The item card also contains the quantity on hand and the quantity available. The quantity available will be less than the quantity on-hand when there are sales orders for the item because Great Plains does not reduce quantity on hand until invoicing the customer. Thus, Great Plains flags quantities mitigating the threat of selling items already promised to a customer.

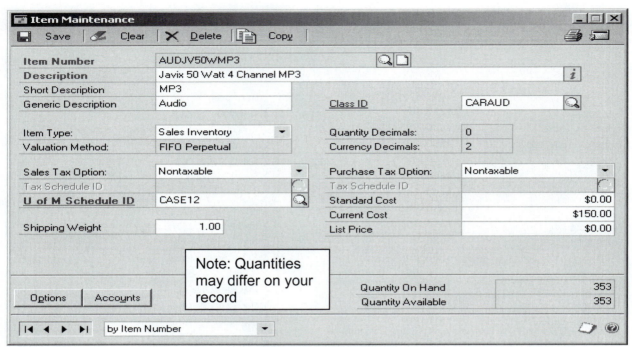

F4:7 Inventory Item Card

Click the Accounts button, revealing the item's default general ledger accounts. These accounts transferred from the item's class. Once again, accounts can be changed for an item without affecting the class. Close the Accounts window.

Next, notice the item's Standard Cost value. When using a standard cost pricing method, the item's standard cost is entered here. S&S does not use standard costing; therefore, the field is empty. There is also a value under the Current Cost field. This value defaults from the last price posted from a vendor's invoice. Under S&S' pricing structure, this cost also affects inventory sales pricing. (Note: It may help to refer back to *T4:1*.)

Click the Options button to open the window shown in *F4:8*. This window contains additional fields relevant to the item. The Maintain History options defaulted from the class and the Allow Back Orders defaulted from inventory setup options. Close this window.

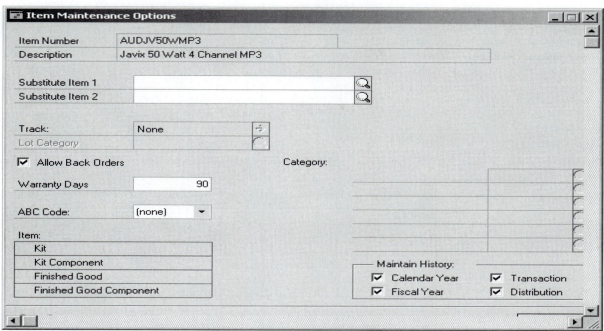

F4:8 Item Maintenance Options Window

The scroll buttons on the lower left of the item window moves to other records in the inventory table. In addition, you can change the default sort of "by Item Number" to a different sort option to change the scrolling method. Take a few minutes to review other items.

INVENTORY PRICING

Click on the *Cards>>Inventory>>Price List* menu to open a pricing record and locate AUDJV50WMP3 (*F4:9*). As previously discussed, S&S uses a percentage markup on current cost to calculate an item's sales price. With this option, the item's price record must supply the markup percent for each price level. WHOLE is the only pricing method used by S&S; therefore, one percentage appears for this item. The $195 selling price for this item is calculated by multiplying item's current cost of $150 by 1.30%. While S&S uses the same pricing method on all items, scroll through the records and notice that the company applies different markup percentages.

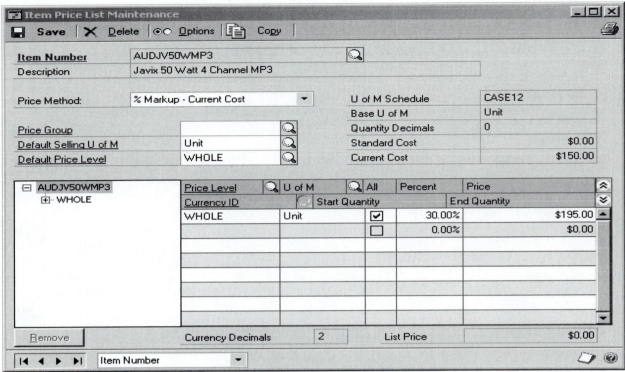

F4:9 Price List Maintenance Window

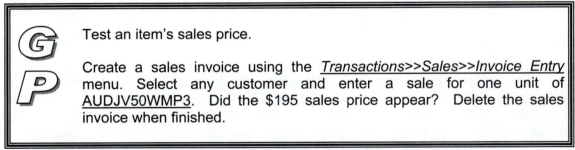

Test an item's sales price.

Create a sales invoice using the *Transactions>>Sales>>Invoice Entry* menu. Select any customer and enter a sale for one unit of AUDJV50WMP3. Did the $195 sales price appear? Delete the sales invoice when finished.

E4:1 Test an Item's Sales Price

INVENTORY VENDORS

S&S links vendors to item records, restricting purchases in the Purchasing Series. The *Cards>>Inventory>>Vendors* menu opens the window used to create this link (*F4:10*). After opening, look up AUDJV50WMP3. Now change the Vendor Lookup option to Assigned and click the vendor lookup icon, finding only one vendor linked to this item. Click Select.

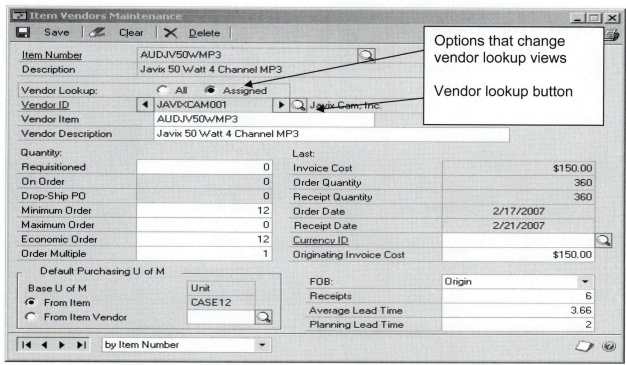

F4:10 Vendor / Item Link

The item-vendor link supplies defaults for orders placed with Javix and information on the last purchase. You can link additional vendors to this item by changing the Vendor Lookup option to All, clicking the vendor lookup button, and selecting another Vendor ID.

Besides linking items to vendors, S&S also creates a preferred vendor link after ranking vendors based on product quality, uniqueness, pricing, and reliability. This link is created by using the *Cards>>Inventory>>Quantities/Sites* menu to open the window shown in ***F4:11***. After opening, set the window's options as illustrated and lookup the item. The window displays the preferred vendor in the item's Primary Vendor ID field.

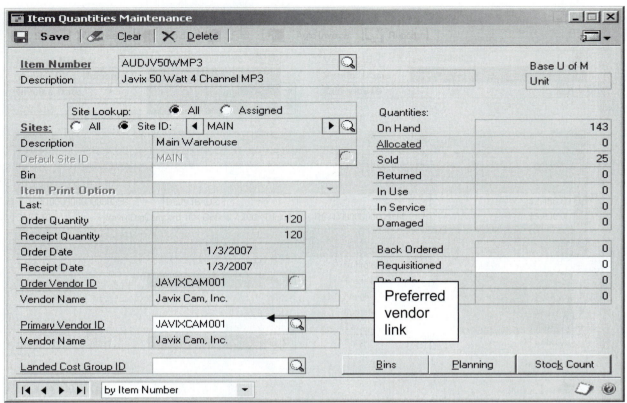

F4:11 Item Preferred Vendor Link

We just illustrated linking an item to vendors and setting the preferred vendor. We could have also set the preferred vendor first and let Great Plains create the item-vendor link. The item-vendor link and preferred vendor settings play different roles in controlling inventory purchases. For instance, when S&S generates a purchase order in the Sales Series, Great Plains assigns the order to the item's preferred vendor. In addition, the item-vendor link restricts item purchases in the Purchasing Series to vendors linked to the items. We revisit these features in Chapters 5 and 6.

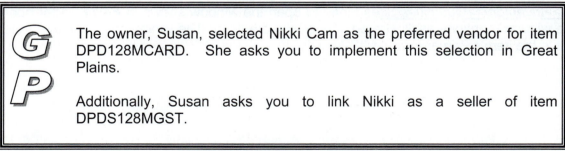

The owner, Susan, selected Nikki Cam as the preferred vendor for item DPD128MCARD. She asks you to implement this selection in Great Plains.

Additionally, Susan asks you to link Nikki as a seller of item DPDS128MGST.

E4:2 Practice Assigning Vendors

INVENTORY ADJUSTMENTS

Inventory quantities primarily adjust through customer sales and vendor purchases. However, on occasion a company adjusts quantities using the Inventory Control Series, particularly after taking a physical inventory or discovering damaged or obsolete items. The *Transactions>>Inventory>>Transaction Entry* or *Batch* menus open the window used to record inventory adjustment and variance transactions (**F4:12**).

Adjustments can be used for adjusting on-hand quantities for changes in inventory after paying a vendor's invoice. For instance, after paying a vendor invoice, you return some of the items. Since the invoice is paid, the vendor issues a credit memo. The credit memo is then posted in the Purchasing Series and the inventory reduction recorded as an adjustment. Adjustments that reduce on-hand quantities are entered as negative amounts.

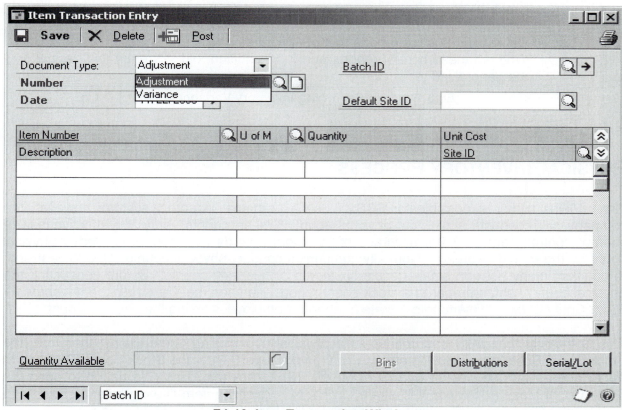

F4:12 Item Transaction Window

On the other hand, variances track changes to on-hand quantities due to damage or obsolescence. These entries are also entered as negative quantities when reducing on-hand inventory; however, Great Plains selects the general ledger account for shrinkage and waste to post the loss.

Lost inventory is another cause for reducing inventory; however, these reductions are often uncovered only after a physical inventory. In the next topic, we record differences identified after a physical count.

On March 18, 2007, Ashton discovered one damaged Nikki digital camcorder. The item number is DCNK4XDZ. Enter this transaction, but before posting, check the default general ledger accounts that will be used for posting. Notice that this entry will post the variance amount to the shrinkage and waste account.

This transaction is an example of when Great Plains selects general ledger accounts from the item card instead of the customer card. However, S&S instructed Great Plains to use customer card general ledger accounts when posting sales of inventory.

Since the accounts are correct, close the window. Always verify a transaction's accounts when recording nonroutine entries. While default accounts serve the majority of entries, the default is not always correct.

Review the posting reports that print after closing the transaction window. Why did these control reports print? In addition, did this entry finalize in the general ledger?

E4:3 Practice Recording Inventory Variance

PHYSICAL INVENTORY PROCESS

Great Plains makes it possible for S&S to use a perpetual inventory system; however, the company still conducts a periodic physical count. These counts verify the effectiveness of internal controls, ensuring the accuracy of inventory records. Ashton scheduled a physical count for the end of February. Normally companies conduct physical counts close to year-end. In addition, many perform smaller scale six-month or quarterly counts. Before conducting the physical count, Ashton prepared a stock count report. He used the *Transactions>>Inventory>> Stock Count Schedule* menu to generate a report for employees taking the physical count.

This is the first time S&S has conducted a physical count using Great Plains; therefore, the Stock Count Schedule window is empty. To create a report, enter the Stock Count ID shown in **F4:13** and assign the Default Site ID of MAIN. Next, click the Mass Add button to open the Stock Count Mass Add window illustrated in **F4:14**. Enter the item filtering criteria shown and click Insert. Click the Add button to add items for the Stock Count Schedule window.

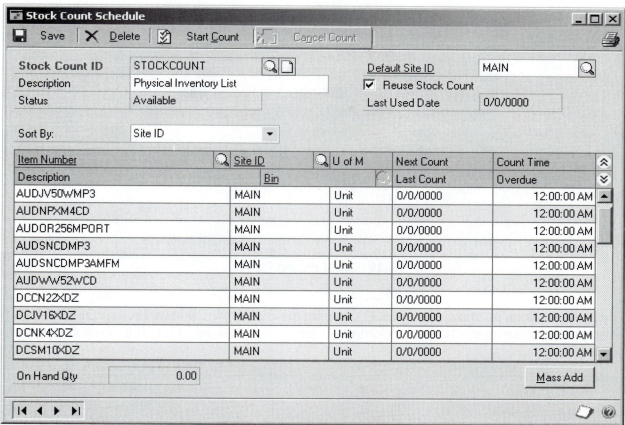

F4:13 Stock Count Schedule Window

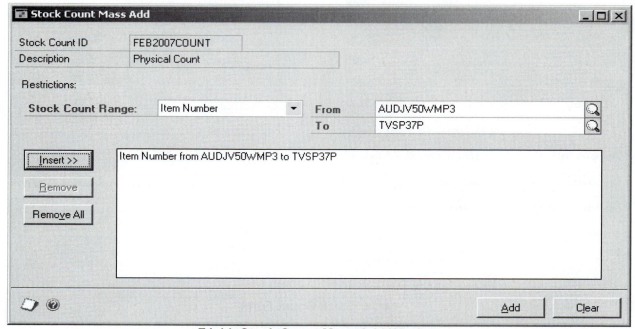

F4:14 Stock Count Mass Add Window

Click Save to store the schedule, then click the Start Count button to schedule the count and generate the stock count report. The Stock Count Print Options window appears in *F4:15*.

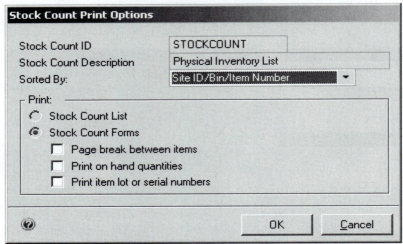

F4:15 Count Report Options

Leave the settings as shown and click OK to print the report. The first report to print confirms no existing exceptions in the Inventory Control Series. Close this report and the Stock Count Form prints (*F4:16*).

```
System:      9/7/2005     12:05:20 AM              S&S, Inc Project DB                    Page:      1
User Date:   9/7/2005                              STOCK COUNT FORM                       User ID:   sa
                                                   Inventory Control

Stock Count ID:    STOCKCOUNT       Physical Inventory List              Counted By:        _____
Status:            Started                                               Count Start Date:    9/7/2005
Reuse Stock Count: Yes                                                   Count Start Time:    12:04:39 AM

Sorted By:    Site ID / Bin / Item Number

Print Options:
              Do not page break between items
              Do not print item lot and serial numbers
              Do not print on hand quantities

Site ID                       Bin
   Item Number                Description              Base U of M       Counted Qty U of M Date Counted Time Counted
      Lot or Serial           Lot/Serial Number                          Counted Lot/Serial Qty
--------------------------------------------------------------------------------------------------------------
MAIN

   AUDJV50WMP3                Javix 50 Watt 4 Channel MP3     Unit        _____ _____ _____ _____

   AUDNPXM4CD                 NeerPio XM Ready 4 Channel CD R/ Unit       _____ _____ _____ _____

   AUDOR256MPORT              ORI 256MG Portable Digital Audio Unit       _____ _____ _____ _____

   AUDSNCDMP3                 Sunyung CD/MP3/ATRAC3           Unit        _____ _____ _____ _____

   AUDSNCDMP3AMFM             Sunyung Portable CD/MP3/AM/FM/TV Unit       _____ _____ _____ _____

   AUDWW52WCD                 WAWA 52 Watt X4 Channel Car Ster Unit       _____ _____ _____ _____

   DCCN22XDZ                  Canyon DigCamcord 22X Optical /  Unit       _____ _____ _____ _____

   DCJV16XDZ                  Javix DigCamcord 16X Optical / 7 Unit       _____ _____ _____ _____
```

F4:16 Stock Count Form

Notice the presence of several control features on this report. First, the items do not reveal the quantities on hand. Consequently, employees must actually count items to enter quantities, thus controlling employee performance. In addition, the report contains an area for initialing and date/time stamping the count, thus implementing employee accountability. Ashton distributes a copy of this report to each employee performing the count. In addition, Ashton could customize this report to show items assigned by employee.

After the count, Ashton inputs employee results using the Stock Count Entry window (*F4:17*). This window is opened using the *Transactions>>Inventory>>Stock Count Entry* menu. Set Great Plains' system date to 3/1/2007 so entries post as of this date, then open the window and lookup the STOCKCOUNT schedule.

The reports turned in by employees indicate two items with quantity discrepancies. The variances occurred in items AUDNPXM4CD (down 5) and AUDSNCDMP3 (down 2). Counted quantities are not provided for you because your numbers may vary based on your activity to date. Therefore, use your window's variance quantities as the counted quantities, except the two items with discrepancies. With these items, make sure the AUDNPXM4CD shows 5 and the AUDSNCDMP3 shows 2 as the variance quantities.

Before posting, select the Autopost Stock Count Variances option and then click the Distribution button to ensure variances will post to the shrinkage and waste account. When finished reviewing, click Process to post and review the posting reports.

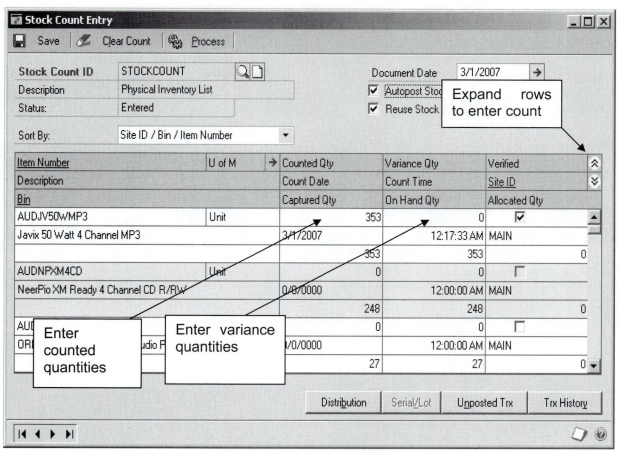

F4:17 Stock Count Entry Window

INVENTORY INQUIRY AND REPORTING

Oftentimes employees need to review inventory to gather information on item receipts, item allocations, and quantities on-hand.   This information is available through the *Inquiry>> Inventory>>Item* menu. (Remember from Chapter 3, inquiry menus are the place to view information.)   Review information that is available through the *Inquiry>>Inventory>>Item* menu (**F4:18**) and the *Inquiry>>Inventory>>Item Allocation* menu (**F4:19**).

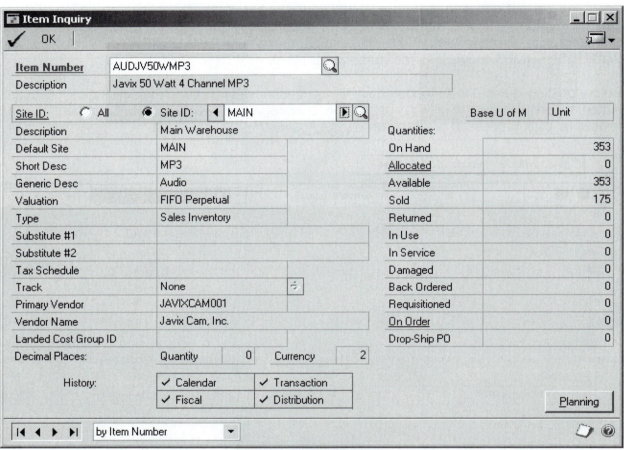

F4:18 Item Information

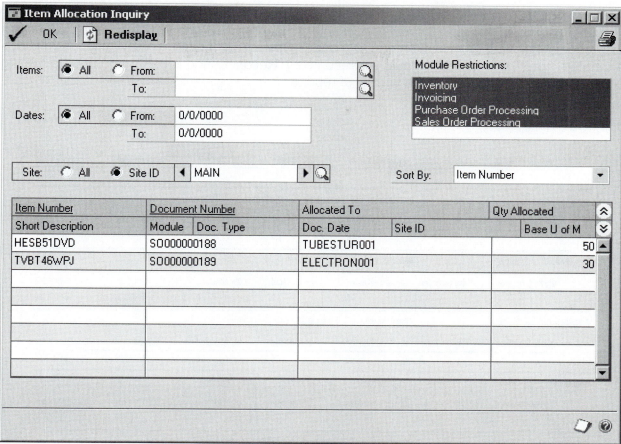

F4:19 Items Allocated to Pending Sales Orders

These windows illustrate the information that can be gathered while using the software. In addition, reports provide output of information for use outside the software. The *Reports>> Inventory* menu groups output by the reporting categories described in **T4:2**.

Inventory Report Category	Information Available
Item	Item details, price lists, and purchasing options
Activity	Stock status, vendor activity, and physical inventory checklist
Analysis	Inventory turnover and other analysis reports
History	Transaction, distribution, and sales history
Posting Journals	Reprints of reports printed after posting
Setup	Reports on item setup, classes, and pricing levels

T4:2 Inventory Report Categories

Use the menu *Reports>>Inventory>>Activity* to access the stock status report. Select the report named StockReport and print. The stock status report is a vital control tool used to reconcile the Inventory Control Series to the inventory general ledger account. Scroll to the last page on the report and locate the total value of inventory for March. (Make sure your system date is set to March.) This total must equal the balance for March's inventory in the general ledger that is viewable using the *Inquiry>>Financial>>Summary* menu. **F4:20** and **F4:21** illustrate reconciling the report's balance to the inventory account. (Note: Your numbers may differ from those illustrated, however, balances should still reconcile.) Reconciliation is performed prior to issuing financial statements to ensure the validity of reports.

Qty Back Ordered	Qty On Order	Qty Requisitioned	Qty On Hand	Qty Allocated	Current Cost	Inventory Value
0	0	0	32	0	$560.00	$17,920.00

Item Number: TVPS60HDTV   **Item Description:** Pasanovic 60 Inch Widescreen HDTV

Qty Back Ordered	Qty On Order	Qty Requisitioned	Qty On Hand	Qty Allocated	Current Cost	Inventory Value
0	0	0	23	0	$1,905.00	$43,815.00

Item Number: TVSB52W   **Item Description:** Subishi 52 Inch Widescreen DLP

Qty Back Ordered	Qty On Order	Qty Requisitioned	Qty On Hand	Qty Allocated	Current Cost	Inventory Value
0	0	0	9	0	$1,860.00	$16,740.00

Item Number: TVSN34W   **Item Description:** Sunyung 34 Inch Widescreen

Qty Back Ordered	Qty On Order	Qty Requisitioned	Qty On Hand	Qty Allocated	Current Cost	Inventory Value
0	0	0	35	0	$2,200.00	$77,000.00

Item Number: TVSN42W   **Item Description:** Sunyung 42 Inch Widescreen Projection

Qty Back Ordered	Qty On Order	Qty Requisitioned	Qty On Hand	Qty Allocated	Current Cost	Inventory Value
0	0	0	7	0	$1,365.00	$9,555.00

Item Number: TVSN50W   **Item Description:** Sunyung 50 Inch Widescreen Projection

Qty Back Ordered	Qty On Order	Qty Requisitioned	Qty On Hand	Qty Allocated	Current Cost	Inventory Value
0	0	0	30	0	$1,610.00	$48,300.00

Item Number: TVSP37P   **Item Description:** SonicPan 37 Inch Plasma

Qty Back Ordered	Qty On Order	Qty Requisitioned	Qty On Hand	Qty Allocated	Current Cost	Inventory Value
0	0	0	10	0	$1,070.00	$10,700.00

	Items	Inventory Value
Grand Totals:	41	$1,065,337.01

F4:20 Last Page of Stock Status Report

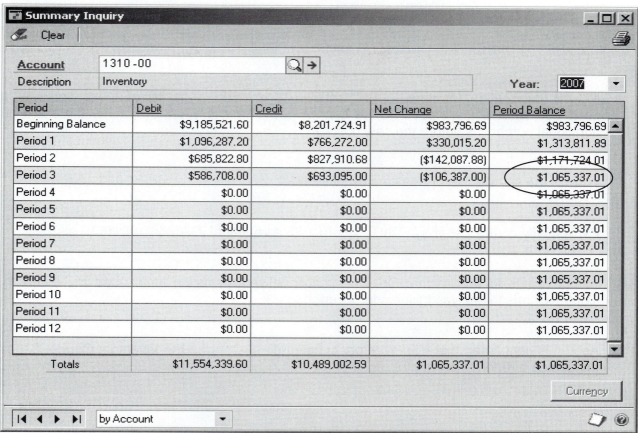

F4:21 Inventory General Ledger Balance

LEVEL ONE AND TWO QUESTIONS

1. Review information for item DCSM10XDZ. When S&S sells 10 of these items to a customer, what amount posts to the cost of goods sold account? (Assume there are no additional purchases before the sale posts.)

2. What is the sales price for one item of TVSP37P?

3. Explain why companies may want to incorporate a variety of inventory pricing levels.

4. Ashton wants to ensure that Ori Corporation delivers items on time. Use the Inventory Control Series to analyze this vendor's performance.

5. Ashton is concerned that idle inventory is tieing up cash. Use the Inventory Control Series to develop a report analyzing his concerns.

CHAPTER 5: REVENUE CYCLE AND GREAT PLAINS SALES SERIES

CHAPTER OVERVIEW

We are now ready to begin processing S&S' sales transactions and perform other revenue cycle activities using Great Plains' Sales Series. This chapter presents information as follows:

> Level One: Use Great Plains to perform revenue cycle activities. We begin with an overview of cycle activities and departments. We then proceed to capturing transactions, posting, and reporting. Along this path, you learn internal control procedures that affect revenue cycle performance.

> Level Two: We shift focus to internal control options selected under Sales Series setup. In addition, we learn month-end and year-end closing procedures for the Sales Series.

Level One covers:
> The Sales Series' menu structure and relationship to the revenue cycle REA data model
> Revenue cycle activities, including customer cards, sales order entry, order fulfillment, invoicing, credit/debit memos, inventory returns, write-offs, and customer payments
> Implementing reports as a control tool over performance and as a trigger for department activities

Level Two covers:
> Implementing internal controls through Sales Series setup
> Implementing addition controls on customer cards
> Month-ending and year-ending the Sales Series

LEVEL ONE

Before using Great Plains to perform revenue cycle activities, we must first understand these activities. *F5:1* depicts revenue cycle activities by departments and the triggers that initiate department activities. Ovals signify the commencement and termination of an activity, rectangles denote activity processes, and parallelograms represent the documents that trigger and control activities. Threats to company performance are listed beneath each department along with internal controls that mitigate these threats. The revenue cycle diagram forms a roadmap for discussions and should be frequently referred to when reading this chapter.

Let's begin at the point where customers place orders with S&S' sales department. This event triggers revenue cycle activities. Throughout the day, sales employees use Great Plains' Sales Series to enter customer orders, assess inventory availability, issue back orders for out-of-stock items, check customer credit, answer customer inquiries, and print sales order documentation. Depending on customer urgency, employees either print sales documentation immediately or print all documentation at day's end. Sales order documentation serves as customer confirmation of the order, as internal control over order processing, and as the trigger for activities in the warehouse.

Upon receipt of a picking ticket, warehouse employees begin filling the order by pulling inventory for the ticket. The ticket provides item descriptions, warehouse locations, and quantities ordered. As employees complete the fulfillment process, they enter fulfilled quantities using terminals that access Great Plains. The owners would like to fully automate the fulfillment process next year with the addition of barcode scanners, but for now, employees must manually enter fulfillment data. After entering this data, warehouse employees print a picking ticket. The ticket and inventory are then sent to the shipping department to trigger customer delivery.

Shipping activities begin with quality and quantity inspections. Employees perform quantity recounts and compare items selected with the picking ticket. In addition, employees spot-check merchandise for noticeable defects. After verifying the order, employees prepare an external bill of lading since Great Plains does not produce this document.[1] Finally, employees retrieve the original sales order from Great Plains, enter any shipping costs from the bill of lading, and print a packing slip. The packing slip is boxed with the inventory and the order placed onto company trucks. The driver carries a copy of the bill of lading for customer signature. Another copy is forwarded to accounts receivable, triggering customer invoicing.[2]

Control over finalizing an order lies with the accounts receivable department. Upon receipt of the bill of lading, department employees independently check shipping department performance by comparing the bill of lading to the original sales order in Great Plains. Employees pull up the fulfilled order, check shipping charges, and then transfer the order to an invoice. The invoice triggers recognition of sales revenue and cost of goods sold. The invoice is then mailed to the customer and all documents cancelled and filed.

---

[1] Great Plains resellers can create a customized report that prints bill of ladings.
[2] While invoicing a customer before actual delivery creates revenue recognition issues, S&S adjusts timing differences by posting adjusting entries prior to issuing financial statements. The cash flow benefits of invoicing at the point of shipping offset any costs of posting adjusting entries.

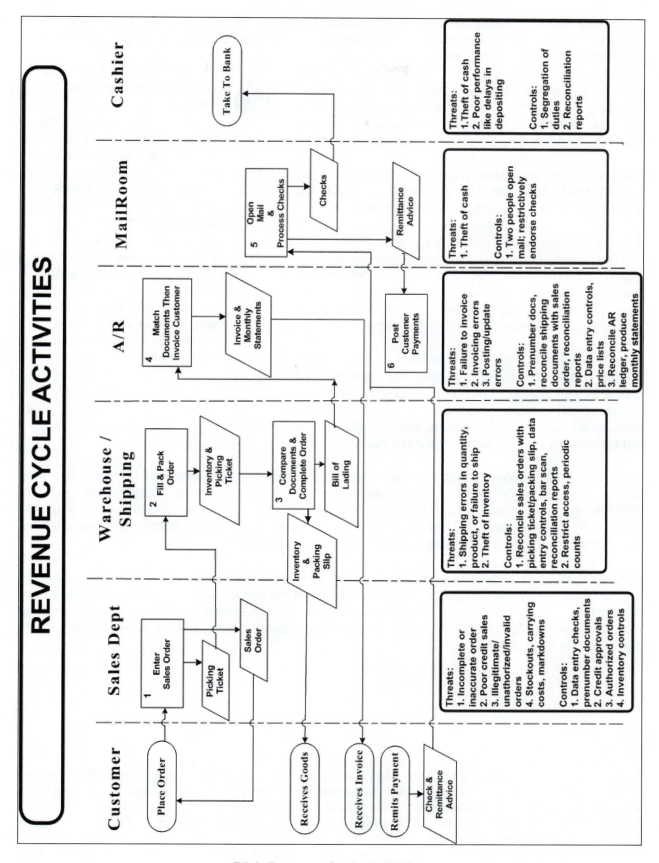

F5:1 Revenue Cycle Activities

Accounts receivable employees are also responsible for mailing monthly statements to the customer, listing customer invoices and payments. These employees also post customer payments. S&S offers most of its customers payment terms of net 30, inferring that invoice payments arrive approximately 30 days after invoicing. S&S pays close attention to cash flow as well as revenue since cash is required to pay vendors for inventory purchases and employees for services. Consequently, any inefficiency in entering, fulfilling, shipping, and/or invoicing orders negatively impact cash flow, which may result in obtaining external financing to meet operating requirements.

> **INTERNAL CONTROL**
> While S&S implements internal controls earlier in the revenue cycle, the shipping department's order inspection is your first encounter with an independent check on performance. This check serves to control order quality, accuracy, and customer satisfaction. In companies with large sales volume, shipping employees do not usually perform an inspection of every order because this would be an inefficient use of employee time. However, these companies institute quality control inspection programs that statistically sample orders throughout the day to control warehouse performance.

After order invoicing, revenue cycle activities shift focus towards collection. Customer payments enter the mailroom for processing. For internal control reasons, S&S always uses two employees to open mail. One employee processes remittance advices while the other processes customer payments.

When payments are sent without a remittance advice, the employee processing remittances prepares a substitute document listing the customer's name, check number, and payment.[3] This employee then totals remittances, sending advices along with control total to the accounts receivable department.

Meanwhile, the second employee restrictively endorses customer checks.[4] Checks are then sent, along with a control total, to the cashier department for depositing. Segregating mailroom activities mitigates threats to cash. In addition, recording customer remittances in accounts receivable and depositing checks through the cashier segregates recording from custody. Recall that Chapter 3 explained the segregation of duties model.[5]

This completes our discussion on the roadmap of revenue cycle activities. We have provided only a glimpse into the flurry of activities performed in the cycle. Moreover, the challenge facing departments using Great Plains is to implement this roadmap, along with implementing strong internal controls. Since cycle activities begin with customer orders, our discussion now turns to Sales Series master records.

---

[3] For customers paying with a two-part check, the top portion of the check normally tears off and serves as the remittance advice. The remittance advice lists the invoices paid by the check. In addition, S&S uses preprinted monthly statements with a tear-off portion that serves as a remittance advice.

[4] Restively endorsing a check means stamping the check's back "For Deposit Only." The stamp includes the bank name and the company's account number.

[5] Additional information on the model is located on page 213 of Marshall Romney and Paul Steinbart, *Accounting Information Systems* (10th ed., Prentice Hall 2006).

BILL OF LADING

The bill of lading is a legal contract between S&S and its customer. This document defines ownership of in-transit inventory and liability for shipping costs.[6] Ownership of in-transit inventory impacts accounting information and liability insurance for losses that occur during shipment.[7] Remember from earlier discussions that S&S transports customer orders, thus S&S is using FOB destination point. In Level Two, we discuss this delivery method's impact on closing procedures. Furthermore, because S&S ships orders, it does not charge customers for delivery unless an order is rush delivered by an outside carrier.

SALES SERIES: CUSTOMER MASTER RECORDS

As we learned in Chapter 2, transaction records link to master records. Consequently, before capturing sales orders, S&S created customer master records. The *Cards>>Sales>>Account* menu opens the window accessing customer accounts. We begin with managing existing customers and then move to creating new customers. Remember, a list of S&S' existing customers is found in Appendix B.

From the Customer Maintenance window, select Rick's Specialty Goods' customer account. The window now displays Rick's permanent information (see **F5:2**). The Customer ID field stores the record's primary key. A primary key enforces entity integrity, helping ensure that customers appear only once in the customer table. However, this works only where companies employ strong controls over creating Customer ID values. Unlike employees having social security numbers that serve as unique identifiers, customer information does not contain information to serve as a candidate primary key. Therefore, most companies implement a primary key assignment scheme.

Remember that you can type RIC in the Customer ID field before launching the look-up. This advances you to the customers beginning with RIC.

Ashton holds responsibility for controlling the assignment of primary keys to customer records. Before instituting an assignment scheme, Ashton remembered that Great Plains speeds customer lookups by typing the first few characters of a record's primary key. Thus, Ashton decides to use the first eight letters of a customer's name as their ID. However, Ashton soon notices this does not ensure uniqueness, for instance, when two customer names contain the same eight letters, such as Alliance International and Alliance Enterprises. Consequently, alphabetic characters alone will not uniquely identify customers.

---

[6] Refer to the bill of lading example in Marshall Romney and Paul Steinbart *Accounting Information Systems* (10th ed., Prentice Hall 2006), p. 366.
[7] Title transfer affects revenue and asset recognition for the selling company and the customer. For the customer, inventory is not capitalized and the liability not recognized until title transfers. For the seller, revenue is not recognized and the inventory remains capitalized until title transfers.

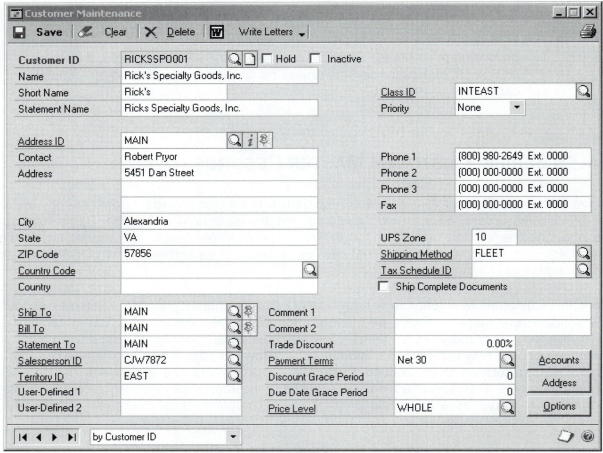

F5:2 Customer Card for Rick's Specialty Goods

Ashton overcomes this conflict by combining a customer's alphabetic identification with a numeric notation. The first customer in an alphabetic sequence will be assigned 001. Subsequent conflicts in alphabetic characters will be assigned 002, 003, . . .#nnn. Applying Ashton's scheme, the Alliance dilemma is resolved by assigning Alliance001 to Alliance International and then Alliance002 to Alliance Enterprises. Review the primary keys assigned to S&S' customers in Appendix B and notice that customer IDs use Ashton's primary key scheme. In addition, review **T5:1**, providing an explanation of other fields appearing on the customer record. Continue to explore Rick's Specialty Goods' customer record, making sure to open the Options and Accounts windows.

Field	Description
Customer ID	Record's primary key that uniquely identifies the customer.
Name, Short Name, and Statement Name	Company name and short name used to speed data entry. Statement name used when customer's name different for statements.
Class ID	Links customer to a class for grouping customers with similar attributes. Classes are also used for reports and to assign defaults such as credit limit, default general ledger accounts, and salesperson. Along with speeding data entry for new customer records, customer classes ensure data consistency among customers with similar attributes. Customer classes are created from the *Tools>>Setup>>Sales>>Customer Class* menu. S&S groups customers by business operations such as big box stores, traditional retailers, and internet sellers.
Multiple Address fields	Address ID used to create multiple customer addresses. for instance, one address for billing and one for deliveries. The customer record is linked to at least one main or primary address. S&S uses the <u>Main</u> ID to identify a customer's primary address. In addition, the Ship To, Bill To, and Statement To fields link to customer addresses.
Shipping Method	Links customer record to shipper records stored under the *Tools>>Setup>>Company>>Shipping Methods* menu. Examples of shipping methods include UPS, FEDEX, or Fleet. Great Plains does not automatically generate shipping costs, thus this link is for informational purposes only.
Tax Schedule ID	Links customer record to sales tax records stored under the *Tools>>Setup>>Company>>Tax Details* menu. Since S&S is a wholesale distributor, customers are not linked to a Tax ID.
Salesperson ID	Links customer record to S&S' salesperson table stored under the *Cards>>Sales>>Salesperson* menu. Salesperson records may be linked to either an Employee ID or a Vendor ID. When linked to a vendor, Great Plains integrates sales commission liabilities with vendor accounts. This integration is not available for employees.
Territory ID	Links customer record to S&S' geographic territories stored under the *Cards>>Sales>>Sales Territory* menu. These territories enable regional sales reporting. S&S uses the East, Mid, and West territories to track sales data.
Payment Terms	Links customer record to S&S' payment terms stored under the *Tools>>Setup>>Company>>Payment Terms* menu. Payment terms are explained later in the chapter.
Price Level	Links customer record to inventory pricing table discussed in Chapter 4.

Accounts Button	Opens window that stores default general ledger accounts used during Sales Series posting. As discussed in Chapter 4, S&S selected the option that defaults Sales Series posting using accounts on the customer card rather than accounts on the inventory card. This option was selected from the *Tools>>Setup>>Sales>>Sales Order Processing* menu.
Address Button	Opens window used to create new and manage existing customer addresses.
Options Button	Opens the window used to store customer controls over credit limit and maximum write-off. Also contains other options such as finance charge defaults.

T5:1 Customer Record Field Descriptions

Changing information on existing customer cards is easy. After retrieving the record, simply type in new data and save the record. The Customer ID is the only field that cannot be modified since it is the record's primary key linked to transaction records.

We must emphasize that opening the Customer Maintenance window is an authorization function; therefore, access should be denied to employees with recording or custody responsibilities. Granting access to unauthorized employees exposes a company to threats from poor credit sales, unauthorized sales, lost inventory, and lost cash. For instance, suppose a salesperson increases a customer's credit limit and then posts sales that boost commissions. The customer subsequently files bankruptcy and S&S is unable to collect payment. Another scenario, the salesperson creates a fraudulent customer containing the salesperson's address and enters a high credit limit and a high write-off amount. The salesperson then enters an order that ships to him and then posts a transaction that writes off the invoice. Here, motivation is theft of inventory instead of commission boosting.

While continued concealment in either scenario depends on lax controls in other areas of the cycle, the best way to mitigate these types of threats is to control access to the Customer Maintenance window. Thus, the departments illustrated in our roadmap should not have access to the Customer Maintenance window because these employees are involved with recording sales (sales department), custody of assets (warehouse/shipping /cashier departments), or recording invoices (accounts receivable department).

 When you close the Customer Maintenance window before saving changes to the customer record, Great Plains prompts you to save, discard, or delete the record. Of course, the Delete button removes a customer record, unless the customer has transaction history. When you inadvertently change information, use either the Clear button on the Customer Maintenance window or close the window using the x icon and click the Discard button when prompted.

1. Giggle Place, Inc. wants to add a new address for shipments. This address is 1865 Illinois Avenue, Nashville, TN 47568. Create the new address and link to the appropriate fields on the customer card. Note: Data pertaining to the UPS zone, shipping method, and salesperson remain the same.

2. Susan has approved increasing the credit limit of Fillards, Inc. to $300,000. In addition, she wants Fillards' payment terms extended to permit a 2% discount on payments made within 10 days. She asks you to make these changes on the customer's card.

3. List three companies in the Midwest region. Which salesperson handles sales to these customers?

4. Which department should have authorization to create new customers and manage existing customer accounts?

5. Which departments' employees should have permission to modify noncritical customer data such as addresses or phone numbers? How can employees change noncritical data without accessing the Cards menu?

E5:1 Practice with Customer Cards

The only difference between managing customer information and creating new customer records appears when assigning a value to the Customer ID field.

Susan Jones, the Controller of Electronic Connections is opening a new account with S&S. The company is located at 35 Park Avenue, Chicago, IL 60609. The phone number is 605-878-9970. Discount wants shipments sent to its warehouse located at 265 West Main Street, Menlo Park, Chicago 60610. The phone number at this location is 605-865-3304 and Alan Keith is the warehouse supervisor.

Discount is a traditional operation located in the Midwest region and is granted an initial credit limit of $100,000. Scott has approved the customer and asks you to create the record using Ashton's primary key scheme for the Customer ID field. Save the customer when finished. Why are default general ledger accounts already present on Discount's record?

E5:2 Add a New Customer

SALES SERIES TRANSACTIONS

After working with customer, you are ready to capture sales transactions. Recall from our roadmap that several departments perform revenue cycle activities. Accordingly, Great Plains groups the Sales Series Transaction menu into tiers that help identify the department originating a cycle activity (see *F5:3*).

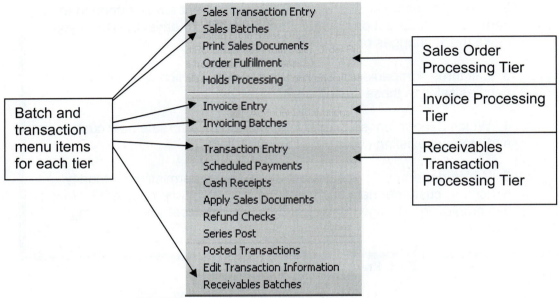

F5:3: Sales Transaction Menu Tiers

Take a moment and become familiar with this tiered structuring. The Sales Order Processing Tier contains menus used to capture sales orders, print order documentation, and fulfill orders. Employees in the sales, warehouse, and shipping departments work primarily in this tier. In addition, accounts receivable employees use this tier to transfer orders to invoices.

The Invoice Processing Tier contains menus that access invoices transferred from the Sales Order Processing Tier. Finally, the Receivables Transaction Processing Tier is used to post payments, credit memos and invoices for noninventoried sales. Accounts receivable employees work primarily within these two tiers.

Notice that each tier contains a separate batch and transaction menu item. The transaction windows opened within each tier function differently and are illustrated in *F5:4*. Take a few minutes to review these transaction windows and notice that each window originates a different document type. All windows contain an invoice document type; however, the Receivables Transaction Entry window does not permit inventory transactions because it lacks an Item Number field. Additionally, the Invoice and Receivables transaction windows do not contain sales order or back order document types. You will understand these distinctions later in the chapter.

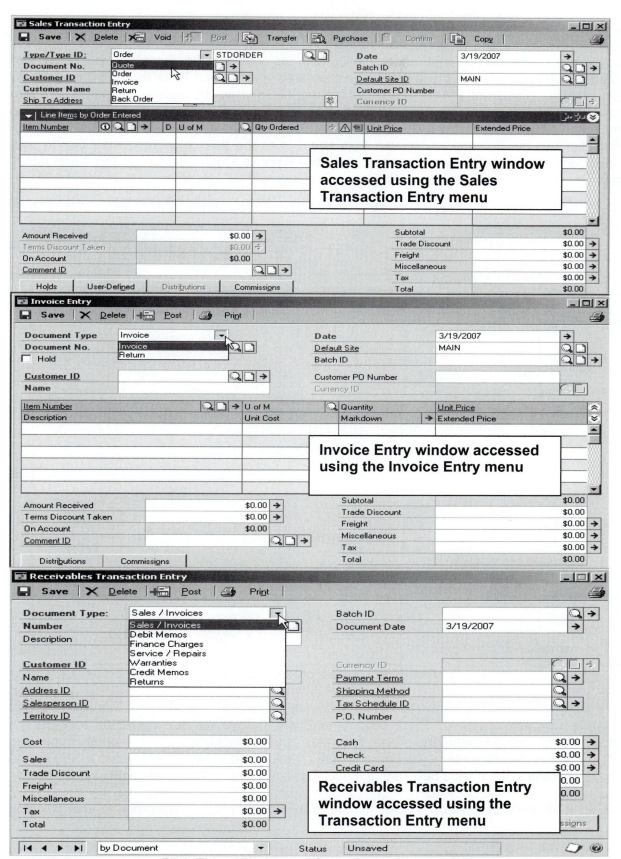

F5:4 Three Windows of Sales Series Transactions

To understand how these tiers function differently, review an REA diagram for the revenue cycle.[8] The layout of this diagram, from left to right, depicts Resources (inventory and cash) and the Events (transactions) that affect Resources, as well as the Agents (employees and customers) participating in the events. The squares and named lines represent a separate entity (table). To Great Plains, resource and agent squares are master tables while event squares are transaction tables. In addition, named lines between resources and events are transaction tables. Thus, the Take Order event uses the Sales Order Processing Tier to link transactions to the Inventory table; the Sale event uses the Invoicing Processing Tier to post transactions linked to the Inventory table; and the Receive Cash event uses the Receivables Transaction Processing Tier to post transactions affecting the Cash table.

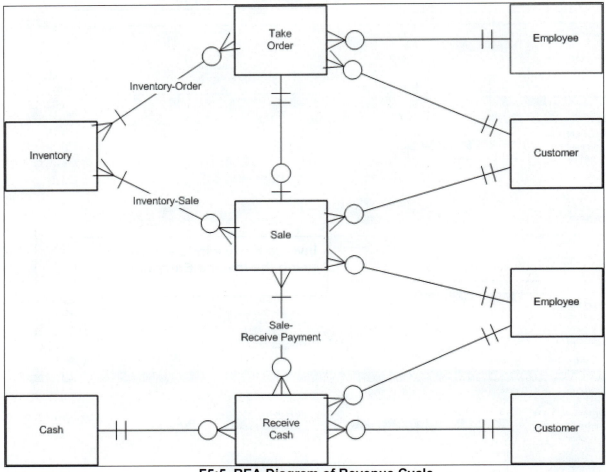

F5:5 REA Diagram of Revenue Cycle

So which transaction window records a customer return of inventory? The Receivables transaction window contains a Returns document type, but we see that the tables accessed by this tier do not include inventory. Thus, that rules out the Receivables Transaction Processing Tier. However, the other tiers' do interact with inventory, so either can be used to record the return. Therefore, the choice becomes a function of operating and internal control policies.

Let's look at internal control policies where a customer returns inventory to the shipping

---

[8] Marshall Romney and Paul Steinbart, *Accounting Information Systems* (10th ed., Prentice Hall 2006), p. 590.

department without notifying the salesperson. (Note: Either of the scenarios that follow are implemented by setting the user access permissions discussed in Chapter 3.)

Scenario One: Policies require shipping employees to enter the return by using the Sales Transaction Entry window. However, permission to post the return is denied. Instead, the accounts receivable department posts returns after contacting the sales department for authorization. In other words, this scenario separates inventory custody, return authorization, and transaction recording. An accounts receivable employee contacts the salesperson for authorization since he or she initiated the sale; therefore holds a stake in protecting commissions and satisfying the customer.

However, you might ask, "Didn't the shipping employee receive the inventory (custody) and also record the return transaction?" Actually, recording does not take place until the transaction posts. The shipping department merely captured the data. Capturing data is a database control that ensures protection of information at the source. In assessing threats, always recognize the possibility of losing control over a transaction. Control policies that capture a return in shipping ensure monitoring a transaction through Great Plains reporting, thus mitigating the threat of lost data.

Scenario Two: Policies require shipping employees to notify the salesperson upon receipt of customer returned inventory. Sales employees use the Sales Transaction Entry window to enter the data while posting remains in the accounts receivable department. However, this policy threatens data loss should the salesperson forget to enter the return. With failure to capture the data, monitoring resides only in the employee's memory. (Note: Policies should require the sales department to enter returns when the customer contacts a sales employee before returning inventory.)

Scenario Three: Policies require shipping employees to notify the accounts receivable department. Accounts receivable clerks enter the return using the Invoice Entry window. Once again, the threat of data loss exists and delays in capturing a transaction expose companies to threats of data loss.

You will better understand Sales Series menu tiers after reading this chapter. For now, know that each tier serves a distinct purpose and that transactions initiated in one tier must be finalized in that tier. For instance, a return entered through the Invoice Processing Tier must be posted using that tier.

SALES DEPARTMENT ACTIVITIES

We are now ready implement Great Plains to effectively manage and support sales department activities. Recall that the sales department serves as the primary point of contact for customers. Sales personnel interact with customers by taking orders and responding to customer inquiries on pricing, inventory availability, anticipated delivery dates, outstanding account balances, payment terms, and pricing discounts. Furthermore, sales personnel analyze sales trends, focus on customer satisfaction, and search for additional ways to enhance company revenue. Given that customer orders initiate revenue cycle activities, we begin with capturing orders before moving on to other sales department activities.

Sales Orders and Batches

Whether capturing customer rush orders or processing routine orders, all sales orders enter Great Plains through batches. To understand the batch requirement, return to an earlier discussion on the revenue recognition principle. Specifically, revenue is recognized when earned or deemed to have been earned. For inventory sales, revenue is recognized when legal title transfers per the bill of lading. In our roadmap, revenue recognition occurred when accounts receivable issued an invoice and these documents are issued upon shipment. Therefore, revenue posts when accounts receivable transfers orders to an invoice and posts. This also means that sales orders cannot post. However, we must capture the order to take it through the departments illustrated in our roadmap. This is where the batch folder comes into play. Sales order batches store orders for processing by the sales, warehouse, and shipping departments. (Recall from Chapter 2 that batches as folders that store transactions until posting.)

One final concept before moving on capturing orders, S&S' customer orders are delivered using FOB destination terms. This means that title does not transfer until received by the customer. This statement contradicts S&S policy that posts invoices upon shipment. However, recall that we also pointed to the importance of focusing on cash flow as well as revenue. With cash flow in focus, the receivable department posts an invoice upon shipment to speed customer collection. Any timing differences that conflict with the revenue recognition principle are adjusted through journal entries prior to issuing financial statements.

Let's begin capturing orders. First, create a sales order batch using the Sales Batches menu on the Sales Order Processing Tier. Refer to **F5:6** to create a batch that will store customer orders for March 16, 2007. S&S employees assign values to the Batch ID by using SO and the batch date. This helps later identify the batch for subsequent processing. In addition, the batch's Origin is set to Sales Transaction Entry and a brief description supplied.

Click the Transactions button to open the Sales Transaction Entry window. Enter the order illustrated in **F5:7**, selling 30 Javix digital camcorders to Better Buy. Click the order detail expansion icon to view item fields (**F5:8**) and review the descriptions for transaction fields in **T5:1**.

 Note that the Distributions button in the Sales Transaction Entry window is grayed out, reinforcing the point that sales orders cannot post to the general ledger.

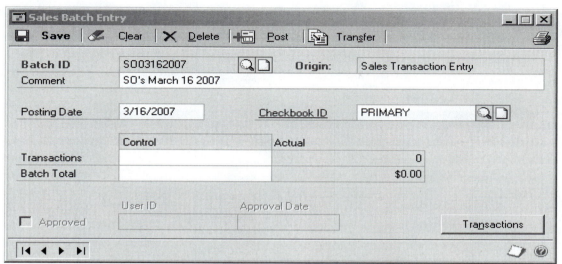

F5:6 Sales Order Batch Window

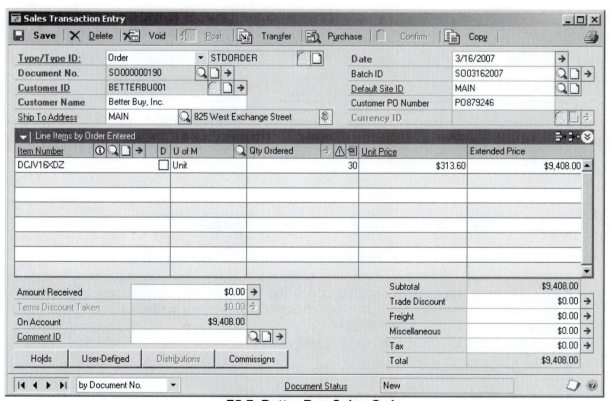

F5:7 Better Buy Sales Order

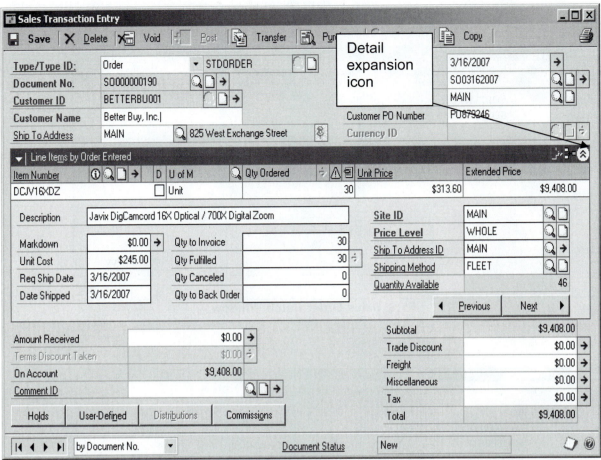

F5:8 Better Buy Inventory Details

 What information is located under the Commissions button?

The Commission window shows the salesperson's commission percentage. The salesperson is defaulted from the customer's card and the commission rate defaults from the records located under the *Cards>>Sales>>Salesperson* menu. The rate and salesperson can be changed on a transaction without affecting defaults.   For an order requiring split commissions, enter the additional salesperson and adjust commission percentages.

Field	Description
Type/ Type ID	Document type determines subsequent transaction processing. The choices are <u>Quote</u>, <u>Order</u>, <u>Invoice</u>, <u>Return</u>, and <u>Back Order</u>. <u>Quote</u> controls sales department information given to customers seeking to place orders and tracks potential sales. These documents can later be transferred to orders or invoices when a customer decides to purchase. <u>Order</u> captures customer purchases that require inventory shipment. After shipping, the document is transferred to an invoice for posting. <u>Invoice</u> captures sales ready for posting. Invoices are created by transferring a quote or shipped order. Additionally, invoices are entered directly for sales not requiring shipment, such as when S&S provides repair services. <u>Return</u> processes customer inventory returns. <u>Back Order</u> stores customer orders for inventory on back order.
Document No.	Uniquely identifies the transaction. Document numbers auto-fill and sequentially increment. Document numbers become part of the transaction's audit trail discussed in Chapter 4.
Customer ID	Customer ID links the transaction record to the customer's record. Transactions can be entered for existing customers or for new customer created "on the fly" (adding customers by entering a new Customer ID). Remember, segregation of duties require customer creation remain separate from transaction recording, so "on the fly" customer creation should be prohibited.
Customer Name	Auto-fills based on the Customer ID selected. This feature is called closed loop verification, meaning that the selection of data for one field automatically generates data for a related field.
Ship To Address	Customer address used to ship inventory. Field is another auto-filled using default on the customer card. The address may be changed on a transaction without affecting the customer's record. To change, click the hyperlink and select another ID from the customer's card.
Date	Stores the order's origination date. This date is used to monitor the time required to process transactions and does not affect posting since orders cannot post.

Batch ID	Identifies the batch folder storing the transaction. Transactions without a Batch ID must be posted immediately. Since orders cannot post, these transactions must be saved with a Batch ID. When creating a batch first and then clicking the Transactions button, the Batch ID is automatically entered to this field. However, a new Batch ID can be created by typing a value. Using this method, Great Plains opens the batch window to complete information and save the batch. Furthermore, a transaction can be transferred to a different batch by looking up an existing Batch ID.
Default Site ID	S&S' location housing inventory used to fill the order. Remember, S&S maintains one location, <u>Main</u>.
Customer PO Number	Stores the customer's purchase order number. S&S always requests customer PO information to validate the order. However, this field is not required because not all customers use a PO system.
Item Number	ID that identifies the item ordered by the customer. Each item is stored in a separate row called line item. The lookup button assists with entering data to this field. A company can permit free-form entry for noninventoried items by selecting options under Sales Series setup (discussed in Level Two). S&S inventories all items, including service charges, and denies entry of noninventoried sales.
D check box	Box checked when drop shipping an item to a customer. Drop shipments are items shipped to the customer by the vendor. Drop shipments used for nonstocked or are out of stock items.
U of M	Links to Unit of Measure table discussed in Chapter 4. Customers generally order items in units, but can also order by cases of 12 or 10, depending on the item.
Qty Ordered	Works in conjunction with the U of M field. For instance, when UOM is Unit, entering quantity of 30 means customer ordered 30 items. However, entering this same quantity when the UOM is Case12 means customer ordered 360 items.
Unit Price	Price per unit defaults from inventory price list discussed in Chapter 4.
Extended Price	Item quantity times item price.
Site ID	Defaults from inventory item; however, ID can be changed when shipping item from a different warehouse.
Price Level	Defaults from customer's card and used to determine sales pricing. The pricing level may be changed for each line item, thus accommodating different pricing structures on the same order.
Ship To Address ID	Defaults from Ship To Address entered in top section of the order. Changing the ID on a line items permits customization of order shipments.
Shipping Method	S&S' shipping method. This defaults from the customer card but can be changed on each line item to customize shipping.
Quantity Available	Quantity available appears after entering the order quantity. This quantity excludes items on outstanding customer orders.

Markdown	Field's arrow opens a window used to enter markdowns on price. Markdowns entered as either a percentage of the sales price or a specific dollar amount.
Unit Cost	Item's cost defaults from the Inventory Control Series. The amount shown does not always equal the cost of goods sold posted when the transaction is invoiced. Inventory costing layers or averages may change between the time of order placement and invoice posting.
Req Ship Date	Ship date required to deliver order on time. S&S strives to ship customer orders on the date placed.
Date Shipped and Qty Fulfilled	Date S&S actually shipped the order and the quantity shipped. For S&S, the Sales Series is set to fulfill orders during order entry. However, many companies use a separate fulfillment process, entering shipment dates and quantities at that time.
Qty Canceled	Used to cancel ordered quantities after the order prints. This field is useful for tracking lost sales due to order cancellations.
Qty to Back Order	Difference between customer's order quantities and inventory's on-hand quantities. The Purchase button on the Sales Transaction Entry window can be used to create a purchase order in the Purchasing Series to process back orders.
Order totals (bottom right)	Subtotal field automatically calculates based on the items ordered. The discounts and other charges require manual entry.

T5:2 Order Field Properties Table

Sales Order Documents

After entering an order, documents can be printed individually by using the *File>>Print* menu while in the Sales Transaction Entry window. On the other hand, the *Transaction>>Sales>> Print Sales Documents* menu prints all orders in a batch. Either method opens the Sales Document Print Options window appearing in *F5:9*. Notice this window contains options for printing all sales documents discussed in our roadmap.

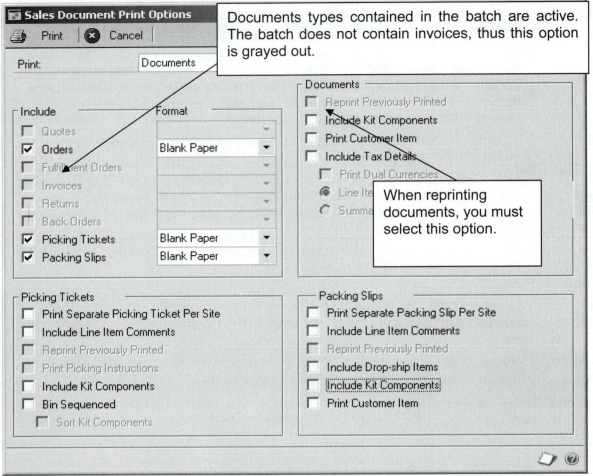

F5:9 Print Sales Documents Window

Modifying Existing Sales Orders

What happens when a customer wants to modify quantities or items on the original order? When the order has not been printed, you can simply reopen the order, enter the changes, and save. However, once printed, order modification may require a password if the company selected this internal control option under sales order setup. (Note: Setup topics are reserved for Level Two.) For now, Ashton has not instituted password controls; therefore, you can change quantities and modify line items on printed orders.

However, what happens when a customer wants to cancel the order? Once the order prints, Great Plains institutes internal controls and blocks access to the Sales Transaction Entry window's Delete button. Printing an order infers customer release of the document; therefore, the order must be voided by clicking the Void button. This feature also provides tracking voided orders. For unprinted orders, the Delete button on the Sales Transaction Entry window removes the order, unless the setup option that denies this feature is selected. Again, as with password protection for changed orders, Ashton has not enforced restrictions on deleting unprinted sales orders.

On March 19, 2007, you are working in the sales department. The following customer places an order for the items listed below. Perform all the sales department steps required to process this order.

Laufmans' order:
  15 Batoshi 46 inch Widescreen Projection
  25 Sunyung 5.1 Home Entertainment Combo DVD/VCR

E5:3 Capturing Sales Orders

Batch and Edit Lists

In our roadmap, we stated that sales orders and picking tickets trigger other activities and now we know how to print these documents. However, we have not discussed an important control over transaction entry. Review the Sales Document Print Options window again, this time as illustrated in *F5:10*. Notice the drop-down menu for the Print option. Besides printing sales documents, there are options that print alignment forms, edit lists, and batch lists.

Alignment forms send test patterns to the printer used to line up sales orders or invoices to preprinted forms. Sending a test page prior to printing documents lets a user review output prior to printing on actual forms.

Edit and batch lists are the reports that control data entry. S&S' internal control procedures require printing both reports and reviewing data prior to printing customer documentation and posting transactions. We know that Sales Series batches can contain any of the document types available in the Sales Transaction Entry window. Therefore, batch lists print every transaction type in a batch. However, edit lists print only transactions ready to post to the general ledger. Consequently, a batch list reports sales orders, back orders, returns, quotes, and invoices in a batch and an edit list reports only invoices and returns. Batch lists display information on the customer account, transaction amounts, salesperson, commissions, markdowns, discounts, and items on transactions. Edit lists print the same information but add the general ledger accounts that will be used for posting.

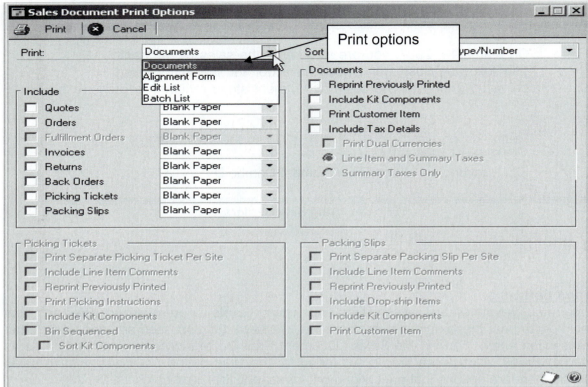

F5:10 Document and Control Reports Print Window

 Print the control report for the Laufmanns transaction entered in **E5:3**. Which report did you select? In addition, describe the internal control functions of this control report.

E5:4 Control Reporting

WAREHOUSE AND SHIPPING ACTIVITIES

When the picking ticket arrives in the warehouse, employees begin filling the order and entering quantities picked onto the ticket. When finished, the inventory and picking ticket are sent to the shipping department.

 To minimize steps when working with chapter exercises, the Sales Series option that automatically enters fulfillment data has been activated. Therefore, after entering an order, the Qty Fulfilled and Date Fulfilled fields already contain data.

Upon receipt in shipping, an employee prepares a bill of lading and checks inventory to verify items to the picking ticket. Then, using the *Transactions>> Sales>>Order Fulfillment* menu, the employee retrieves the order and enters the Qty Fulfilled, Date Fulfilled, and shipping costs, when applicable (see **F5:11**). The employee prints the packing slip (**F5:12**) and boxes the slip with the inventory. The order is then placed on company trucks and a copy of the bill of lading sent to the accounts receivable department, triggering invoicing.

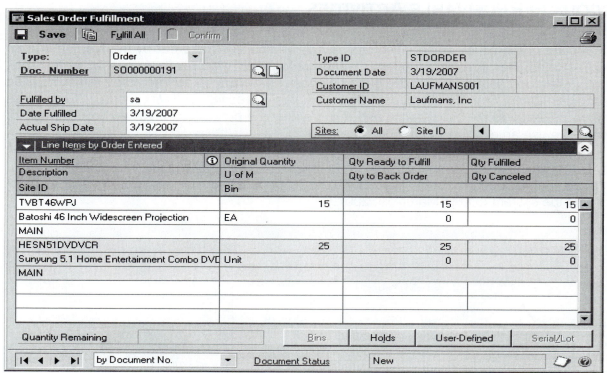

F5:11 Order Fulfillment Window

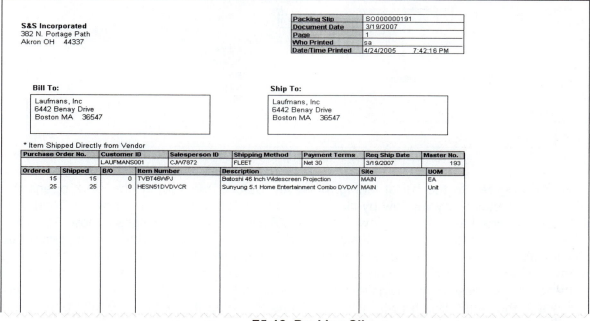

F5:12 Packing Slip

ACCOUNTS RECEIVABLE ACTIVITIES

Upon receipt of the bill of lading, accounts receivable finalizes the order by transferring it to an invoice. Remember, invoicing triggers revenue recognition (i.e., revenue, cost of goods sold, and other related charges post in the general ledger.) Invoicing is performed by retrieving filled sales order using the *Transactions>>Sales>>Sales Transaction Entry* menu. Employees compare the order to the bill of lading and then transfer the order to an invoice. To illustrate this process, we use an existing sales order.

This order was placed by the customer on March 17 and fulfilled on March 19. Therefore, before opening order SO000000188 to Tubes and Turners (*F5:13*), the clerk sets the system date to March 19, 2007.

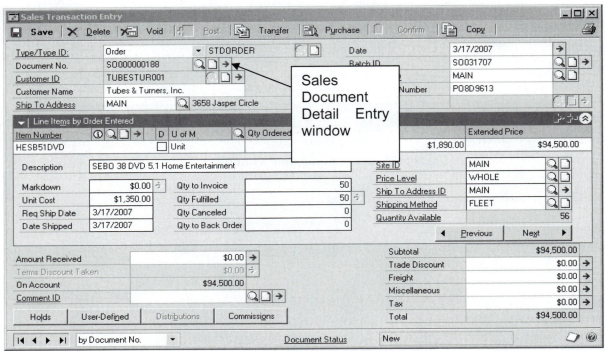

F5:13 Tubes and Turner Sales Order

The transaction agrees to the bill of lading; however, before transferring, the clerk opens the Sales Document Detail Entry window by clicking the arrow located to the right of the Document No. field. This opens the batch window shown in *F5:14*. The clerk assigns a new Batch ID, instructing Great Plains to place the transferred order in a new batch. Without completing this step, the invoice remains in the current batch, while changing the batch avoids commingling documents. In addition, a new batch ensures accuracy of the posting date. As the figure shows, the clerk will assign the transferred invoice to Batch ID INV03192007. Type in this information and the Sales Batch Entry window opens to create the batch (*F5:15*). Make sure the posting date is correct, then save and close the batch window. Now, click OK on the Sales Document Detail Entry window.

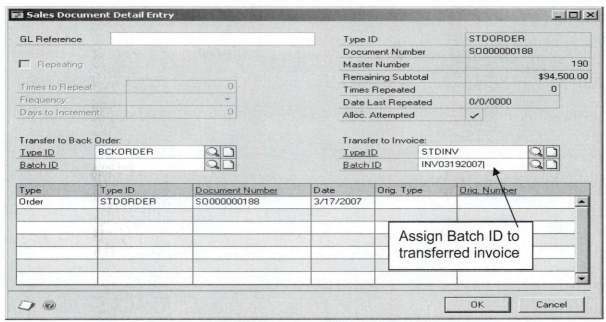

F5:14 Sales Document Detail Entry Window

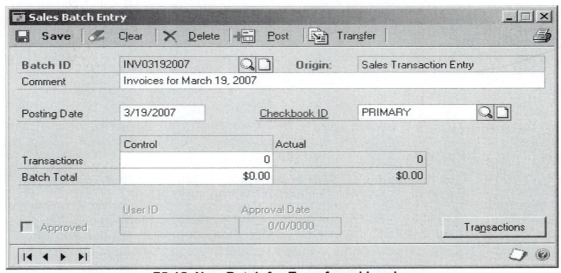

F5:15 New Batch for Transferred Invoice

While in the Sales Transaction Entry window, the clerk clicks the Transfer button, opening the Sales Transfer Documents window shown in **F5:16**. Review **T5:3** for information on this window's options. Set the options as illustrated and then click Transfer to print a log (**F5:17**) for the transferred order. Transfer logs indicate when errors occur during transfer. Errors require corrections before orders successfully transfer. When there is an error, the transfer process is restarted after correcting the error.

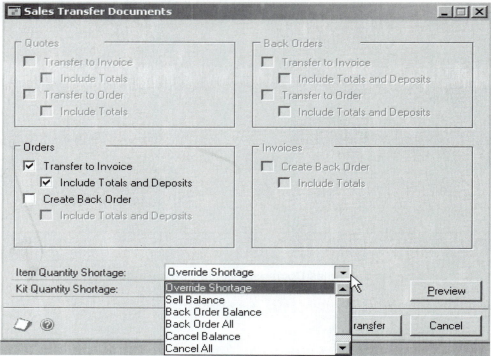

F5:16 Transfer Documents Window

Options	Purpose
Transfer to Invoice	Option appears for each document type. Options are grayed out for document types not included in the transfer.
Include Totals and Deposits	This option transfers shipping and miscellaneous charges entered on sales orders to the invoice. When the document being transferred contains these items, failure to select this option means data must be reentered after transferring. In addition, selecting this option updates a customer's record for advance deposits; however, general ledger accounts do not update until the invoice posts.
Create Back Order	When documents being transferred contain an inventory shortage, selecting this option generates a back order. The back order is placed in the back order batch selected in the Sales Document Detail Entry window. Back orders are then printed and sent to the customer and purchasing department as notification of inventory shortages.

| Quantity Shortage Handling | With inventory shortages on orders, Great Plains requires instructions for handling the shortage. An option under Sales Series setup selects whether to prompt for allocation instructions during line item entry or to wait for instructions during order transfer. S&S chose to prompt for instructions during line item entry. While this option may slow data entry because employees must immediately address inventory shortages, it enhances customer service because employees can provide customers with information on shortages. More importantly, line item allocation immediately flags inventory, thus items are unavailable to subsequent orders. Once allocated by line item, the quantity shortage option in the Sales Transfer Documents window does not override previous allocations. Therefore, S&S' does not select this option when transferring orders. We will illustrate inventory shortages later in the chapter. |

T5:3 Sales Transfer Documents Attributes

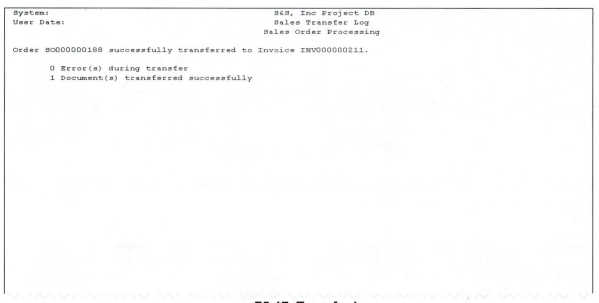

```
System:                                      S&S, Inc Project DB
User Date:                                   Sales Transfer Log
                                          Sales Order Processing

Order SO000000188 successfully transferred to Invoice INV000000211.

      0 Error(s) during transfer
      1 Document(s) transferred successfully
```

F5:17 Transfer Log

Thus far, we have illustrated transfers performed in the Sales Transaction Entry window. However, this is not always efficient. With multiple orders, the clerk updates the orders as previously shown, saves the changes, and closes the Sales Transaction Entry window. He then reopens the batch and clicks the Transfer button on the Sales Batch window. A word of caution when using this method, updated orders along with **all** orders containing fulfilled quantities transfer. There is no method for identifying orders or selecting a range of orders to transfer. Consequently, before using the Transfer button on the batch window, make sure all orders are ready for transfer. On the other hand, there is an advantage to using the batch Transfer button. Great Plains deletes the empty batch after transfer. Otherwise, the single order transfer method eventually leaves an empty batch folder requiring manual deletion.

After successful transfer of the Tubes order, the Sales Transaction Entry window (**F5:18**) displays an invoice. Notice the changed document type and number as well as the existence of the new Batch ID. Close the Sales Transaction Entry window and open the Sales Batch Entry window. Retrieve Batch ID INV03192007 and print the Tubes and Turners invoice using the *File>>Print* menu (**F5:9**) and selecting the Invoices option.

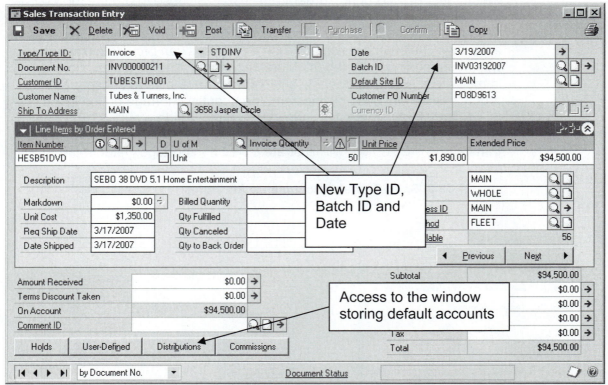

F5:18 Tubes and Turner Invoice

Before posting, an edit list should be printed and reviewed. Posted invoices are finalized and ready for processing customer payments.

Laufmans' order from **E5:3** is ready for invoicing. Update the order for invoicing and transfer the invoice to batch INV03202007. Explain how the clerk could change the default general ledger posting accounts prior to posting.

Post the invoice and list accounts posted to as well as control reports printed. Explain the internal control features of these reports. Should other control reports have been printed prior to posting the invoice? If yes, please explain.

E5:5 Transfer Laufmans' Order to Invoice

Posting Payments on Account

Along with posting invoices, accounts receivable posts customer payments. Recall that the mailroom processes remittances, sending these documents and a control total to accounts receivable. Since S&S offers customers payment terms, the company selected the customer card option of Open Item instead of Balance Forward. The Open Item option is required when offering payment terms because it permits application of payments to specific invoices whereas the Balance Forward option deducts payments from the customer's outstanding balance, a method used by credit card companies. You can imagine how important dates are when posting cash receipts using the Open Item method. Plus or minus one day can mean the difference between accepting or denying a discount.

The Cash Receipts menu on the Receivables Transaction Processing Tier opens the Cash Receipts window that posts customer payments. Set the system date to March 26, 2007 before opening this window. We are going to record a cash receipt for the Tubes and Turner invoice posted in the last topic. Tubes remitted check number 896912 for $94,500 (*F5:19*).

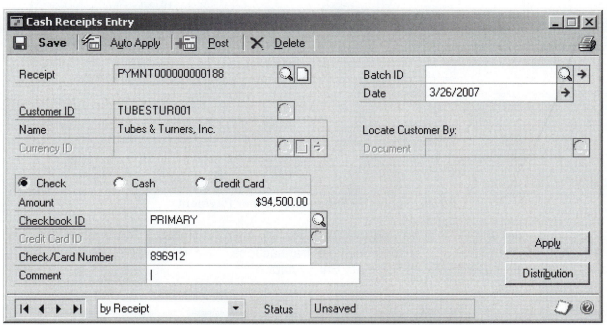

F5:19 Tubes and Turner Cash Receipt Entry

Enter this information and click Apply to open the Apply Sales Documents window shown in *F5:20*. There is only one open invoice, so check the invoice's Apply to box and then OK. (Note: Your document numbers will vary if other transactions have been posted.)

Auto Apply Warning

Be very careful when using the Auto Apply button in the Apply window because payment applications may not behave as intended. With customers having multiple outstanding invoices, Auto Apply selects invoices for payment by either the oldest due date or the earliest document number, depending on Sales Series setup. This may not always correspond to the invoice a customer intended to pay.

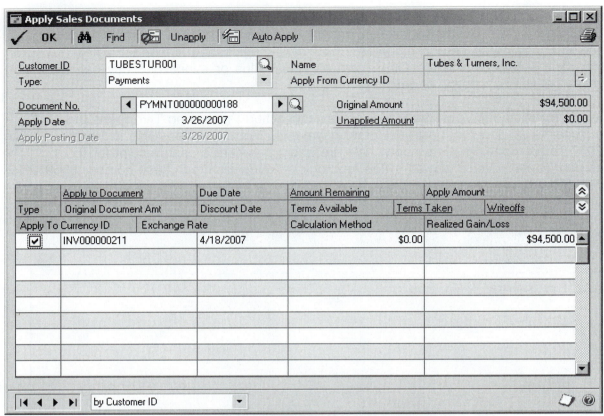

F5:20 Apply the Tubes and Turner Payment

After applying, click the Post button on the Cash Receipts Entry window. Remember: Batches are an alternative method for posting multiple transactions. The Receivables Batches menu creates batches that use the Cash Receipts Entry window.

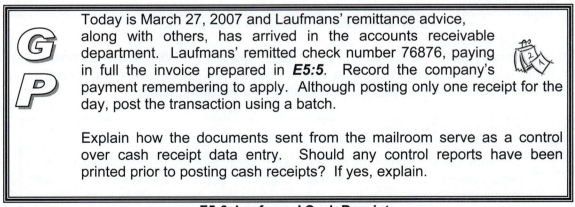

Today is March 27, 2007 and Laufmans' remittance advice, along with others, has arrived in the accounts receivable department. Laufmans' remitted check number 76876, paying in full the invoice prepared in *E5:5*. Record the company's payment remembering to apply. Although posting only one receipt for the day, post the transaction using a batch.

Explain how the documents sent from the mailroom serve as a control over cash receipt data entry. Should any control reports have been printed prior to posting cash receipts? If yes, explain.

E5:6 Laufmans' Cash Receipt

Preparing Customer Statements

Customer statements is another activity performed by the accounts receivable department. Great Plains permits companies to cycle bill, meaning customers can be grouped so that statements are sent throughout the month to manage cash flow. Customers are placed into billing cycles using the customer's card. S&S does not use cycle billing, thus statements are mailed once a month.

Prior to issuing statements, customer accounts are aged using the *Tools>>Routines>>Sales>> Aging* menu. In addition, employees review suspended transactions using the *Transactions>> Sales>>Series Post* menu.[9] Aging customer accounts is straightforward (see *F5:21*). Select the options illustrated and click Process.

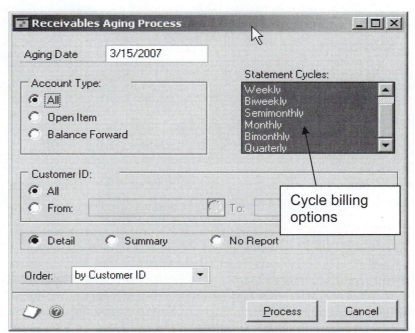

F5:21 Receivables Aging Process Window

After aging, customers statements are prepared by selecting the *Tools>>Routines>>Sales>> Statements* menu. The Customer Statements window in *F5:22* displays the window after choosing the <u>Regular</u> statement ID. Additional report IDs can be created, such as <u>BI-WEEKLY</u>, for storing options that print bi-weekly statements. You can also insert restrictions to select ranges of Customer IDs and Statement Cycles. Click Print on the statement window and review the output.

_____

[9] For a refresher on the Master Posting and Series Posting windows, see the Posting Setup topic in Chapter 3.

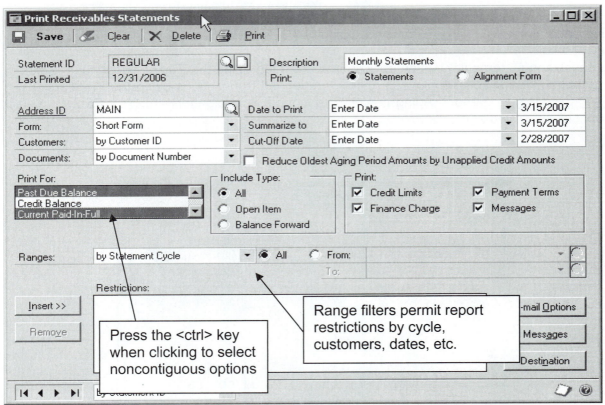

F5:22 Receivables Statement Window

This concludes the life cycle of a sales order. If only life were this straightforward. We did not encounter one bump along the way, such as orders for out-of-stock inventory, customer returns of inventory, customer credit/debit memos, and customer write-offs. We discuss these items later in the chapter. Before that, let's review some of the basic Sales Series reports.

SALES SERIES: BASIC REPORTING

Companies require a variety of analysis, control, and status reports from their general ledger packages. This topic focuses on a few of the basic reports printed under the *Reports>>Sales* menu. Reporting falls into the Trial Balance, History, Analysis, Posting Journals, Commissions, Setup, and Activity categories. The History, Commissions, and Analysis categories provide information on customer sales trends, payment discounts, item gross profit analysis, and salesperson performance. The Posting Journal category reprints control reports printed after posting. The setup category reports internal control options created under Sales Series setup. The remaining categories, Trial Balance and Activity, are the focus of this topic.

Accounts Receivable Trial Balance Report
The Trial Balance category contains a variety of options for printing accounts receivable aging reports. Employees responsible for credit and collection, sales transaction posting, internal controls, and financial statement preparation rely on aging reports. It is important to prepare and review aging reports at least once a month, if not more frequently. The report lists customer payment statuses, account balances, delinquencies, and cash flow expectations.

Additionally, aging reports serve as an internal control tool used to reconcile the Sales Series to the Financial Series. When reconciling these Series, the balance at the end of the aging report **must** equal the net balance of the Accounts Receivable and Sales Discounts Available accounts in the general ledger. To illustrate this concept, print the Hist AR Aging report found under the *Reports>>Sales>>Trial Balance* menu's Historical Aged Trial Balance category (**F5:23**). Refer to the reporting topic in Chapter 1 should you need a refresher on running reports.

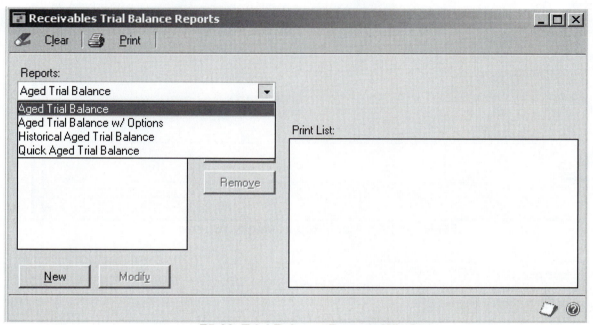

F5:23 Trial Balance Reports Window

Next, highlight the report and click the Modify button. Note that the In Detail option is unchecked (**F5:24**), thus the report will run as a summary of customer accounts. In addition, the report date is set to print outstanding accounts as of 02/28/2007. Change this date to March 31, 2007 and click the Print button. (Remember the Destination button is set to print the report to the screen.) Scroll to the last page of the report and note the ending balance (your balance may vary from the report illustrated in **F5:25**).

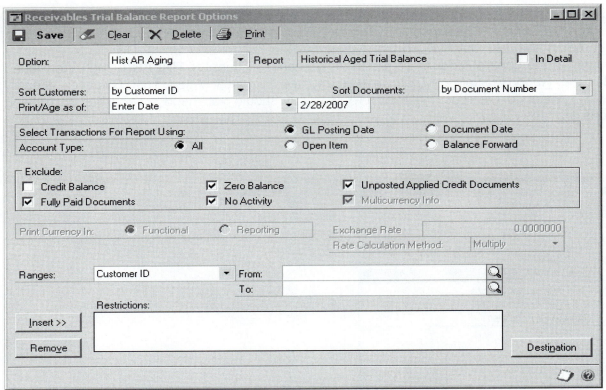

F5:24 Hist AR Aging Report Modify Window

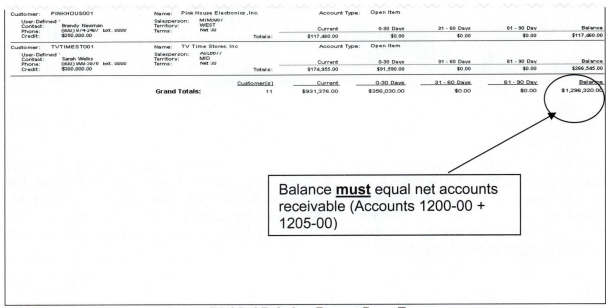

Balance **must** equal net accounts receivable (Accounts 1200-00 + 1205-00)

F5:25 AR Aging Report Page Two

What is account 1205-00, Sales Discounts Available?

When selecting the option to track discounts available in Sales Series setup, Great Plains tracks potential customer discounts on invoices that offer discount terms. Thus, Great Plains records the potential discount to a contra Accounts Receivable account, reflecting the net outstanding receivables if all customers were to take advantage of the discount.

Great Plains makes appropriate entries to the Accounts Receivable account and discount taken (contra revenue account) when customer payments are recorded within the discount period.

The next step to reconciling requires a review of the general ledger accounts, Accounts Receivable and Sales Discounts Available. To check these balances, use the *Inquiry>>Financial>>Summary* menu, pull up each account, and total the account balances for March. The sum of the accounts must equal the aging balance or the Series are "out of balance." There are times when two Series become "out of balance." This usually occurs when employees don't follow proper procedures to correct posting errors or post transactions to the wrong accounts.

With an out-of-balance condition, an investigation ensues to uncover the discrepancy. Hopefully the Series have been reconciled monthly, therefore the condition occurred in the current period. When this is not the case, you must pinpoint the period by repeatedly running earlier month-end aging reports, and comparing balances to the general ledger accounts.

After identifying the initial period of discrepancy, you then review detailed postings in the general ledger accounts for that period. This review is performed by printing the detailed general ledger trial balance discussed in Chapter 2. You are searching for audit trail codes not originating from the Sales Series.[10] Upon discovery of an out-of-place code, you have located the problem.

A code originating from the Financial Series indicates someone probably attempted to fix an error in the Sales Series with a journal entry in the Financial Series. As stated previously, improper procedures for correcting errors often produce the out-of-balance condition.[11] It cannot be overstated that all errors originating in one Series must be corrected in that Series, unless the correction involves reclassifying an entry from one revenue or expense account to different revenue or expense accounts. When audit trail codes originate from a Series other than Financial, reconcile that Series to its general ledger control account to help locate the discrepancy.[12]

When the audit trail fails to pinpoint the problem, the next method relies on the Smart List.[13] This reconciling method can be time consuming. You begin by selecting the Accounts Transactions Smart List category. The Current Financials Journal report is then customized to filter for entries posted to the two accounts receivable accounts. To do this:

1. Add the Originating Master Name as a column because it contains the Customer ID. In addition, add the TRX Source to locate the general ledger audit trail code associated with the transactions.

---

[10] Refer to the audit trail discussion in Chapter 3.
[11] Appendix C lists proper procedures for correcting errors in each Series.
[12] Each Series contains trial balance reports that must reconcile to the control account for the Series.
[13] Refer to the Smart List topic in Chapter 2.

2. Click Search to filter the report for the 1200-00 and 1210-00 accounts. In addition, enter the date ranges pertaining to the out-of-balance period.

3. Add the customized report to the Favorites list for future use.

The results are then exported to Excel. In Excel, the data is grouped and subtotaled by customer. The spreadsheet then serves as the backdrop for determining what the Financial Series indicates as a customer's ending balance and comparing the amounts to the customer's balance on the aging report. You will also need to enter customer ending balances from the last reconciled aging (or export using the Smart List) into your spreadsheet to determine Financial Series ending balances.

We do not illustrate the full process here because this exercise is reserved for end-of-chapter assessment. The point of this discussion is to emphasize the importance of reconciling the Series at least monthly. Imagine reconciling an out-of-balance condition going back six months or a year. Moreover, the integrity of financial statements and loss of customer trust is threatened when Series are out of balance.

Activity Reporting
The Activity Report category (*F5:26*) prints control reports for sales activities. For some companies, these reports replace document triggers. Instead of waiting for a sales order to arrive in shipping, the Sales Open Order report (*F5:27*) prints outstanding orders. The warehouse or shipping departments can review this report daily and begin order fulfillment prior to receipt of the sales order. Likewise, fulfillment reports can trigger the shipping or billing processes.

The Sales Document Status report monitors sales order processing. Daily review of this report can pinpoint order processing delays that improve revenue cycle efficiencies.

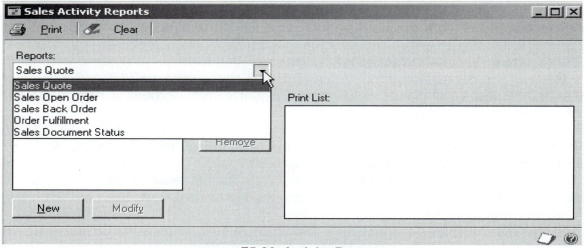

F5:26 Activity Reports

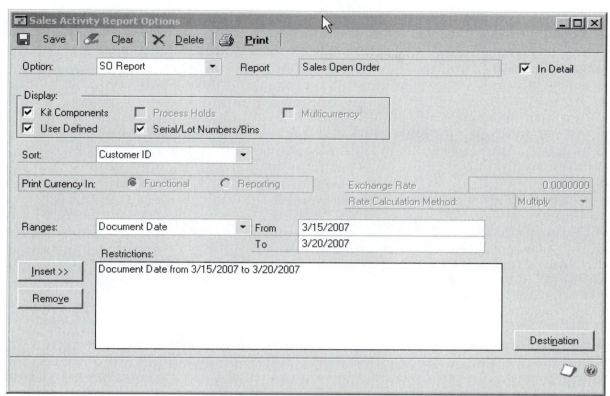

F5:27 Sales Open Order Report

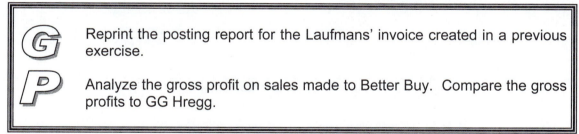

Reprint the posting report for the Laufmans' invoice created in a previous exercise.

Analyze the gross profit on sales made to Better Buy. Compare the gross profits to GG Hregg.

E5:7 Sales Series Reporting Practice

RECEIVABLES SALES SERIES TRANSACTIONS

In this section, we explore orders with inventory shortages, customer returns of inventory, credit/debit memos, and customer write-offs.

Customer Returns and Credit/Debit Memos
We look first at customer returns of inventory and credit/debit memos. Customers return inventory for various reasons such as damage to items, wrong items, or unwanted items. As discussed earlier in the chapter, returns may be captured in either the Invoicing or Sales Order Processing Tiers. S&S requires the accounts receivable department to enter returns and clerks use either the *Transactions>>Sales>>Invoice Entry* or *Invoicing Batches* menu. The data entry process is similar to sales orders, except the document type is Return. Since returns occur infrequently, transactions are recorded and posted immediately.

For our example, we refer to a previous invoice for Candy Bowl Catalog. In November 2006, the company purchased several items. Among these were 95 MaYaha 7.1 Channel audio receivers. On March 16, 2007, Candy Bowl returns 16 defective receivers for credit. Capture the entry as shown in *F5:28*.

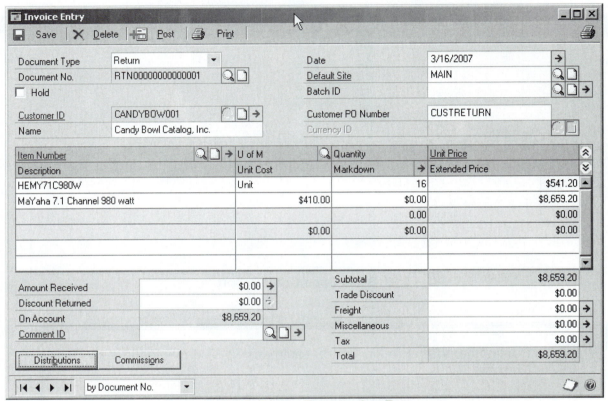

F5:28 Return Transaction Entry

After entering the quantity returned, the window in *F5:29* opens, requesting the status of this inventory. The On Hand field stores the quantity to be restocked and available for future sales. The remaining boxes, other than Damaged, signify inventory quantities not restocked, but viable for other purposes such as demos, salvage, or repair. The quantity returned by Candy Bowl goes in the Damaged box, signifying a write-off of inventory to the damage expense account. Enter 16 in the Damaged field, then click OK. Before posting this transaction, ensure that inventory costs will post to the 4530-00 account by clicking the Distribution button (see *F5:30*).

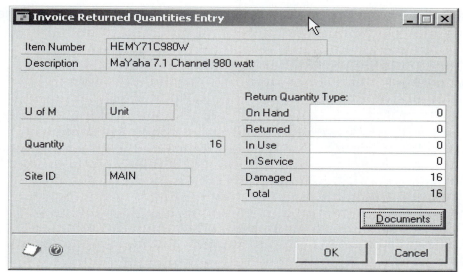

F5:29 Returned Inventory Disposition

F5:30 Return General Ledger Distribution

The distribution window shows an entry to reduce accounts receivable (1200-00), to reverse revenue and commissions (4100-01, 5200-00, 2230-00), and to transfer cost of goods sold (4530-00) to damage expense (4500-01).

After posting the return, apply this document against Candy Bowl's invoice using the *Transactions>>Sales>>Apply Sales Documents* menu. In the Apply Sales Documents window (**F5:31**), pull up Candy Bowl's account, and select Returns as the Type. Next, lookup the return document in the Document No. field. Check that both apply dates are correct, then select the original invoice to apply the return. After selecting, the Original Amount becomes $254.80. This balance remains due. In addition, the Unapplied Amount shows zero, indicating the return was fully applied.

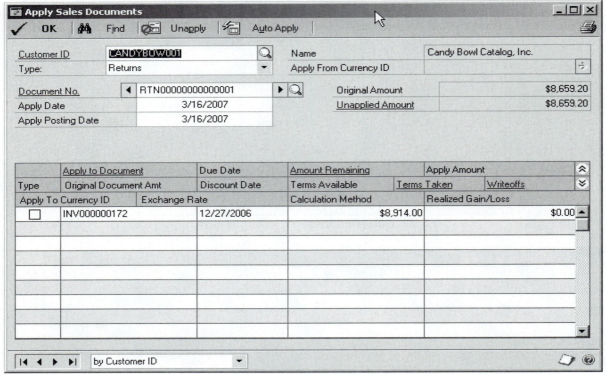

F5:31 Apply Window

There are other situations requiring the Apply Sales Documents window. For instance, after reviewing an aging report, you notice payments or credit/debit memos have not been applied against invoices. Since S&S uses the open invoice method, these documents must be applied to reduce outstanding invoices; otherwise, invoices remain suspended on the customer's account.

The previous example illustrated returns that reduced a customer's account. Credit memos also reduce account balances for reasons other than inventory returns. Sometimes credit is given to customers that are dissatisfied with an item, but are satisfied when offered an after-invoice price reduction. Perhaps a delivery was delayed, so S&S issued a credit memo compensating the customer.

On the other hand, debit memos increase account balances by recording additional charges such as additional delivery fees not on the original invoice. Regardless the reason, credit and debit memos adjust customer balances after invoicing and do not involve inventory. Both document types reside in the transaction window opened from the *Transaction Entry* menu. The data is entered as illustrated in our return example with the exception of selecting either the Debit or Credit document type. In addition, credit memos must be applied to reduce an invoice's balance.

Two final points before leaving this topic. First, the credit department (S&S' owners) authorizes all credit memos. Second, credit and debit memos occur for various reasons, therefore the Distribution window should be checked prior to posting and an explanation stored in the Description field of the line item.

Customer Write-Offs

All sales carry the threat of failure to collect. When a company implements strong credit authorization controls, these situations arise infrequently. However, no procedure ensures total protection. Therefore, companies write off an account after exhausting other collection remedies. For illustrative purposes, we will write off the remaining $254.80 balance for Candy Bowl. There are two methods for entering this write-off.

The first method writes off invoices when applying payments. Refer back to the Apply Sales Documents window (*F5:20*), noting the appearance of a write-off field in the second row. Hence, when applying Candy Bowl's return, we could have clicked the line item expansion button, opening the second row, and entered the write-off amount. If the amount exceeded the maximum write-off set for Candy Bowl's customer card, Great Plains would have prompted for entry of an authorization password. S&S uses the password of <u>PASSWORD</u>.

To understand why S&S sets a write-off password, we must remember that write-offs are an authorization function and authorization falls into two categories, general and specific. Great Plains provides two locations for authorizing write-offs. The first appears under the customer card's maximum write-off field. This field stores the general authorization for write-offs. The second location appears under the Receivables setup menu where Great Plains stores an override password that specifically authorizes write-offs exceeding the customer maximum.

The second method for writing off an invoice is accessed from the *Tools>>Routines>> Sales>>Write Off Documents* menu. Open the window appearing in *F5:32*. This window searches customer records based on screening criteria, which is especially useful when several customers have minimal balances. For instance, when there are ten customers with balances under $2. Entering $2 in the Writeoff Limit field and omitting specific customer filters processes these write-offs with one click. However, before processing, it is wise to run a Preview report (*F5:33*) because processing posts write off amounts.

Use this method to write-off CandyBowl's balance. When processed, the posting control report appearing in *F5:34* prints.

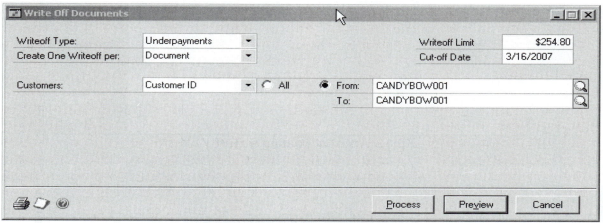

F5:32 Write Off Documents Window

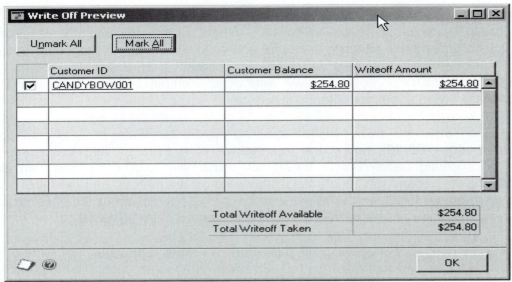

F5:33 Write Off Preview Window

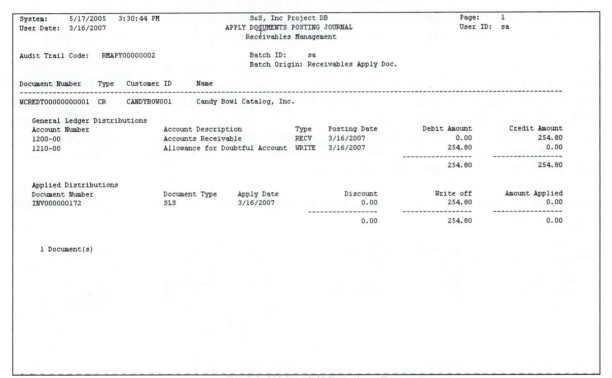

F5:34 Write Off Posting Report

Review the report in **F5:34** and explain why Great Plains used accounts 1200-00 and 1210-00 to record the write-off. Provide generally accepted accounting principles (GAAP) justification for using these accounts.

E5:8 Write-Off Posting Accounts

Orders and Out-of-Stock Inventory

In previous sales order examples, there was always enough inventory stock to fill customer orders. However, this is not always the case. Let's process an order to Better Buy where the quantity requested exceeds the quantity on-hand.

Enter the order from Better Buy (*F5:35*) placed on March 28, 2007 for fifty 34" widescreen televisions made by Sunyung, item number TVSN34W.

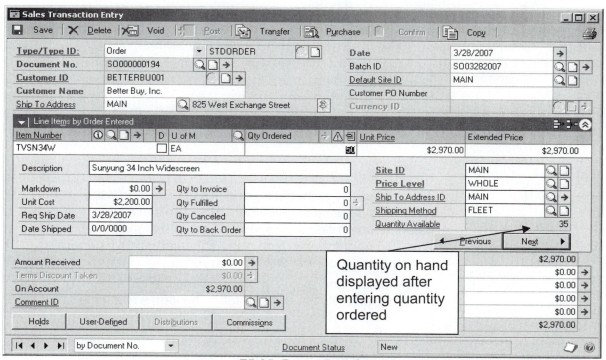

F5:35 Better Buy Order

Upon entering the quantity, Great Plains opens the Sales Quantity Shortage Options window (*F5:36*), requesting instructions on allocating the inventory shortage. To understand why this window opened, we need information on setup options.

Sales Order setup contains an option for defaulting allocation of inventory shortages. This option has been set to allocate by line item. Therefore, the software prompted for allocation instructions on the line item that created the shortage. Great Plains offers a variety of methods for allocating shortages; refer to *T5:4*. When reviewing this table it is helpful to remember that sales orders flag inventory, marking it unavailable to subsequent orders. The entry that actually reduces inventory does not record until invoice posting.

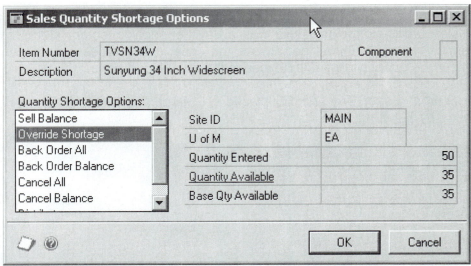

F5:36 Sales Quantity Shortage Options Window

Method	Description
Sell Balance	This method flags inventory and fills the order with the remaining balance in inventory. The item's available balance then reflects zero. However, with this method, a back order for the shortage does not automatically generate during sales order transfer.
Override Shortage	This method ignores the shortage, flags the balance on-hand, and fills the order in full. The item's available balance then reflects a negative quantity. Again, back orders do not generate during transfer.
Back Order All	This method back orders the entire order quantity, thus no items of inventory are flagged or filled. Back orders are generated during transfer of sales orders.
Back Order Balance	This method is a combination of Sell Balance and Back Order All. The items on-hand are flagged and the order quantity filled. Back orders generate during transfer.
Cancel All	This method cancels the entire order.
Cancel Balance	This method flags inventory and fills the order with the on-hand balance. The remaining balance is cancelled.
Distribute	This method is used when companies maintain multiple sites. The order quantity is distributed, according to availability, among multiple locations.

T5:4 Inventory Shortage Allocation Methods

Select Back Order Balance in the Quantity Shortage Options field, then click OK. Notice the quantity available changes to zero in the Sales Order window (*F5:37*) and the QtyFulfilled contains 35, the amount that was on-hand.

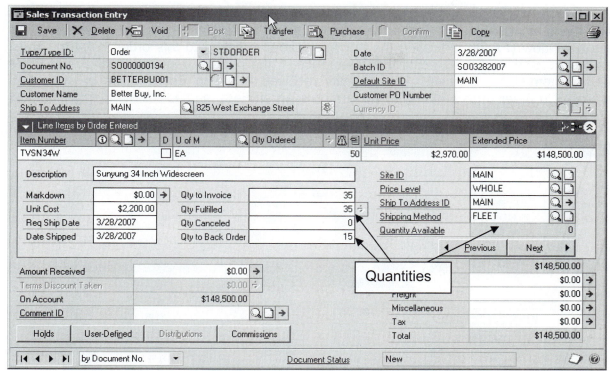

F5:37 Better Buy Order After Allocation

Instead of waiting to send a back order request to the purchasing department, let's generate a purchase order by clicking the Purchase button. This opens the PO Generator window (**F5:38**). Select the Item tab and change the quantity on the order to 30. This restocks inventory above the order shortage. Click the Generate button and the order is assigned to the preferred vendor shown on the left. (Preferred vendors were discussed in Chapter 4.) Open the inventory item's card, noticing Sunyung is the preferred vendor.

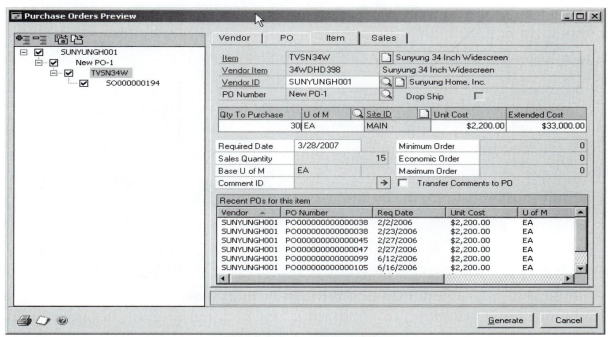

F5:38 PO Generator Window

Now return to the order entry screen and reopen Better Buy's order. Notice the paperclip beside the quantity amount. Place the cursor inside the field and click the paperclip. This opens a window (*F5:39*) indicating the purchase order is linked to this order (*F5:40*). Thus, when the Purchasing Series posts the items' receipt, the quantity required to fill Better Buy's order is automatically flagged. The quantity received linked to Better Buy's order is thus unavailable to other orders. The PO generator is an efficient method for managing inventory shortages.

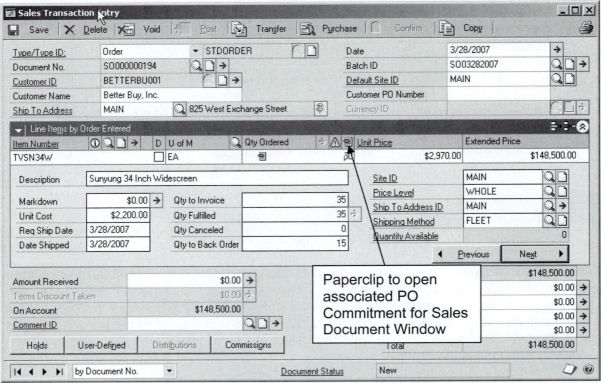

F5:39 Better Buy PO with Associated PO

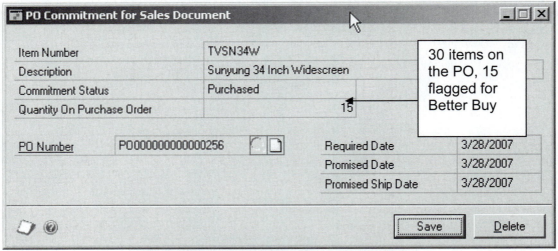

F5:40 PO Associated to Better Buy's Order

LEVEL TWO

Level Two focuses on Sales Series setup. In the revenue cycle, internal control begins at understanding Sales Series options that assist in meeting internal control objectives. Sales Series options are pervasive controls over activities performed in the Series.

SALES SERIES SETUP AND INTERNAL CONTROLS

From discussions in Level One, you understand that Sales Series activities segment into sales order processing, invoicing, and receivables. Accordingly, each segment contains individual setup options.

Receivables Setup

We begin with Receivables setup options because this segment contains options that function as pervasive controls for the Sales Series as well as options for activities performed in the Receivables Transaction Processing Tier. The Receivables Management Setup window (**F5:41**) is accessed using *Tools>>Setup>>Sales>>Receivables* menu. Receivables setup controls divide into five primary sections, Aging Periods, Options, Passwords, Apply by, and Defaults. Explanation for each section follows.

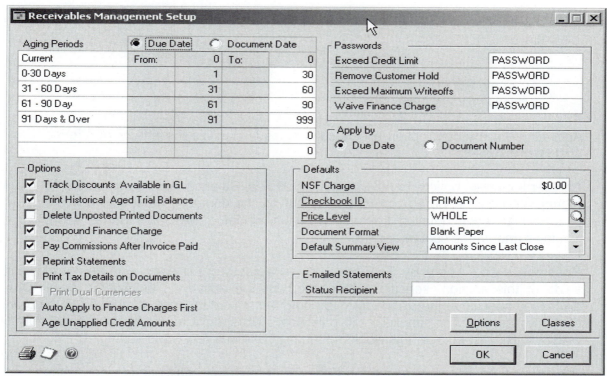

F5:41 Receivables Management Setup Window

Aging Periods Section: Aging periods control sales document aging and age brackets. The choice to age by either document or due date affects age bracket balances reflected on aging reports. Documents that age include invoices, returns, credit/debit memos, finance charges, and payments.

Options Section: Many of the items in the Options section are self-explanatory; however, the option to Track Discounts Available in GL requires explanation. As discussed in Level One, activating discount tracking instructs Great Plains to record the accounts receivable amount net of the potential discount offered to customers.

For instance, an invoice posts for $1,000 to a customer offered a 2/10, Net 30 discount. The entry recorded is:

	Debit	Credit
Accounts Receivable	$ 980	
Sales Discounts Available	$ 20	
Sales Revenue		$1,000

When the customer pays within the discount period the entry is:

	Debit	Credit
Cash	$ 980	
Sales Discounts Taken	$ 20	
Accounts Receivable		$980
Sales Discounts Available		$20

When customer pays outside the discount period the entry is:

	Debit	Credit
Cash	$1,000	
Accounts Receivable		$980
Sales Discounts Available		$20

Activating the discount option allows companies to analyze the effects of offering customer discounts.

Another important option, Print Historical Aged Trial Balance, allows companies to regenerate prior period aging reports. However, the company must also activate options that retain detailed transaction history under other Sales Series setup windows and on the customer card.

Passwords and Apply By Sections: When a password is entered in any of the four fields of this section, specific authorization for the activity is activated. Level One discussed specific authorization for overriding the maximum write-off amount entered on customer cards. For simplicity, all passwords on specific controls have been set to PASSWORD. Of course, this would not be the case in a real world setting.

The Apply by option determines the behavior of payment applications when using the Auto Apply button in the Apply Sales Documents window. When auto-applying payments, the Due Date option applies payments to the oldest invoice. The Apply Sales Documents window and the Auto Apply button were discussed in Level One.

Defaults Section: The options listed set default behavior for specific activities performed in the Sales Series. The Checkbook ID and Price Level defaults apply to transactions where the customer or inventory cards fail to assign a default. For S&S, the Checkbook ID defaults the cash entry for payments to the general ledger account associated with the Primary checking account.

In addition, the Receivables Management Setup window (*F5:41*) contains buttons accessing the Customer Class Setup window and Receivables Setup Options window (*F5:42*). The Customer Class window was discussed in Level One; therefore, we move on to the Receivables Setup Options window.

Type	Description	Code	Next Number
Sales / Invoices	Sales / Invoices	SLS	SALES000000000018
Scheduled Payments	Scheduled Payments	SCH	SCHED000000000001
Debit Memos	Debit Memos	DR	DEBIT000000000002
Writeoff Debit Memos			WDEBIT00000000001
Finance Charges	Finance Charges	FIN	FCHRG000000000003
Service / Repairs	Service / Repairs	SVC	SRVCE000000000001
Warranties	Warranties	WRN	WRNTY000000000001
Credit Memos	Credit Memos	CR	CREDT000000000001
Writeoff Credit Memos			WCREDT00000000002
Returns	Returns	RTN	RETRN000000000001
Cash Receipts	Payments	PMT	PYMNT000000000190

Date of Last:

		Default Tax Schedule IDs:	
Finance Charge	8/31/2006	Sales	
Statements Printed	12/31/2006	Freight	
Balance Forward Accounts Aged	0/0/0000	Miscellaneous	
Open Items Accounts Aged	3/15/2007		
Paid Transactions Removal	0/0/0000	User-Defined 1	User-Defined 1
		User-Defined 2	User-Defined 2

Sales History Includes:
☑ Sales   ☑ Discount   ☑ Freight   ☑ Miscellaneous   ☑ Tax

OK

F5:42 Receivables Setup Options

This window applies only to entries made in the Receivables Transactions Processing Tier. The window stores document numbers for transactions. Remember, these codes and sequence numbers form the audit trail discussed in Chapter 3. In addition, the window stores the last date certain receivable activities were performed and the option to maintain receivables history. The remaining fields are self-explanatory.

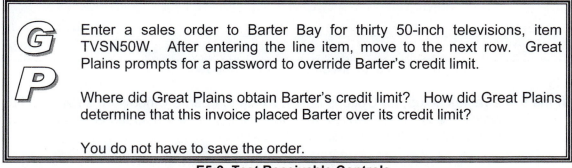

Enter a sales order to Barter Bay for thirty 50-inch televisions, item TVSN50W. After entering the line item, move to the next row. Great Plains prompts for a password to override Barter's credit limit.

Where did Great Plains obtain Barter's credit limit? How did Great Plains determine that this invoice placed Barter over its credit limit?

You do not have to save the order.

E5:9 Test Receivable Controls

Invoicing Setup

Controls over activities performed in the Invoice Processing Tier are separate from receivable controls. The *Tools>>Setup>>Sales>>Invoicing* menu opens the Invoicing Setup window (***F5:43***). Many options are self-explanatory; however, a few require explanation.

The first concerns Great Plains' selection of default posting accounts. In Chapter 3, we accepted the fact that Ashton defaulted general ledger accounts from a customer's card. The Customer option under Posting Accounts from explains why this is true.

Second, note the section storing document numbers. These numbers are different from the numbers used in Receivables, as well as those we will see in Sales Orders Processing setup. Each Sales Series setup window associates distinct audit trail numbers to identify transaction origination. This is a good time to point out that not only must an error be corrected in the Series originating the transaction, the error must be corrected in the Series tier originating it. This is because of the way Series options are setup. Appendix C covers error correction by Series and document type.

Finally, we see an option to track voided transactions. This feature, coupled with the option that bars deletion of printed documents under Receivables setup, implements internal controls over data entry. In addition, tracking voided documents lets companies analyze customer sales performance.

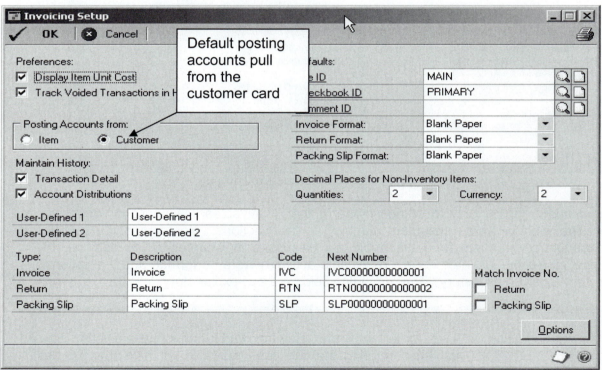

F5:43 Invoicing Setup Window

As with the Receivables setup, an Options button exists to open a window for setting additional controls over invoicing activities. Notice that the Invoicing Setup Options window (***F5:44***) provides an extensive list of specific authorization controls.

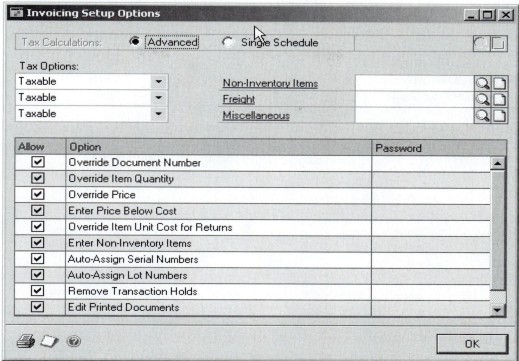

F5:44 Invoicing Setup Options Window

Sales Order Processing Setup

Sales Order Processing setup options are accessed under the *Tools>> Setup>>Sales>>Sales Order Processing* menu. Setup options for activities performed in the Sales Order Processing Tier are similar to those in Invoicing setup. However, there is an added layer of complexity. Remember sales orders interface with inventory. In addition, sales order entry uses a variety of source documents. Therefore, aside from the basic options, the Sales Order Processing Setup window contains buttons accessing options by document type. We also see the familiar Options button. Our discussion focuses on the options that may not be self-explanatory.

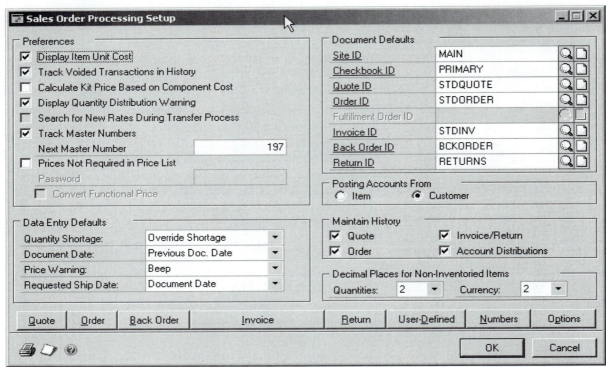

F5:45 Sales Order Processing Setup

Preferences Section: We discuss only a few of these options, in particular:

❖ **Display Item Unit Cost:** Determines whether an item's inventory cost displays during transaction line item entry.

❖ **Track Voided Transactions in History:** Functions the same as in the Invoicing Setup window.

❖ **Prices Not Required in Price List:** Controls item pricing on orders. Left unchecked, this option prevents employees from inserting prices not maintained in a price list. Therefore, all inventories must appear and be priced in the Inventory Control Series. Companies that customarily sell nonpriced items of inventory will need to activate the preference, then assign a password that prevents entry of unauthorized prices. In addition, this feature must be activated when a company requires entry of noninventoried items.

Data Entry Defaults Section: Data entry defaults determine field defaults during transaction entry. Here we find the default for handling inventory allocations discussed in Level One. Additionally, we find the option to default a customer requested ship date from the sales order date.

Posting Accounts From: We saw this setting in Invoicing Setup. The location of default general ledger posting accounts can be set differently for transactions originating in the Sales Order Processing Tier. Companies have different reasons for selecting either Customer of Item. For instance, a manufacturer needs to use the item option to determine the general ledger accounts based on whether the item is raw materials, work-in-process, or finished goods. S&S uses the customer option to record sales and costs of goods sold by department.

Document Defaults Section, Document Buttons, and Option Button: Document defaults determine the document type selected when entering transactions in the Sales Order Processing Tier. The default is by transaction type. For instance, for order entry the document defaults to the STDORDER form. When the order transfers to an invoice, the document used is STDINV. These documents, or forms, determine the format of printed output. However, these documents do more than control the appearance of printed output. The document sets internal controls over data entry. To see this, click the Order button at the bottom of the Sales Order Setup window. This action opens the window illustrated in *F5:46*.

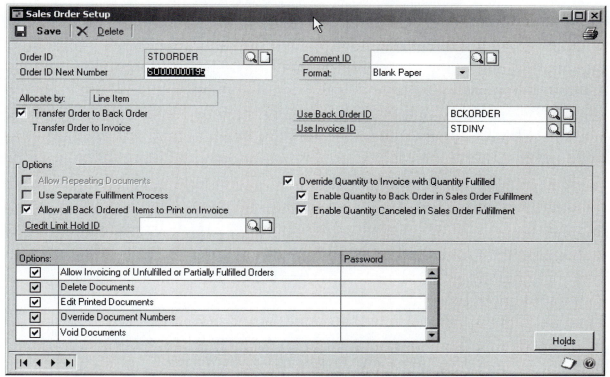

F5:46 Sales Order Document Control Window

Use the Order ID lookup to open the control settings for a STDORDER. We find that the STDORDER transfers inventory back orders to the BCKORDER form and invoices to the STDINV form. We also see two Options sections that control data entry on this form. Both sections deny the action when left unchecked. However, the lower options also permits specific authorization passwords for checked items. (Note: All options are active to facilitate discussions.)

A couple of controls receive special mention. The Edit Printed Documents option protects output. Usually this option remains checked but passworded, to restrict editing printed documents. The Override Document Numbers denies overriding source document numbers that form the audit trail. Usually this option is left unchecked.

S&S uses only the STDORDER; however, companies often use multiple document types based on the order. For instance, a company may use DRPSHP for orders that are drop shipped to the customer. Options must be set on each document.

Close the Sales Order Setup window, then take a few minutes to explore the windows beneath the Back Order, Return, and Invoice buttons. You will find similar controls in each window.

Finally, we find look at the familiar Options window. Click the Options button to open the window illustrated in *F5:47*. The fields displayed in this window pertain to data entry regardless document type. In other words, these controls and options apply to all activities performed in the Sales Order Processing Tier.

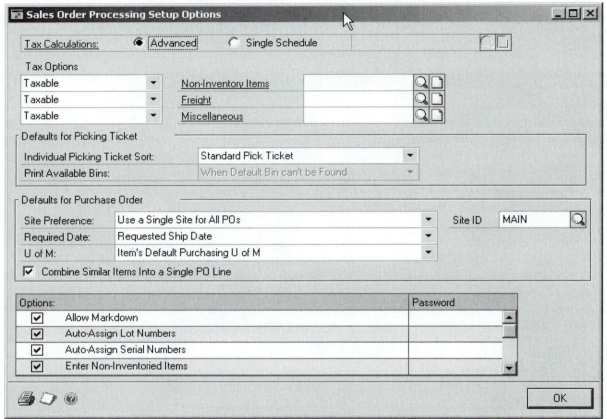

F5:47 Sales Order Processing Options Window

CUSTOMER CARD INTERNAL CONTROLS

In Level One we covered customer card default settings. Defaults serve as data entry controls by auto-filling fields containing general ledger accounts, credit limits, write-off maximums, and other features. However, we did not discuss denying employees the ability to add new customers during transaction entry (referred to as creating customers "on-the-fly"). Remember, creating customers is an authorization function and violates internal controls when performed during data entry (recording). The Advanced Security menu discussed in Chapter 3 is the only way to prevent "on the fly" customer creation.

Another data entry control involves entering sales to customers with past due accounts. This threat is controlled by opening the customer's card and checking the Hold feature. This prevents new sales orders and invoices to customers placed on hold. In addition, the

Receivables Management Setup window's specific authorization password for removing holds should be instituted.

SALES REPORTING AS A CONTROL TOOL

In Level One we discussed all Sales Series report categories except Setup. In addition, we looked at reports from an internal control aspect. The Setup category of reports documents Sales Series settings selected under each setup menu. This category of reports is vital to instituting and documenting compliance with internal control policies.

SALES SERIES: MONTH-END AND YEAR-END CLOSING PROCEDURES

No discussion on internal controls is complete without looking at closing procedures. Closing procedures involve several steps. The accounting department focuses on three areas when closing a period. First, accountants institute posting procedures that ensure transaction posts to the proper accounting period. Second, accountants verify all transactions for the month or year finalized and posted according to GAAP. Finally, accountants verify that the Sales Series reconciles with the Financial Series.

Verify Transactions Record to Proper Period

Ashton instituted period-end posting procedures to protect data integrity. These procedures focus on controls over batch processing. For instance, at the beginning of March, S&S employees process both February and March transactions. Since S&S set the Sales Series to post by Batch Date, Ashton must ensure that transactions for March are stored to a batch separate from February transactions. Without period-end procedures, commingled transactions post to the month of the batch.

In addition, Ashton sets a March cutoff date for stopping processing of transactions in February. Cutoff dates establish the last day for processing a prior month's transactions. After this date, Ashton records sales for February using accrual entries created in the Financial Series. However, this does not mean that the actual transactions never post through the Sales Series. Rather, actual transactions post through March-dated batches with a February transaction date. The February transaction date is necessary to preserve the true date of the transaction.

Verify Completed Postings

Aside from time period concerns, Ashton must verify all valid February transactions recorded. The first step Ashton performs is a review of cycle activity reports, looking for fulfilled orders not yet invoiced. Next, Ashton checks the Sales Series Post window for suspended transactions. Finally, Ashton reviews shipment logs for in-process deliveries. Remember from discussions in the invoicing topic that S&S invoices orders before actual customer delivery for cash flow reasons. This invoicing procedure is GAAP compliant when the company ships FOB shipping point. However, S&S uses FOB destination; therefore, title does not transfer until customer receipt, meaning revenue should not be recognized until customer delivery. Therefore, Ashton posts an entry in the Financial Series to adjust invoice revenue and cost of goods sold for shipments in-transit.

Sales Series Reconciliation, Reporting, and Period Ending Procedures

The process for verifying Series reconciliation was discussed in Level One. After reconciling, Ashton runs month-end reports (and year-end reports when applicable), then performs either a month-end or year-end close of the Sales Series.

To close a month, Ashton follows the process discussed in the Company Fiscal Periods topic in Chapter 2. This topic told us that the *Tools>>Setup>>Company>>Fiscal Periods* menu places a check mark in the Series Closed column to close and open periods. Remember, closing a month denies additional postings to the month, thus protecting financial statement integrity.

At year-end, Ashton follows the same procedures for closing the month, including placing a check mark in the December Series Closed column under the Fiscal Periods window. However, the year-ending involves more than a fiscal period checkmark to the Series. The Series must be year-ended using the *Tools>>Routines>>Sales>>Year End Close* menu, ***F5:48***.

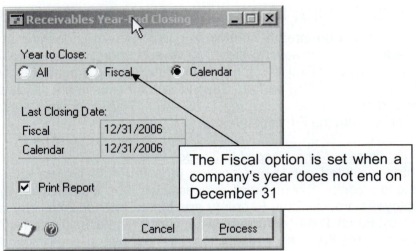

F5:48: Year-End Closing Window

Year-ending the Sales Series significantly alters data files. During year-end, the current year's closed transactions move to history files. In addition, when setup does not retain transaction history, detailed information on closed transactions is deleted; therefore, printing detailed reports is critical. Finally, year-ending removes customer cards marked temporary and updates the Last Year totals on customer records.

Given the changes to data files, Ashton performs a backup prior to closing. Additionally, Ashton sets different transaction processing procedures for December and January transactions. He still sets a January cutoff date; however, this cutoff date means transactions for the new year are entered but not posted until after closing the prior year.

LEVEL ONE QUESTIONS

1. a. Create the following customer:

Company Name:	Best Home Electronics
Main Address:	PO Box 174, Kent, OH 44323
Shipping Address:	378 North Main Street, Kent, OH 44323
Co. Contact:	Ms Sue Smith
Phone:	(330) 775-7777
Location:	Midwest Customer

   b. View the default posting accounts for the new customer. Explain why these accounts are already assigned.

   c. Set the customer's credit limit to $70,000. For S&S, which employee(s) should perform this function?

   d. Turn in the Sales Series Setup report for customers listing your entries. You must customize the existing Customer Setup report to print in detail and show only the record for Best Home.

2. When completing this question, keep all entries in March 2007. The new customer from the previous question is purchasing:

   15 of item TVSN42W
   50 of item TVBT46WPJ

   a. Record the entries from order to invoicing, producing all required documentation for revenue cycle activities. Explain how revenue cycle departments used your documentation.

   b. Note any exceptions that appear during data entry. When encountering inventory shortages, choose to override shortages. Explain procedures for handling exceptions.

3. Print a customer statement for the new customer as of March 31, 2007.

4. Record the new customer's payment in-full received on April 10. Turn in the posting reports.

5. Assume an out-of balance condition exists requiring the Smart List's assistance in reconciling the Sales Series to the Financial Series. Export the Smart List report to Excel and develop a worksheet to show the Series is in-balance.

LEVEL TWO QUESTIONS

1. Explain how the Sales Series implements pricing controls. How does this control minimize threats outlined in the Sales Cycle Activities diagram?

2. Why does Great Plains deny sales order posting? (Justify your answer using the Conceptual Framework.)

3. Implement Sales Series batch controls and explain the steps taken.

4. Sales order employees are overriding invoice numbers assigned to transferred sales orders. Explain your solution to the problem, including tests on the solution.

5. The owners want the ability to sell an item below cost, but do not want this option available to employees. Explain how you would provide the owners this flexibility.

6. Explain why strong internal controls deny the ability to edit a printed document. How would you implement this control for sales orders?

7. One of the threats companies face is the failure to bill customers. Explain specific features of Great Plains that detect and minimize this threat.

8. The revenue cycle faces a threat of credit sales to customers with poor or limited credit histories. Explain Great Plain's preventative tools that mitigate this threat.

9. Select one of the threats on the Sales Cycle Activities diagram not listed in previous questions and explain how Great Plains helps control that threat.

CHAPTER 6: EXPENDITURE CYCLE AND GREAT PLAINS PURCHASING SERIES

CHAPTER OVERVIEW

With knowledge on revenue cycle activities, we move to the matching side of revenue. This chapter focuses on expenditure cycle[1] activities and using the Great Plains Purchasing Series to process, report, and control cycle activities.

> ➢ Level One focuses on using Great Plains for transaction processing. After an overview of expenditure cycle activities, you learn to process transactions by department. In addition, you learn internal controls over transaction processing, including purchasing documentation and reporting.

> ➢ Level Two focuses on configuring pervasive internal controls using Purchasing Series setup. Month-end and year-end closing procedures are also covered.

Level One covers:
> ➢ The Purchasing Series menu structure and the expenditure cycle REA data model
> ➢ Aspects of handling day-to-day expenditure cycle activities, including vendor cards, purchase orders, inventory receipts, vendor invoicing, credit memos, inventory returns, and vendor payments
> ➢ Using reporting as a control tool and activity trigger

Level Two covers:
> ➢ Implementing internal controls through Purchasing Series setup
> ➢ Performing Series month-end and year-end closing

---

[1] A deeper understanding of expenditure cycle activities is found in Chapter 11 of Marshall Romney and Paul Steinbart, _Accounting Information Systems_ (10th ed., Prentice Hall 2006), p. 410-425.

LEVEL ONE

As in Chapter 5, we begin with interpreting expenditure cycle activities. We see the familiar activity diagram in *F6:1*. Departments trigger cycle activities by sending requisitions for goods, supplies, or services to the purchasing department. Requisitions internally control purchases, mitigating overstocking and unauthorized purchases. We also notice that the purchasing department receives the back orders, discussed in the previous chapter, from the sales department.

Great Plains does not offer purchase requisitions; however, it does include Purchase Order Enhancements that require PO approval prior to printing. This approval feature allows department managers to input purchase orders without violating internal controls, thus creating cycle efficiencies. We will see in the purchase order topic how PO Enhancements implement controls over releasing PO documents.[2]

As indicated in the activity diagram (*F6:1*) the purchasing department authorizes POs before release. Purchasing is assigned responsibility for ensuring document release to authorized vendors.[3] At day's end, purchasing reviews POs entered by department managers to verify purchasing efficiencies and compliance with purchasing controls. For instance, purchasing employees verify, using the PO status report, that POs to the same vendor are combined into one, POs are to preferred vendors, and quantities purchased maximize vendor price breaks. After review, purchasing authorizes and then prints (releases) POs, sending a signed copy to the vendor. As with sales orders, purchase orders do not post. (For S&S, purchasing employees are the owners, Scott Parry and Susan Gonzalez.)

The diagram illustrates next that vendor shipments arrive in receiving. Receiving employees must determine whether arriving shipments have authorized Pos; therefore run daily PO status reports containing details on issued POs. In addition, employees use Great Plains to look up information on outstanding purchase orders and to enter receiving data.

After verifying receipt authorization, the receiving department inspects package contents for item quality and comparison with the vendor packing slip. Employees input receipt quantities to Great Plains. Inventoried goods are sent to the warehouse, while noninventoried goods are sent directly to departments. Back order journals are sent to the sales department as notification of inventory arrivals on pending customer orders. Receiving employees also send a receiving report and vendor packing slips to the accounts payable department. Sometimes vendors enclose an invoice in lieu of the packing slip. These are also sent to accounts payable to trigger payment.

When not enclosed with the shipment, vendor invoices arrive in S&S' accounts payable department from the mailroom, triggering the invoice posting process. Employees enter invoices against received POs. Besides posting vendor invoices, accounts payable employees prepare vendor invoice aging reports, sending reports to the controller and cashier. The cashier reviews S&S' cash position and then selects vendors for payment. When selecting, the cashier focuses on taking advantage of vendor discounts when cash flow permits.

---

[2] Great Plains also offers the Purchase Order Generator add-in, which automatically generates inventory purchase orders based on stock levels. This add-in is not included with the student version.
[3] Recall that vendor assignment to inventory items was in Chapter 4

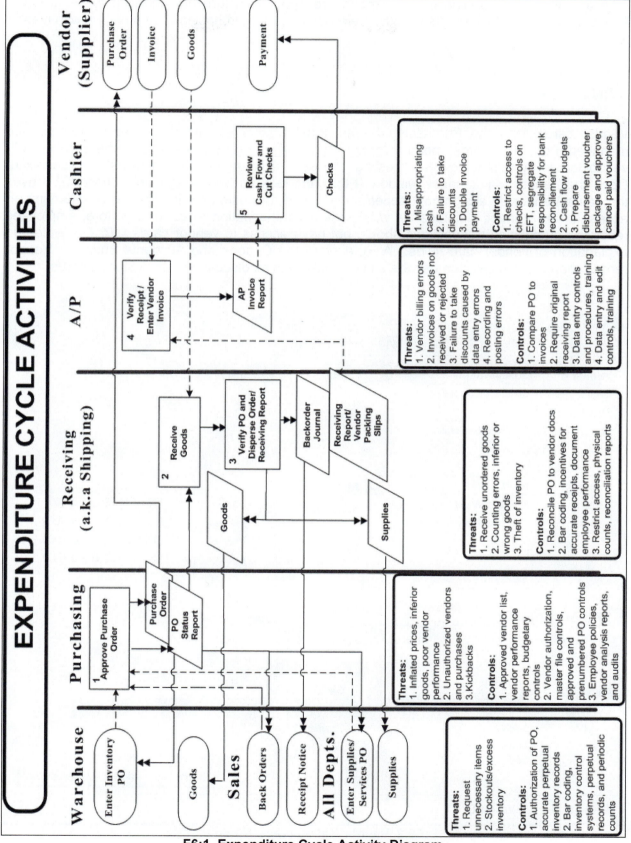

F6:1 Expenditure Cycle Activity Diagram

With a basic understanding of the expenditure cycle, let's turn our attention to using Great Plains to perform activities. As with the Sales Series, the Purchasing Series begins with master records.

VENDORS

Vendor cards form the Purchasing Series' master records. Vendors, like customers, are managed from the Cards menu, *Cards>>Purchasing>>Vendor*. We become familiar with vendor cards by managing S&S' existing vendors. A list of vendors appears in Appendix B. Open the Vendor Maintenance window (*F6:2*) and look up SumSang Corporation. S&S uses the same Vendor ID assignment scheme discussed for customers in Chapter 5. Remember, access to the Vendor Maintenance window is an authorization function; therefore, employees recording purchasing transactions should not have access to vendor cards. *T6:1* provides an explanation of vendor card fields. Also, explore the Options and Accounts Buttons. Vendor record changes and creation use the same procedures as discussed with customer cards.

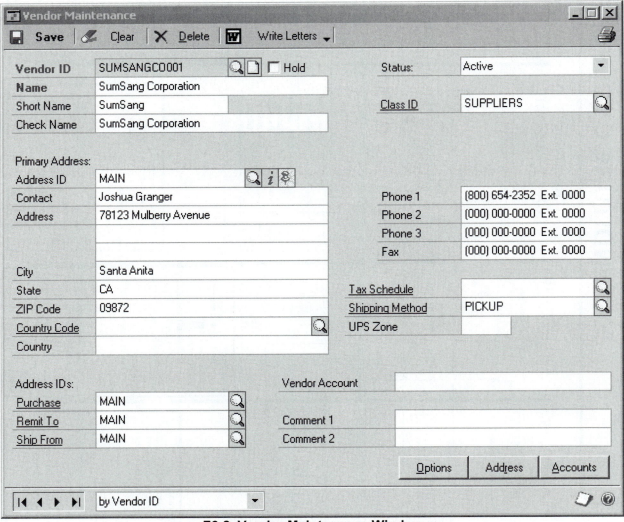

F6:2 Vendor Maintenance Window

Field	Description
Vendor ID	Vendor record's primary key used to link vendor records with transactions. In addition, Vendor IDs ensure entity integrity.
Name	Full company name, may also assign a short name to speed data entry.
Status	Vendor flag denoting the card as active, inactive, or temporary.
Class ID	Class IDs for vendors function similar to customer classes in the Sales Series. Vendor classes are setup using the *Tools>>Setup>> Purchasing>>Vendor Class* menu. S&S uses the vendor classes Marketing, Pay/Adm, R&M, Suppliers, Utilities, and Other to assist in analyzing purchases.
Address ID	The Address ID associates multiple vendor addresses with a vendor card. All vendors must have at least one main or primary address identifier.
Shipping Method	The Shipping Method links to the same shipper table discussed in the Sales Series. However, the selection here refers to the shipping method used by the vendor.
Tax Schedule	Vendor field linked to S&S' sales tax table maintained under the *Tools>>Setup>> Company>>Tax Details* menu. As a wholesaler, S&S does not pay taxes on inventory purchases.
Purchase, Remit To, Ship From	The Address ID in these fields refer to S&S' locations that vendors use to ship inventory and mail invoices.
Vendor Account	The account number assigned to S&S by the vendor.
Accounts Button	Default general ledger distribution accounts used for posting purchase transactions. However, when purchasing inventory, Great Plains selects default accounts on the inventory card.
Address Button	Opens the address window used to view and maintain multiple vendor addresses.
Options Button	Window that accesses payment terms, credit limits, and other options, including the option to trigger vendor 1099 tax reporting.

T6:1 Vendor Card Fields

Now is a good time to review default posting accounts on transactions involving inventory.

First, Great Plains looks to Sales Series setup to determine whether the customer or item option controls inventory posting. Remember from Chapter 5, S&S defaults posting accounts from customer cards; therefore, sales revenue and inventory expense (cost of goods sold) posts using the accounts on the customer's card.

When the customer card fails to provide a default expense account, Great Plains looks for defaults on the inventory card. When not present here, Great Plains looks for a default expense account on the vendor card. (When the transaction involves the purchase of noninventoried items, Great Plains always looks to default expense accounts on the vendor card.)

Finally, when all other sources fail to assign a default, Great Plains looks to accounts stored under the *Tools>>Setup>>Posting>>Posting Accounts* menu. When a default is not present, Great Plains suspends the transaction, producing the error appearing in Appendix A. This error is corrected using the procedures found in Appendix A.

So how does Ashton know when posting did not use the customer card defaults? Remember, S&S posts revenue and expense transactions to an account containing the 01, 02, or 03 department segment. Consequently, the defaults on item cards, vendor cards, and posting setup use accounts with the 00 segment. Ashton performs a monthly review of general ledger transactions, thus errors are easily identified when accounts with the 00 segment contain entries.

1. S&S' owners, Scott and Susan, have access to vendor cards. Scott holds primary responsibility for selecting and entering new vendors and has identified a new vendor for Lipsphi and Pasanovic widescreen televisions (items TVLP42HD and TVPS60HDTV.) The vendor's information follows. Scott asks you to create the vendor card, accepting the defaults supplied by the SUPPLIERS class. However, change the delivery method to Local Delivery.

Bright Electronics Supply
757 Lakeshore Blvd.
Cleveland, OH 44107
Joe Swain, Sales Director
(216) 754-3261

2. Review the vendor cards in Appendix B. SumSang Corporation's Vendor ID does not follow Ashton's primary key assignment rules. Identify the problem. Also, can this error be corrected?

E6:1 Practice with Vendor Cards

PURCHASING SERIES TRANSACTIONS

With vendor cards under our belt, let's begin capturing purchasing transactions. Once again, like in the Sales Series, the Purchasing Series has a tiered menu structure as shown in *F6:3*. The first tier initiates transactions interfacing with Inventory Control. The second tier processes all other Purchasing Series transactions such as noninventory invoices and vendor payments.

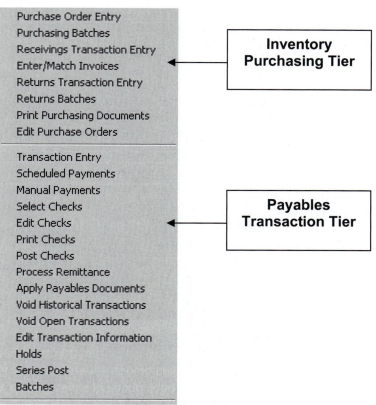

F6:3 Purchasing Transaction Menu

To understand each tier's interaction with data files, review the REA data model in *F6:4*. We see that Order Goods and Receive Goods interfaces with the Inventory table. We also know from our activity diagram that purchase orders initiate inventory purchases. Therefore, we can safely assume that the first tier initiates transactions involving inventory.

Now look at the menu commands in the first tier. The *Purchase Order Entry* menu creates POs. Keep in mind that POs are commitments to purchase; therefore, capturing POs is a database function at this point. Theoretical justification for not posting POs is found in GAAP's matching principle.[4] This principle requires expenses be matched (recognized) against earnings and earnings are recognized under the revenue recognition principle.[5] Additionally, the liability for inventory purchases does not arise until inventory title passes. This means that the purchase liability is booked (posted) when S&S receives the inventory. Consequently, an event for financial statement purposes has not occurred at the point of PO capture.

---

[4] The matching principle recognizes expenses using a direct relationship, period cost, or rational allocation method. For inventory, the applicable method is direct relationship, meaning inventory costs are directly related to inventory sales.

[5] The revenue recognition principle was discussed in Chapter 5.

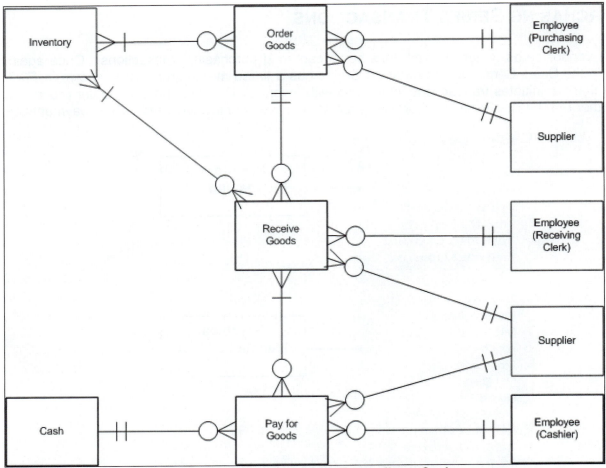

F6:4 REA Data Model for Expenditure Cycle

While POs are entered individually, receipts and/or invoices applied against POs are entered using the *Purchasing Batches* menu.   Review the window in ***F6:5***, noting the Origin field. Setting the Origin field to Receivings TRX opens the Receivings Transaction Entry window (***F6:6***) when clicking the Transactions button. This window is also opened using the *Receivings Transaction Entry* menu. The *Receivings Transaction Entry* menu is used when entering single receipts of inventory while the *Purchasing Batches* menu is more efficient for multiple receipts and permits batch control.

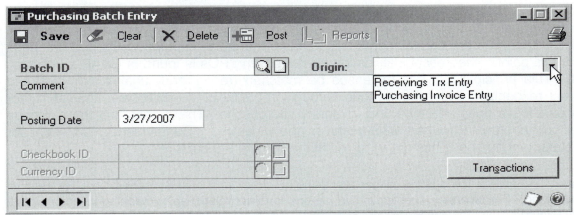

F6:5 Purchasing Batch Entry Window

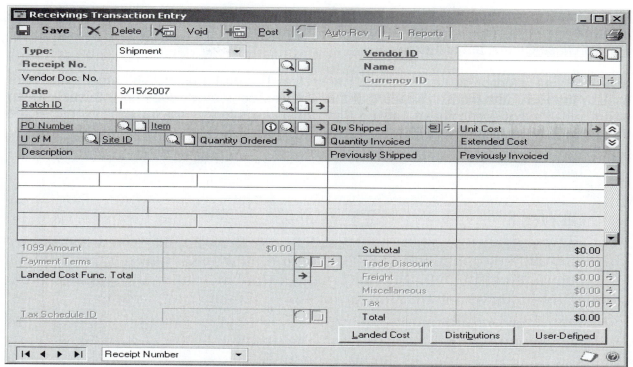

F6:6 Receivings Transaction Entry Window

The *Purchasing Batches* menu works similarly when recording vendor invoices for inventory receipts. With the Origin of Purchasing Invoice Entry, the Transactions button opens the Purchasing Invoice Entry window (*F6:7*). This window is also opened by using the *Enter/Match Invoices* menu.

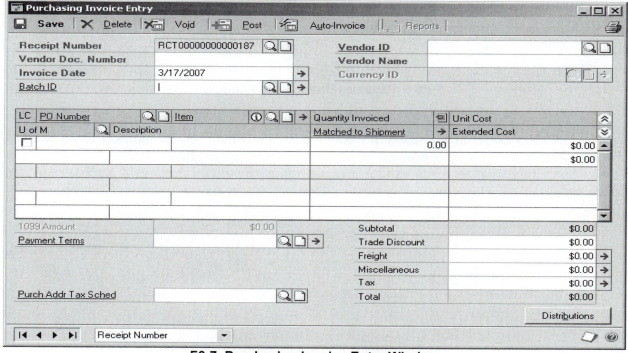

F6:7 Purchasing Invoice Entry Window

The menu items *Returns Batches* and *Returns Transaction Entry* record inventory that is received and later returned to the vendor. The menu items, *Print Purchasing Documents* and *Edit Purchase Orders*, are self-explanatory.

Now turn your attention to the Payables Transaction Tier of the purchasing menus and refer back to the REA data model. Notice that the Pay for Goods event does not interact with the Inventory table, but does interact with the Cash table. Let's look at the transactions processed using this tier's *Batches* menu (**F6:8**).

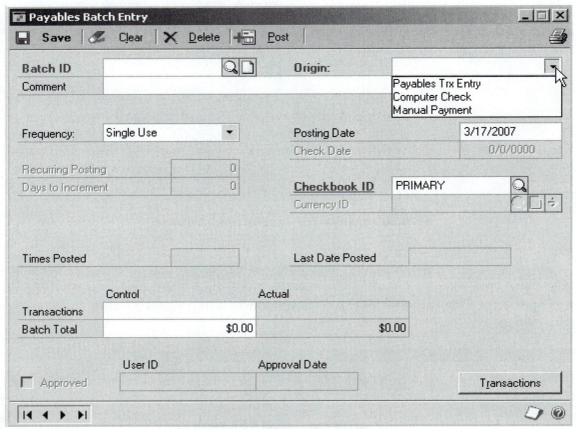

F6:8 Payables Batch Entry Window

Batches with the origin of Payables Trx Entry open the Payables Transaction Entry window (**F6:9**). This window is also opened by using the *Transaction Entry* menu. The Payables Transaction Entry window posts vendor invoices for noninventory purchases such as utilities, travel, and supplies. Remember, this window does not interface with Inventory Control.

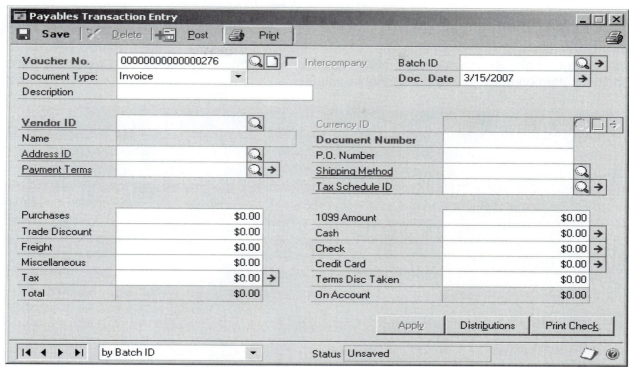

F6:9 Payables Transaction Entry Window

Batches with the origin of Computer Check opens the Select Payables Checks window (***F6:10***), which can also be opened by using the *Select Checks* menu. The Select Payables Checks window parses existing invoices and selects invoices for payment based upon user supplied screening criteria.

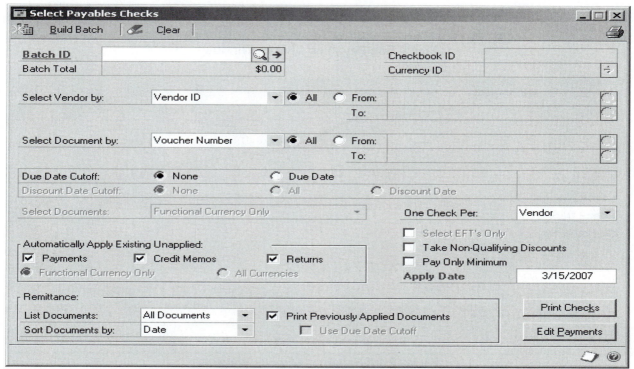

F6:10 Select Payables Checks Window

Once invoices are selected for payment, the _Edit Checks_ menu opens the Edit Payables Checks window (**F6:11**) used to delete selected and add additional invoices for payment. After editing selections, the _Print Checks_ menu opens the Print Payables Checks window (**F6:12**) to print computer checks to vendors. (Note: You can also open this window by clicking the Print Checks button on the Edit Payables Checks window.)

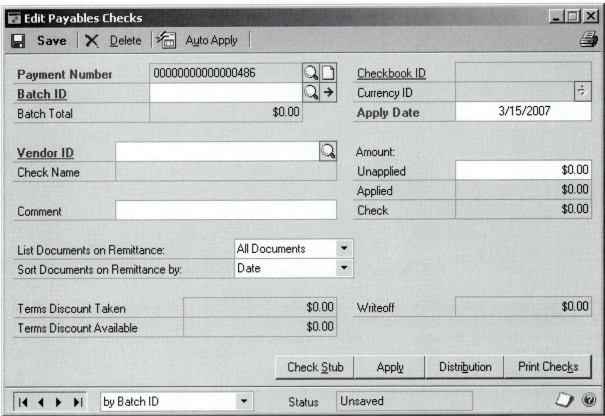

F6:11 Edit Payables Checks Window

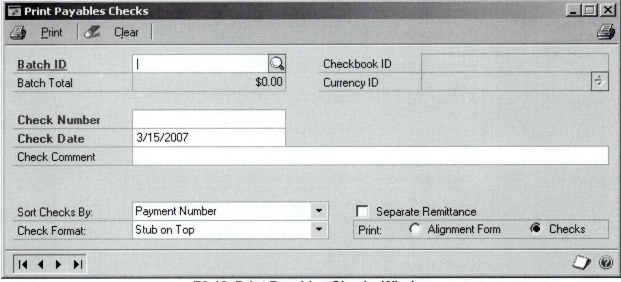

F6:12 Print Payables Checks Window

Computer checks are different from manual payments. The _Manual Payments_ menu opens a Payables Manual Payment Entry window (**F6:13**) to post handwritten checks, cash payments, or credit card payments to vendors.

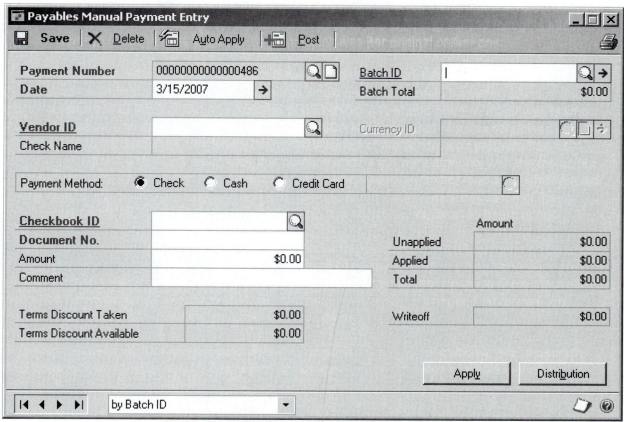

F6:13 Payables Manual Payment Entry Window

Finally, the _Post Checks_ menu is used to posts checks printed through the Print Payables Checks window, while _Process Remittance_ prints remittance advices for vendor checks. Now that you know the menu locations for executing transactions, we move on to processing cycle activities using Great Plains.

PURCHASING AND DEPARTMENTAL ACTIVITIES

For S&S, POs trigger cycle activities. Department managers input noninventory POs while purchasing, sales, and warehouse employees input inventory POs. Let's begin with an inventory PO to Javix Corporation, then build on the process (see **F6:14**). First, review the transaction window's contents, referring to **T6:2** for an explanation on nonfamiliar fields.

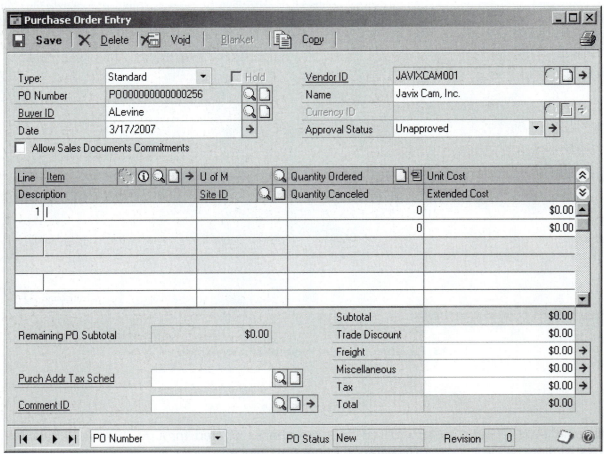

F6:14 Javix Purchase Order

PO Field	Description
Type	Types include Standard, Drop-Ship, Blanket, and Drop-Ship Blanket. The default is standard. Drop-Ship sends inventory directly to customers, meaning inventory does not arrive at S&S' warehouse. Instead items are shipped directly to customers. Drop-Ship is used to speed customer delivery for out-of-stock and nonstocked items. Sometimes companies issue blanket purchase orders, especially when there is a contract with the vendor. Blanket POs authorize a maximum spending limit covering a specific time period. POs applied against the blanket do not require additional authorization and Great Plains tracks purchases against the PO.
PO Number	A document control number generated by Great Plains. Strong internal controls track PO numbers and verify authorization.
Buyer ID	Links an employee's Great Plains User ID with the PO.
Vendor ID	Links a PO to the vendor table. Refer to the REA diagram noting that the Order Goods table associates records to records in the Supplier table. S&S has the same "on the fly" vendor creation issue discussed with customers. S&S prevents vendor creation during PO entry by denying access using advanced security features discussed in Chapter 3.
Approval Status	With Purchase Order Enhancements, POs must be approved prior to printing.
Line	Displays the number of line items on the order. A line item contains two rows of fields. The default view shows information for both rows; however, remember the expansion button expands and contracts line item information.
Item	Links line items to the Inventory table. Great Plains permits line item entry without linking to items, for instance, where a PO authorizes services. In addition, the lookup view for the item field may be customized in Purchase Order Setup to display only items linked to vendor cards in the Inventory Control Series. Recall from Chapter 4 that associating vendors to items is performed from the *Cards>>Inventory>>Vendors* menu.
U of M	Links to the unit of measure table created in the Inventory Control Series. S&S purchases most of its inventory by Case 10 or Case 12. This link defaults from the item card.
Unit Cost	Defaults from the price last paid the vendor on the item card.
Quantity Cancelled	Used to cancel quantities on printed POs. Remember, Great Plains assumes printed POs have been released to vendors, thus limits changes.
Remaining PO Subtotal	When using a blanket PO, the remaining balance appears in this field.

T6:2 Purchase Order Fields

A lookup to the Buyer ID tables finds no existing buyers. Therefore, click on the Buyer ID hyperlink and look up April Levine's User ID, selecting her ID as shown in *F6:15*.

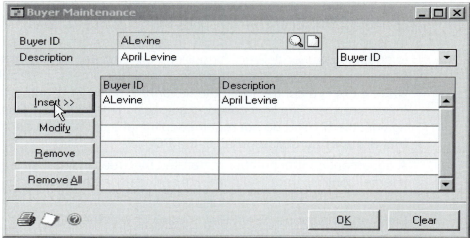

F6:15 Purchasing Buyer Table

Now enter items to the Javix PO. Launch the lookup window into Inventory Control. Look at the next few windows (*F6:16* through *F6:18*) for some ideas on inventory lookups. The first shows the basic inventory lookup. The next shows the view after selecting the additional sort of Description. The final window shows information after clicking the Details Expansion icon.

Item Number	Short Description	Additional Sorts...
AUDJV50WMP3	MP3	
AUDNPXM4CD	SatRadio	
AUDOR256MPORT	PortAud	
AUDSNCDMP3	MP3	
AUDSNCDMP3AMFM	PortAud	
AUDWW52WCD	CarAud	
DCCN22XDZ	Camcord	
DCJV16XDZ	Camcord	
DCNK4XDZ	Camcord	
DCSM10XDZ	Camcord	
DCSM18XDZ	Camcord	
DP0Y4MG3XD	DigiCam	

All Items with no search criteria.

F6:16 Initial Lookup of Item

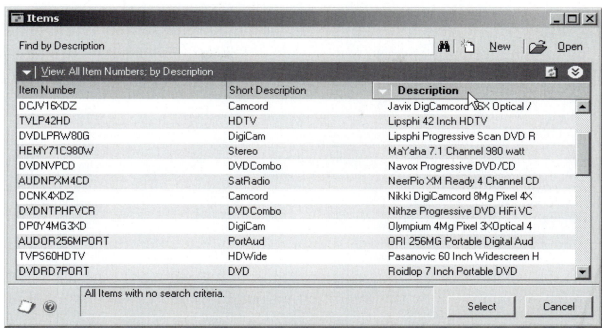

F6:17 Lookup with Item Description

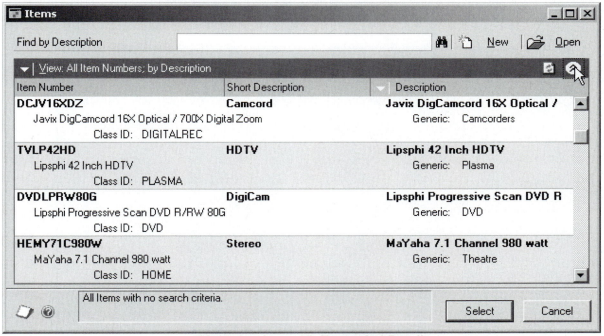

F6:18 Lookup with Expanded Details

The Javix PO contains two line items. Complete the window as shown in **F6:19**. Return to the item field of Line Item 2 and look up information on purchase orders for this item (use the ⓘ symbol). The lookup displays the status of outstanding purchase orders (see *F6:20*). Also, notice the paperclip symbol 🔲 above the Quantity Ordered field. Do you remember seeing this symbol when placing sales orders? The paperclip shows purchase order commitments for outstanding sales orders.

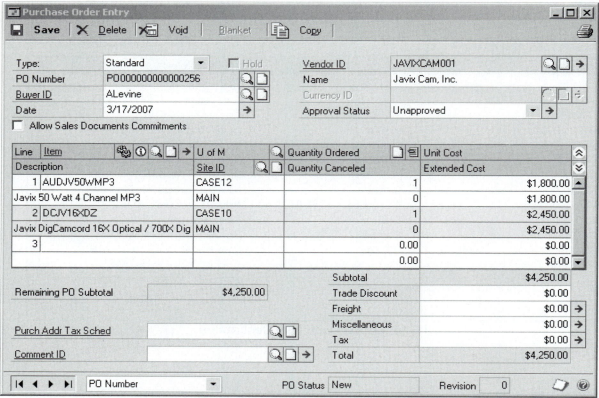

F6:19 Javix PO with Inventory Items

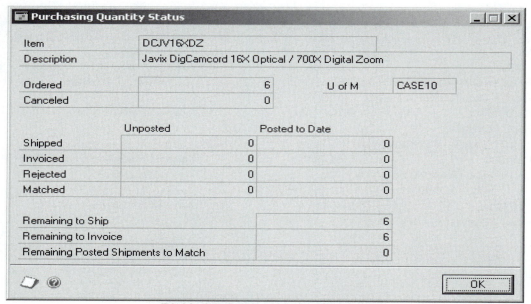

F6:20 PO Status Inquiry Window

Unlike sales orders, POs are not entered in batches. Instead, Pos are saved and then printed individually or in groups. To print POs individually, use the printer icon in the Purchase Order Entry window. Multiple orders are printed by using the *Print Purchasing Documents* menu. Save the PO, then print while inside the entry window.

Since the order has not been approved, the message in **F6:21** appears. Change the PO's status to Approved and the message in *F6:22* appears.

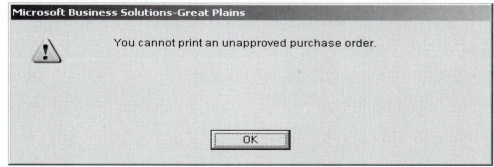

F6:21 PO Not Approved Warning

F6:22 Approval Exceeds Authorization Warning

Open PO Enhancements by using the *Tools>>Setup>>Purchasing>>Purchase Orders Enhancements* menu and see why this occurs. The window in *F6:23* opens. Click Approval Setup to open the window in *F6:24*. Highlight April Levine and find her authorization level is $5,000 without approval. So why are we getting the exceeds approval message when the Javix order is below $5,000?

F6:23 PO Approval Menu

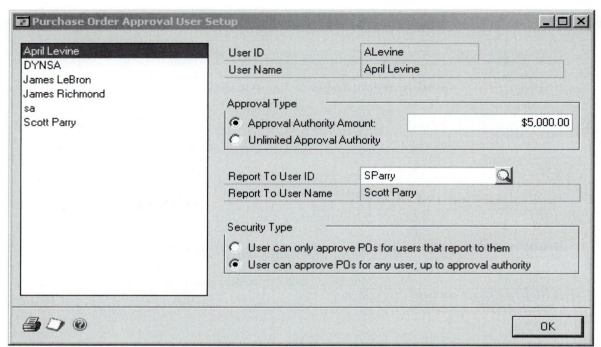

F6:24 PO Authorization Setup

Great Plains bases approval status on the user's login ID. You are logged in as <u>sa</u>, not April Levine. Select the <u>sa</u> ID and notice the approval amount is zero. Set the approval amount to unlimited and save the changes. Now click the printer icon in the PO window and the Purchase Order Print Options window opens as shown in **F6:25.** The Combine Similar Items option is a nice feature for when a PO contains multiple line items for the same inventory item and the U of M is equivalent. This option tells Great Plains to combine line items before printing. After printing, review the PO and notice an authorization signature line for validating the order.

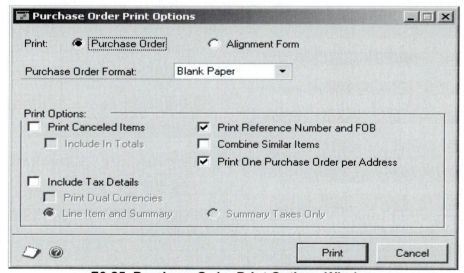

F6:25 Purchase Order Print Options Window

This exercise shows us that despite April being the PO Buyer, the PO approval looks to the user logged into Great Plains to ascertain authorization for releasing the order. In addition, this shows us that PO Enhancements instituted requisition controls over the PO process.

Reopen the Javix PO. Once printed, the POs status changes to Released (view the lower right portion of the window). For internal control reasons, Great Plains restricts the ability to alter released POs. Move to Line Item 2 and select the *Edit>>Delete* command on the main menu. A message appears informing you that this function is denied for released POs.

However, you can still cancel items on a released PO by entering a quantity to the Quantity Canceled field. In addition, you can add additional line items to the order. Let's try this, increase the quantity for Line Item 2 by three, save the order, and close the PO entry window. Upon closing the window, the PO approval audit report prints.

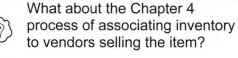

What about the Chapter 4 process of associating inventory to vendors selling the item?

Try entering a PO to WAWA Company for item AUDJV50WMP3 and Great Plains prompts to associate the item with a vendor. Level 2 discusses instituting controls over this feature.

Next, use the *Edit Purchase Orders* menu and retrieve the Javix PO. This window reports two statuses for the order (*F6:26*). The first shows the status for the entire PO and the second shows status by line item. The status types shown on line items is self-explanatory. Notice that Line Item 2 has the Change Order status resulting from the quantity increase. When the order is reprinted, Line 2's status changes to released.

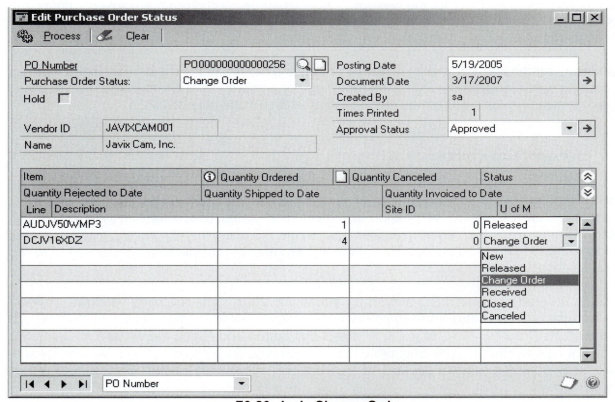

F6:26 Javix Change Order

While editing a PO, you can manually adjust line item statuses, this is usually unnecessary because Great Plains changes statuses as the PO processes. However, this window is the only way to cancel line items on a released POs (see the drop down list beside the PO status).

You should be asking an internal control question at this point. How does S&S ensure changed POs release to vendors? Great Plains has an answer for that and the answer is reporting. Accountants with internal control questions often monitor performance by relying on reporting. Open the PO Status report located under the Analysis category of purchasing reports. Modify the report to show New and Changed PO statuses and run the report.

1. Open the Purchase Order Entry window and identify an internal control master file access weakness based on S&S' current permissions (other than the ability to add vendors on-the-fly.) How would you correct this weakness?

2. When running the PO status report, we selected New and Changed statuses. Why was New included?

3. Now that you have worked with POs, can you identify features of Great Plains that permits department supervisors, sales employees, and the warehouse to enter POs without violating segregation of duties?

E6:2 Working with Purchase Orders

Regardless of whether POs are entered by departments or as back orders, the purchasing department releases POs to the vendor. After release, purchasing employees notify the requisitioner. One way to notify is by sending a copy of the PO. Another way is by sending a PO status report or having departments run this report.

In addition, purchasing must notify receiving of pending orders. Using the old-fashioned method, purchasing sent a copy of the PO to the receiving department. With Great Plains, the receiving department can run daily PO status reports listing released and changed POs.

RECEIVING DEPARTMENT ACTIVITIES

When inventory arrives from the vendor, receiving department employees follow internal control procedures that require PO verification and inspection of the goods for quality and quantity. Receiving employees then enter quantities against the PO using the *Purchasing Batches* menu, selecting the Origin of Receivings Trx Entry. Afterwards, vendor packing slips are sent to the accounts payable department.

All items ordered on Javix's PO arrived on March 22, 2007. The following windows walk you through the steps used to process the receipt. First, create a batch to store March 22nd receipts (*F6:27*). Next, click the Transactions button and notice the window contains two document types (*F6:28*). The Shipment/Invoice type records both receipt and vendor invoice. Since S&S requires accounts payable to record all vendor invoices, select Shipment to record only the receipt.

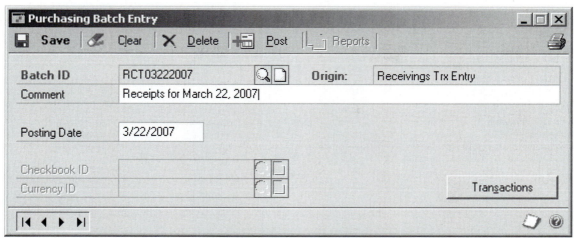

F6:27 March 22 Receipt Batch

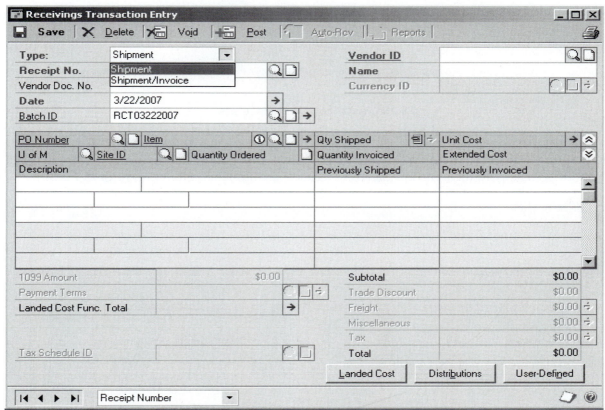

F6:28 Receivings Transaction Entry Window

Referring to *F6:29,* tab through and complete the fields in the top section. The value for the Receipt No. field is auto-filled. Remember, this is a document control that automatically increments; therefore, your number may differ from the one displayed. The Vendor Doc. field stores the vendor's packing slip number. (Note: This field stores the vendor's invoice number when the type is Shipment/Invoice).

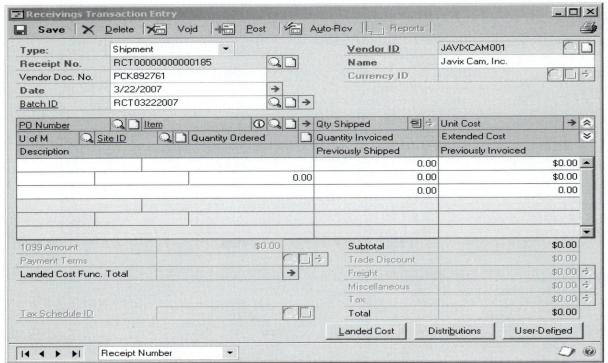

F6:29 Javix Inventory Receipts

After entering the information, we need to complete the quantities received. The quickest method for selecting items is using Auto-Rcv. Click the Auto-Rcv button and refer to **F6:30**.

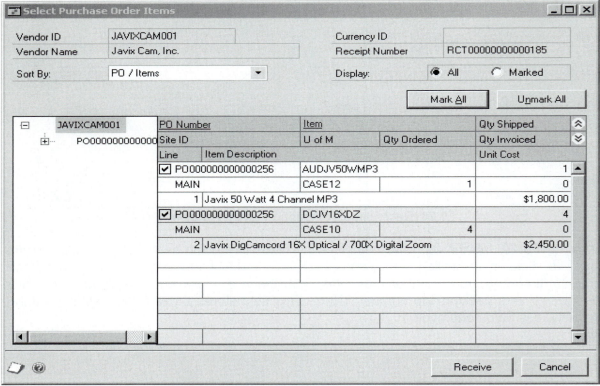

F6:30 Select Purchase Order Items for Javix PO

The Select Purchase Order Items window on the left lists all outstanding POs for Javix. You can click the Mark All button to select all items on a PO or individually check mark items. Click Mark All and then click the Receive button to enter selections in the Receivings Transaction Entry window. Next, click the Distribution button and view the general ledger accounts that will be used during posting (*F6:31*). Review the accounts, noting that the entry will post an amount to the inventory asset account and an amount to the accrued payables liability account. These entries comply with GAAP because inventory title transferred upon receipt. (Remember, the expense for inventory posts through sales invoicing.)

However, are you wondering why the liability posts to accrued payables and not to accounts payable? This occurs because accounts payable is the control account for the Purchasing Series (just like accounts receivable is the control account the Sales Series). Since we did not record an invoice, Javix's balance in the Purchasing Series remains unaffected. Yet GAAP requires recording an asset and liability upon receipt. Thus, the accrued payables account stores the liability to comply with GAAP and to protect Series' reconciliation. In the next topic, we see that the when the invoice for this receipt posts, Great Plains reclasses the accrued payables entry to accounts payable.

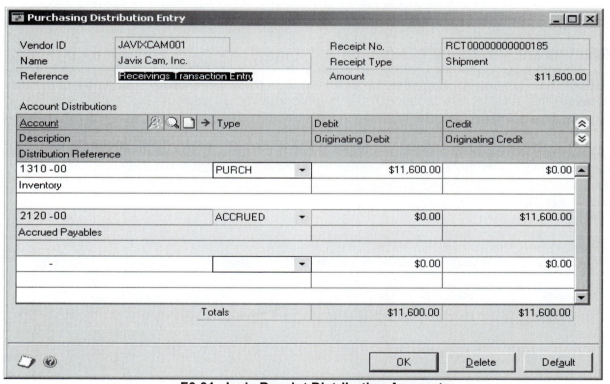

F6:31 Javix Receipt Distribution Accounts

Return to the *Purchasing Batches* menu and post the Javix receipt. Review the control reports that print. Before moving on, return to the *Edit Purchase Orders* menu and look up the PO. Notice the PO's status has changed to Received. Now move on to activities performed by the accounts payable department.

During every step of activity processing, an accountant asks, "How do I control performance?"

By now, we possess the skills to know that Great Plains' reports serve as controls over activities. Therefore, explain how Ashton monitors performance in accounts payable to control the processing of vendor invoices on received inventory.

E6:3 Control Reporting

ACCOUNTS PAYABLE DEPARTMENT ACTIVITIES

The accounts payable department performs several activities, including processing vendor invoices. The trigger for invoice processing is receipt of a vendor's invoice. Clerks post invoices for receipts against POs using the Inventory Purchasing Tier. However, when vendor invoices arrive and are not on a PO, posting occurs in the Payables Transaction Tier. Our discussion now turns to posting invoices with and without a PO.

Vendor Invoices Originating on a PO
We begin with posting invoices where the transaction originated on a PO. Posting is performed by using the *Purchasing Batches* menu in the Inventory Purchasing Tier. By now, you understand that this tier interfaces with the Inventory table. In addition, since a PO originated the transaction using this tier, the invoice must also be matched in this tier.

On March 28, Javix's invoice arrives. Create a batch to store the transaction (***F6:32***), remembering to select the Origin of Purchasing Invoice Entry. Click the Transactions button to open the Purchasing Invoice Entry window. Complete the top portion as shown in ***F6:33.***

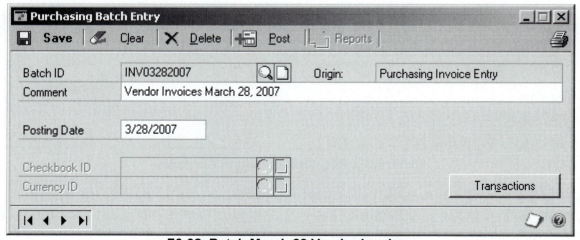

F6:32 Batch March 28 Vendor Invoices

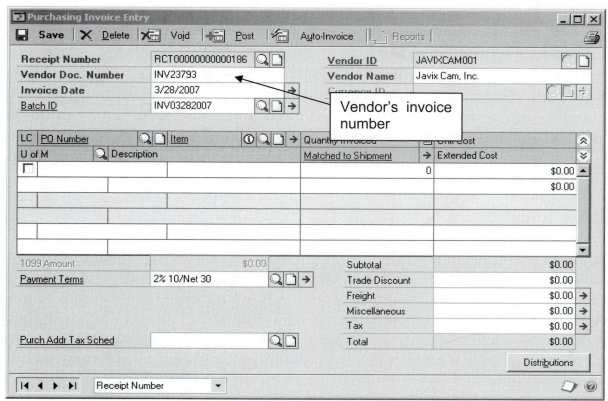

F6:33 Javix Invoice

Next, click the Auto-Invoice button to invoice all items on the receipt (*F6:34*) and then click the Invoice button to return to the Purchasing Invoice Entry window (*F6:35*).

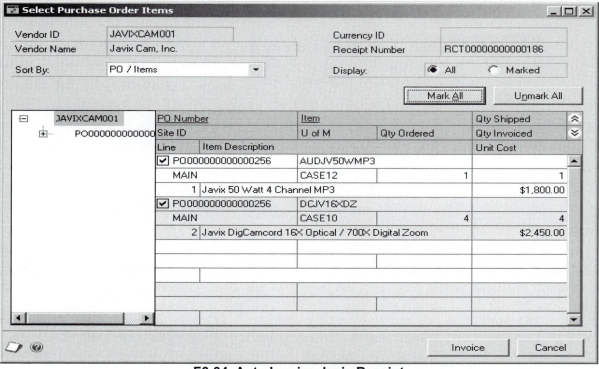

F6:34 Auto Invoice Javix Receipt

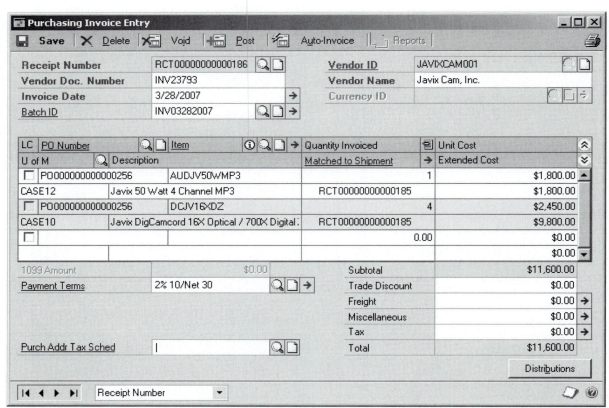

F6:35 Javix Invoice Entry with Items

Notice the PO displays $1,800 as the cost for Line Item 1. However, Javix's invoice reflects $2,000 for these items. Change the amount, then tab off the item. A warning message appears (**F6:36**) because the invoice cost varies from the PO cost. Remember, PO costs were approved by the purchasing department.

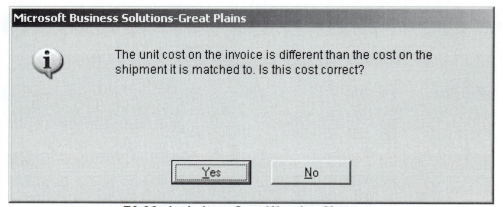

F6:36 Javix Item Cost Warning Message

Click Yes to accept the cost adjustment and the transaction window now contains a variance indicator on the Line Item's cost field (**F6:37**). We will see in Level Two that the Purchasing Series provides password protection that prevents overriding costs in the receiving department. However, this control is not available during invoicing. Consequently, Ashton implements control procedures outside Great Plains. These procedures require accounts payable clerks to notify purchasing of cost variances. In addition, Ashton reviews cost variance reports generated by invoice posting.

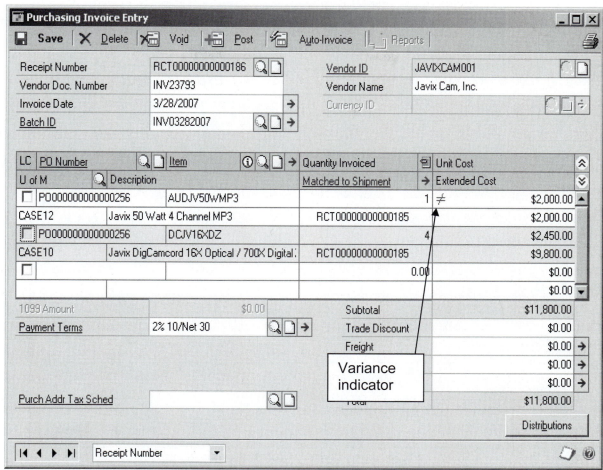

F6:37 Javix Invoice with Price Variance

Click the Distributions button (*F6:38*). Note the reclassification entry that transfers the liability amount posted during item receipt processing from accrued liabilities to accounts payable. In addition, we see an entry to Purchase Discounts Available. This entry results from selection of the payables setup option to track purchase discounts. Therefore, potential vendor discounts posts to a contra-liability account that offsets the accounts payable amount. We saw this feature implemented for customer discounts in Chapter 5.

Finally, notice the $200 entry to Inventory that posts the cost variance ($2,000 minus $1,800). Why did the variance amount post to an asset account instead of the expense account 4510-00 Purchases Variance? More importantly, how does this affect inventory pricing?

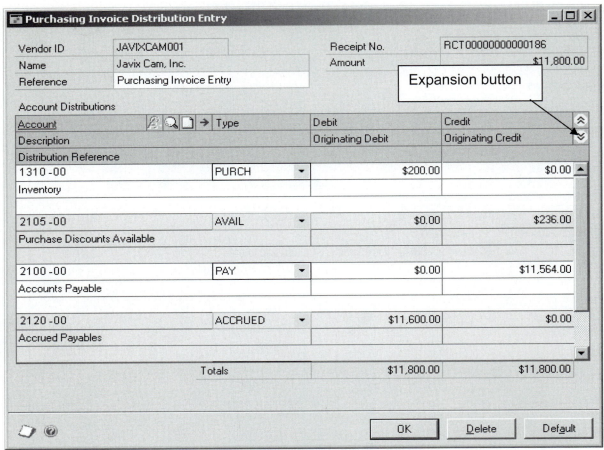

F6:38 Javix Invoice Distributions

For answers to these questions, we return to topics discussed in Chapter 4. Open the inventory item's class using the _Tools>>Setup>>Inventory>>Item Class_ menu. Look up the CARAUD class (**F6:39**) and note the variance tolerance percentage that repricess inventory. This invoice's cost variance is over 5% and the reason Great Plains recorded an inventory increase of $200.

So what effect does this have on inventory pricing? Remember from Chapter 4, S&S uses a percentage of cost method for pricing. Consequently, increases in cost affect sales pricing. With this in mind, you understand the importance of controlling accounts payables invoice processing.   One strong method to control invoice processing is by implementing batch approval. Recall that batch approval is selected under Posting setup. With batch approval, Great Plains denies posting until approved by entering a password. Given the potential for widespread negative effects on financial data, Ashton would be wise to implement batch approval over vendor invoices.

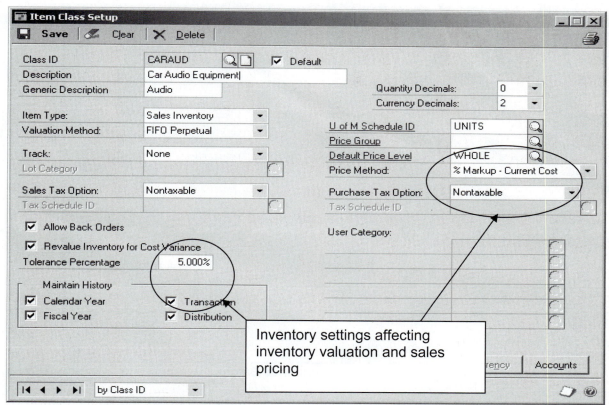

F6:39 Item Class for AUDJV50WMP3

Finally, return to the *Purchasing Batches* menu and post the batch. Review the control reports, especially the variance report.

The Inventory Purchasing Tier is also used to post invoices when PO receipts do not involve inventory. POs are sometimes issued for noninventoried purchases such as services or supplies because the PO serves as authorization. The steps just illustrated are used whenever a PO originates the transaction.

Vendor Invoices Not Originating on a PO

The posting process for vendor invoices not originating on a PO uses the *Batches* and *Transaction Entry* menus on the Payables Transaction Tier. These invoices are normally for expenses such as postage, utilities, insurance, and other recurring business charges.

Many of these charges recur monthly; therefore, invoices are saved to recurring batches. Open the *Batches* menu and look up the HEALTH recurring batch (*F6:40*). Notice that the Frequency field is set to Monthly. Look at the Frequency dropdown list to find there are several timeframes offered. When the frequency is set to Single Use, the folder disappears after posting. This the frequency we have worked with up to this point. However, use one of the other frequencies and the batch, along with transactions, remains available for subsequent postings. Although not discussed in Chapter 5, this feature is also available in the Sales Series.

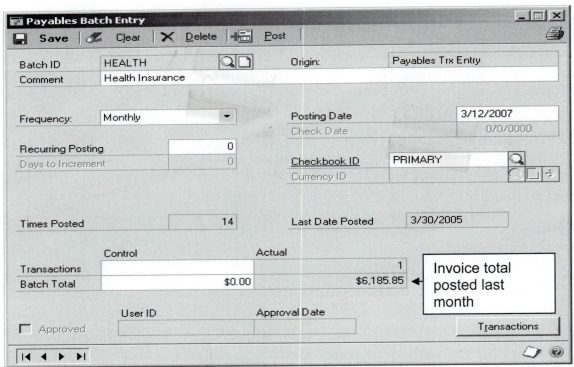

F6:40 Health Insurance Batch

The batch's posting date is 3/12/2007, indicating S&S normally processes the health insurance invoice around the 12th of every month. The batch also indicates one transaction exists, totaling $6,185.85. Click the Transactions button and look up this transaction (**F6:41**).

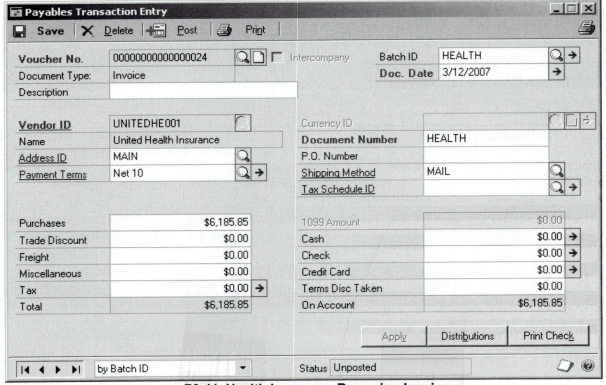

F6:41 Health Insurance Recurring Invoice

Recurring batches simplify posting by retaining the vendor, amount, and account distributions from previous postings. Although invoice charges often change, new amounts are quickly entered to the transaction.

The transaction window also contains 3/12/2007. However, this month's invoice is dated 3/14/2007, so change the Doc Date to match the invoice date. (Remember, the date on the batch determines the date for posting the general ledger amount, while the Doc Date determines the date for posting to the vendor's account. The Doc Date should always be changed to match the invoice date.) There are no other changes to the invoice so click Save. The health insurance transaction often requires minimal changes, especially when S&S experiences no employee turnover, new hires, or plan changes.

Now look up the INTER recurring batch (*F7:42*). Before opening the transaction, notice this batch contains two transactions and is used to post monthly interest on bank loans around the 5th of every month.

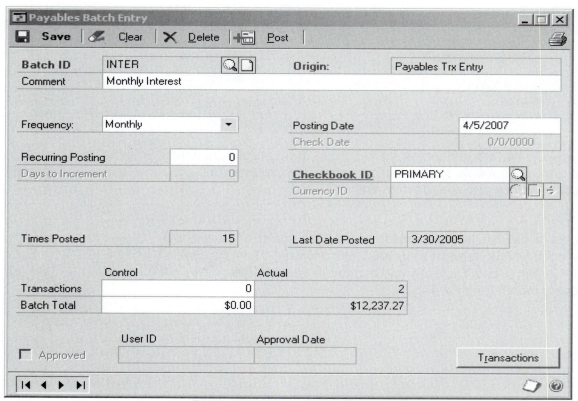

F7:42 Monthly Interest Recuring Batch

Now look up the First National Bank transaction stored in this batch (*F6:43*). (The second transaction is to Bank America.) The transaction tells us that the last invoice from this vendor posted $11,723.63 on March 3rd; therefore, the expense is already posted for March.

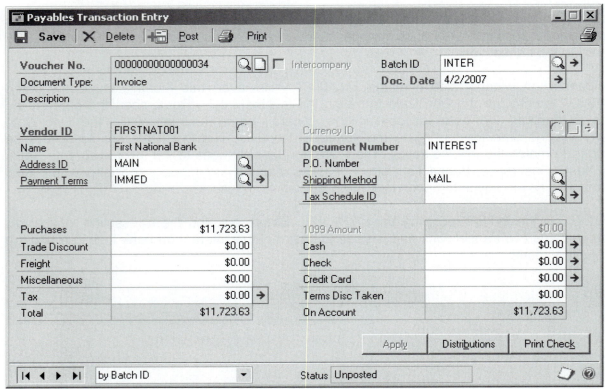

F6:43 First National Bank Invoice

Interest payments are examples of recurring transactions requiring a monthly change in amounts and adjustments to distribution accounts. Despite these change, the recurring entry ensures consistency and speeds data entry.

Let's create a new recurring batch to store S&S' monthly electric bill. Close the transaction currently open. Now, return to the batch window and enter the Batch ID of ELECTRIC. Let's create a 12-month batch to storing the monthly electric bills. This bill is received around the 19th of every month (see *F6:44*).

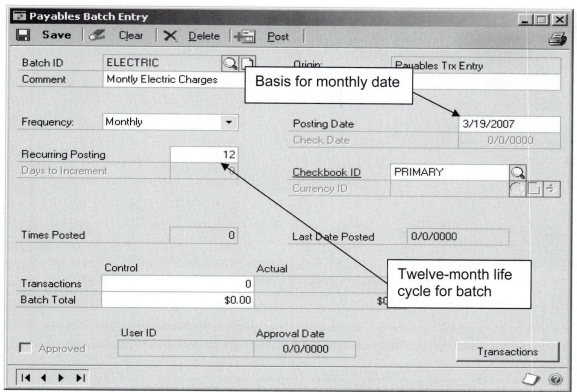

F6:44 Electric Recurring Batch Folder

When entering 12 to the Recurring Posting field, Great Plains deletes this batch after the twelfth posting. Therefore, Accounts Payable must review batches prior to posting and determine whether to increase the batch's life span. Save the batch and click on Transactions.

Complete the electric transaction as illustrated in *F6:45.* Pay close attention to the Doc Date. Open the Distribution window and notice account 5610-05 that defaulted from the vendor's card S&S does not have a department labeled 05. Instead, this segment number identifies the account as an allocation account, discussed in Chapter 2. Therefore, when the transaction posts, electric expense will be allocated to every department's electric expense account based on the percentages values stored in the Fixed Allocation Account window opened with the *Cards>>Financial>>Fixed Allocation* menu. When companies use cost centers, fixed and variable allocation accounts accommodate cost spreading to centers. S&S uses fixed allocation accounts as the default expense account for all utility vendors.

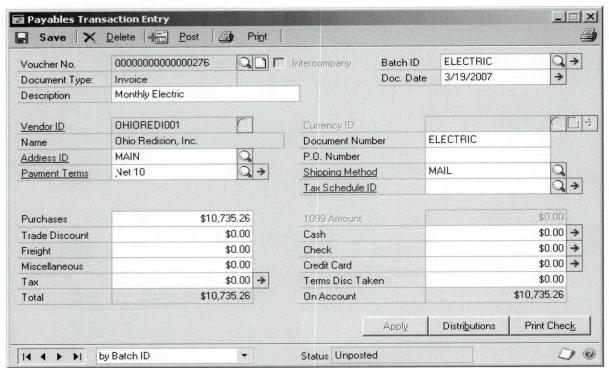

F6:45 Electric Transaction

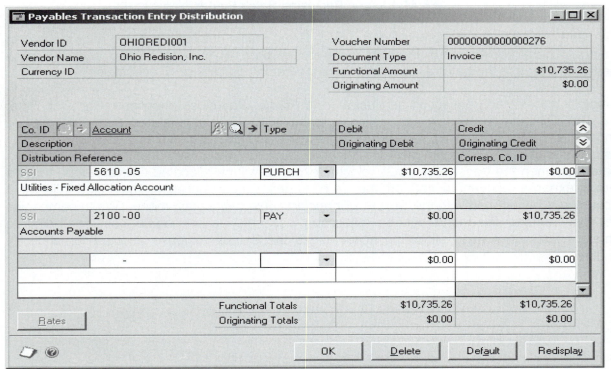

F6:46 Electric Transaction Distribution

Save the electric transaction and close both windows. Instead of posting the batch from the batch window, use the *Transactions>>Purchasing>>Series Post* menu to open the Purchasing Series Posting window in **F6:47**. Recall, we worked with the Sales Series Posting window for in Chapter 5.

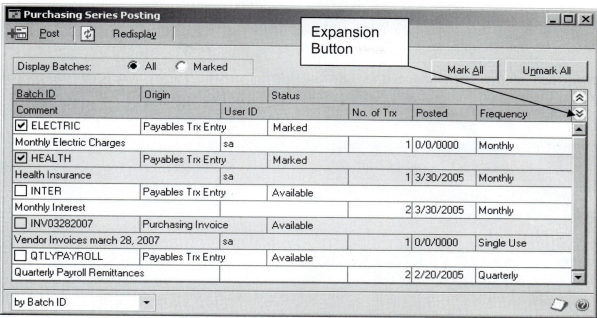

F6:47 Purchasing Series Posting Window

Mark the HEALTH and ELECTRIC batch for posting and then click Post. Notice that the General Posting Journal (*F6:48*) lists the electric invoice as spread to departmental utility expenses.

```
System:     9/12/2005  12:03:12 PM              S&S, Incorporated                    Page:    1
User Date:  3/28/2007                        GENERAL POSTING JOURNAL               User ID: sa
                                                General Ledger

* Voided Journal Entry


Batch ID:      PMTRX00000160
Batch Comment: Monthly Electric Charges


Approved:        No          Batch Total Actual:      $21,470.52     Batch Total Control:      $0.00
Approved by:                 Trx Total Actual:              1        Trx Total Control:           0
Approval Date:


   Journal     Transaction  Transaction  Reversing   Source    Transaction                Audit Trail    Reversing Audit
   Entry          Type         Date        Date     Document    Reference                    Code         Trail Code
   -----------------------------------------------------------------------------------------------------------------------
    1,698       Standard     3/19/2007               PMTRX     Payables Trx Entry          GLTRX00000642


              Account               Description                              Debit           Credit
              ----------------      -------------------------           ----------------  ----------------
              5610-01               Utilities - East                      $2,898.52
              5610-02               Utilities - MidWest                   $2,898.52
              5610-03               Utilities - West                      $2,898.52
              5610-04               Utilities - Administrative            $2,039.70
              2100-00               Accounts Payable                                        $10,735.26
                                                                        ----------------  ----------------
```

F6:48 General Journal Report on Electric

Return to the Payables Batch Entry window, look up the electric batch, and notice that the date has changed for the next posting. We will now pay vendors.

Paying Vendor Invoices

As discussed at the beginning of this chapter, vendor payments are processed using the Payables Transaction Tier. Open the Payables Batch Entry window and set the Origin to Computer Check (see *F6:49*).

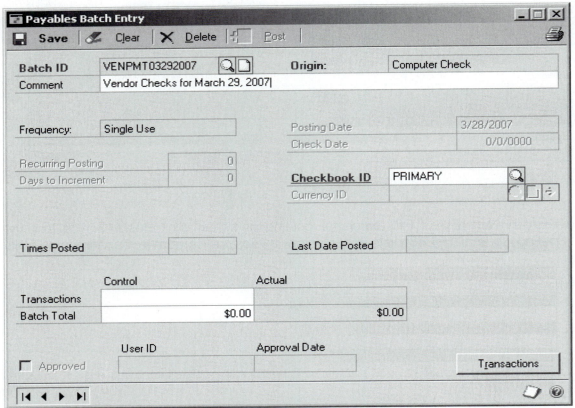

F6:49 Vendor Checks Batch

S&S pays vendors weekly, either on Thursday or Friday. You might think why didn't we create a recurring batch for these payments; however, then you notice that the Computer Check Origin does not accommodate recurring batches.

Click the Transactions button and Great Plains prompts you to select the transaction type (*F6:50*). The choices are Select Payables Checks, Edit Payables Checks, or Print Payables Checks. This list corresponds to the individual transaction entry menus on the Payables Transaction tier. Choose Select Payables Checks, then click Go To to open the window used to select vendors for payment.

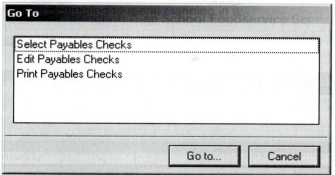

F6:50 Transaction Window Selection

The Select Payables Checks window contains fields used to query outstanding invoices. Since S&S processes payments weekly, enter the screening criteria shown in **F6:51**. Based on these entries, the Build Batch button will select invoices due before April 5th and invoices with discount dates prior to April 11th. In addition, when the checks print, the payment applies against the invoice as of March 29.

 What about the edit list for other purchasing transaction activities?

Although we did not print an edit list for any of the preceding transactions, an edit list should always be printed and compared to external documentation prior to posting.

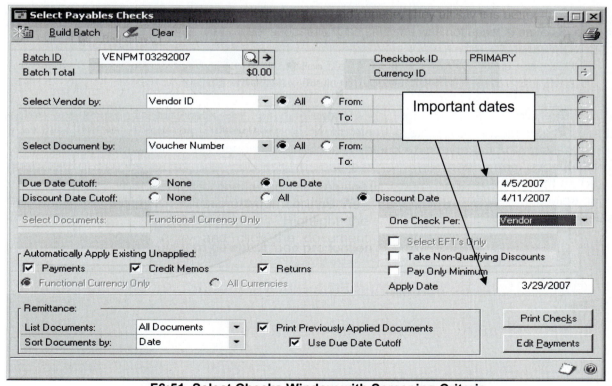

F6:51 Select Checks Window with Screening Criteria

Click the Build Batch button. When finished, the Batch Total field shows the selection of invoices totaling $476,493.52 (*F6:52*).   (Note: Your results may differ when you posted additional transactions.)

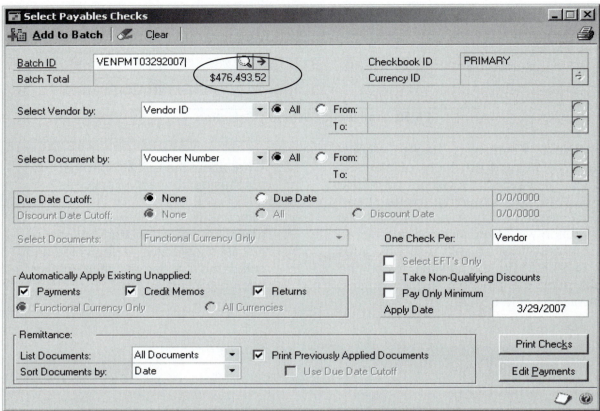

F6:52 Select Checks Window after Build

Red flags should be going up right about now. Do you see the Print Checks button at the bottom of the window? Accounts payable clerks record transactions, and therefore should not have permission to print checks (a custody function). Although this window provides the ability to print checks, permissions in advanced security can deny the clerks access to the menu opened by the Print Checks button. Therefore, internal controls dictate that clerks perform the vendor selection process and produce the edit list shown in **F6:53**, sending the list to the cashier.

```
System:      5/20/2005   12:56:14 PM                S&S, Incorporated                      Page:      1
User Date:   3/29/2007                           COMPUTER CHECKS EDIT LIST                 User ID: sa
                                                   Payables Management

Batch ID:       VENPMT03292007                                                    Batch Frequency:  Single Use
Batch Comment:  Vendor Payments March 29, 2007                                    Audit Trail Code:
                                                                                  Posting Date:     3/29/2007
              Count          Totals        Approved:      No
Control:        0            $0.00         Approved By:                           Checkbook ID:     PRIMARY
Actual:         9         $476,493.52      Approval Date:  0/0/0000

Batch Error Messages:


----------------------------------------------------------------------------------------------------------
Check Number:
   Payment Number:    00000000000000486    Terms Disc Available:      $236.00    Check Total:       $11,564.00
   Document Date:     3/29/2007            Voided:
   Vendor ID:         JAVIXCAM001
   Vendor Check Name: Javix Cam, Inc.

   Messages:


   General Ledger Distributions
     Account           Account Description        Account Type     Debit Amount      Credit Amount
     1100-00           Cash                       CASH                    0.00          11,564.00
     2105-00           Purchase Discounts Available  AVAIL              236.00              0.00
     2100-00           Accounts Payable           PAY                11,564.00              0.00
     4600-00           Purchase Discounts Taken   TAKEN                   0.00             236.00
                                                                  ------------------  ------------------
                                                                      11,800.00          11,800.00

   Applied to Check
     Document Type      Voucher Number       App Date       Discount        Writeoff      Amount Applied
     Invoice            00000000000000275    3/29/2007        236.00            0.00          11,564.00
                                                           ------------------  -----------  ------------------
                                                                236.00            0.00          11,564.00

   Documents Included on Check
     Document Type      Voucher Number       Doc Date         Amount     Amount Paid            Net
     Invoice            00000000000000275    3/28/2007      11,800.00      11,800.00        11,564.00
                                                           ------------------  ------------------  ------------------
                                                             11,800.00      11,800.00        11,564.00
```

F6:53 Select Checks Edit List

CASHIER DEPARTMENT ACTIVITIES

The cashier prints vendor checks after reviewing cash flow reports from accounts receivable and accounts payable, payroll projections, and other cash needs. The cashier also reviews the edit list sent by accounts payable, paying close attention to discounts. The list shows nine vendors selected for payment and Javix's invoice carries a discount.

The owner, Susan, functions as S&S' cashier. She determines that cash flow projections do not permit paying all the invoices. Therefore, she decides to eliminate the payment to Ohio Redision. The vendor card triggered the payment as due immediately, but Susan knows that the invoice can wait until next week.

To delete this invoice from the batch of selected invoices, click the *Edit Checks* menu to open the window shown in *F6:54*. Next, look up the Batch ID and then the vendor, Ohio Redision. Click the Delete button to remove the invoice and reduce the batch total.

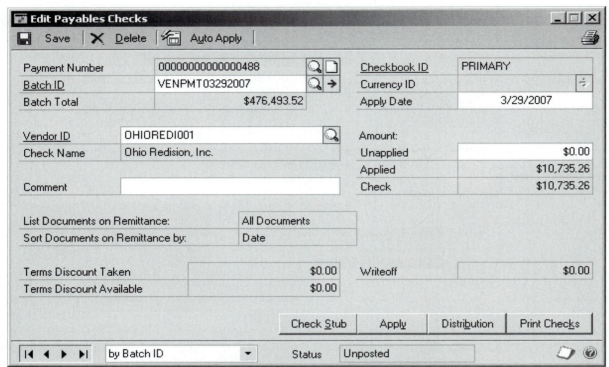

F6:54 Edit Payables Checks Window

After deleting, Susan reprints the edit list to verify accuracy. She then uses the Print Checks button at the bottom of the Edit Payables Checks window. (She could also use the *Print Checks* menu.) The Print checks button opens the window in ***F6:55***. Susan reviews critical aspects of the window prior to printing. First, she verifies that the check number agrees with the checks placed in the printer. Any discrepancy in numbers signals an internal control problem with custody over checks.

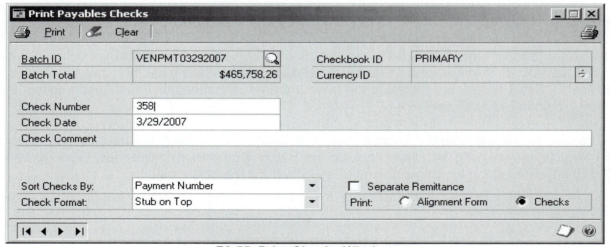

F6:55 Print Checks Window

Next, Susan makes sure to change the Alignment option to Checks. She could also select the Separate Remittance option to print remittances after checks printing; however, S&S' uses two-part checks with the top stub serving as the remittance advice. After completing her review, she clicks the Print button. Upon printing, the Post Payables Checks window appears (***F6:56***).

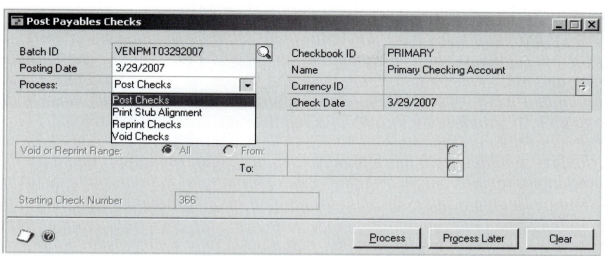

F6:56 Post Payables Checks Window

Susan makes sure the checks printed properly clicking Process in case a printer error occurs during printing. Should an error occur, she can always reprint the checks by waiting to process after reviewing output. She could also close this window by clicking the Process Later button and return to processing later by using the *Post Checks* menu. Click the Process button to post the checks and review the posting reports.

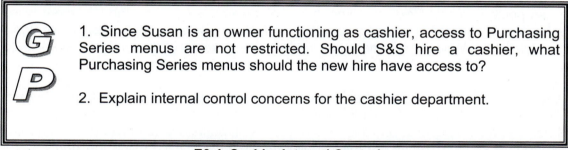

1. Since Susan is an owner functioning as cashier, access to Purchasing Series menus are not restricted. Should S&S hire a cashier, what Purchasing Series menus should the new hire have access to?

2. Explain internal control concerns for the cashier department.

E6:4 Cashier Internal Controls

OTHER PURCHASING SERIES TRANSACTIONS

In this section, we look at processing nonroutine transactions, such as returns of goods to vendors and credit memos.

Return of Vendor Goods
Recall that employees inspect vendor shipments before entering receipts. At times, goods are rejected due to damage, inferior quality, or items received do not match the PO. The *Returns Batches* or *Returns Transaction Entry* menus record inventory returned to vendors. Return transactions are entered using the types shown in *F6:57*.

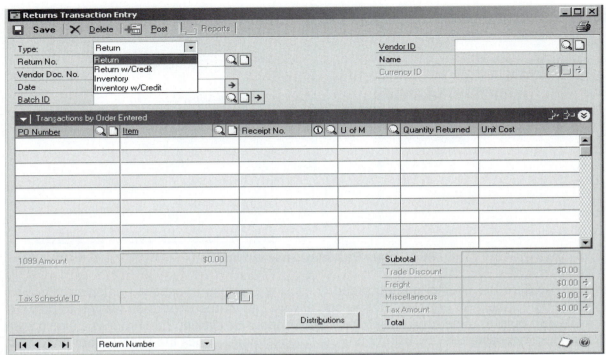

F6:57 Returns Transaction Entry Window

These types fall into two categories, Return and Inventory. The Return type is used when a receipt has posted against Post, meaning the receipt was posted using the Shipment type and the invoice has not posted in accounts payable. A Return reverses the entries to inventory and accrued payables. When the vendor will replace the inventory, then a new PO should be issued.

The Return w/Credit type is used when both a receipt and invoice has posted. In other words, the receipt was posted using the Shipment/Invoice type, or using the Shipment type and the invoice has posted in accounts payable. Return w/Credit posts a credit towards the invoice and reduces the item's cost. Credits are then applied against the invoice using the _Apply Payables Documents_ menu.

The two inventory types apply to either intercompany transfers of inventory posted in the Inventory Control Series or drop shipments returned by customers. Again, Inventory w/Credit means the vendor is giving credit against the invoice, while Inventory means the vendor will replace the inventory.

Try your hand at a return of goods. First, receive the item on PO 254 issued to WAWA Company using Shipment type. Post the receipt. Next, open the Returns Transaction Entry window and return two of the items received. Since this is a return prior to invoicing, use the Return type.

E6:5 Practice a Return

Credit memos
Let's say that an invoice has been paid; however, it is later discovered that an overcharge was

billed so the vendor issues a credit memo. Credit memos are posted using the *Transaction Entry* menu, assigning the Credit Memo Document Type to the transaction. However, since this tier does not interface with inventory, credits adjusting the cost paid for an item must also be posted as an inventory adjustment in the Inventory Controls Series (see Chapter 4).

Credit memos also apply to other situations such as when vendors reduce charges because of late delivery, etc.

S&S received a credit memo for $300 from Channel Oxe for advertising that ran last month. Enter the credit, distributing the amount evenly to each sales department's advertising expense.

When you posted the transaction, did the General Posting Journal print? If not, this transaction is suspended. Locate the suspended transaction and post.

E6:6 Credit Memo Practice

The Purchasing Series does not contain a debit memo document type. Instead, additional vendor charges are recorded using the Misc Charge document type.

PURCHASING SERIES: BASIC REPORTING

We previously discussed a few of the Purchasing Series' control reports.[6] This topic focuses on the aging report. Like in the Sales Series, the aging report for vendors must reconcile to the accounts payable control accounts located in the Financial Series. As with the Sales Series, Purchasing Series reports are grouped into categories and aging reports are located under the Trial Balance category.

Another important report is the check register. The check register was one of the control reports that printed after paying vendor invoices. Auditors usually request companies to print a check register listing checks issued during the year and review the list looking for large payments and out of sequence checks. The check register report is located in the Check Information category.

1. Reconcile the Purchasing Series to the Financial Series.

2. Prepare a check register listing the checks printed in this Chapter.

E6:7 Practice on Purchasing Series Reporting

---

[6] More information on expenditure cycle reporting is available in Chapter 11 of Marshall Romney and Paul Steinbart, *Accounting Information Systems* (10th ed., Prentice Hall 2006), p. 435-437.

LEVEL TWO

Level Two focuses on internal controls over Purchasing Series activities. The controls set here assist with enforcing internal controls over expenditure cycle activities.[7]

PURCHASING SERIES SETUP AND INTERNAL CONTROLS

The expenditure cycle activity diagram listed threats to the cycle. Keep these threats in mind as you read this topic. Just as this Series' menu divides into two tiers, there are two setup items under the *Tools>>Setup>>Purchasing* menu, namely *Purchasing Order Processing* and *Payables*. We begin with *Payables*.

The Payables Management Setup window (**F6:58**) contains some already familiar settings. The following explains the settings by window section.

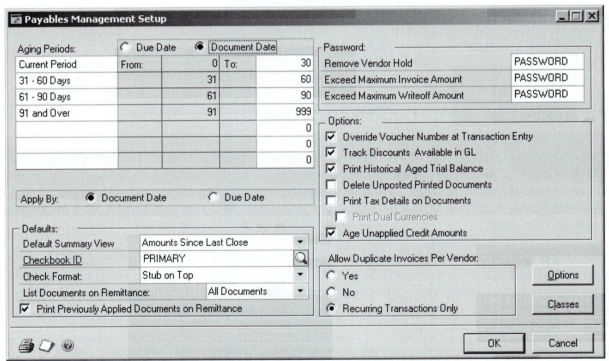

F6:58 Payables Management Setup Window

Aging Periods Section: Similar to Receivables setup, the Aging Periods Section controls vendor invoice aging. The choices are age by Due Date or by Document Date and. These choices affect vendor aging reports. Assume an invoice dated June 15 with a due date of July 15, on July 17th this invoice is 32 days old when aged by document date versus 2 days old when aged by due date.

---

[7] For an in-depth understanding of expenditure cycle control activities, refer to Chapter 11 of Marshall Romney and Paul Steinbart, *Accounting Information Systems* (10th ed., Prentice Hall 2006), p. 425-435.

Defaults Section: When not defaulted on a vendor card, vendor payments post to the general ledger account linked to the PRIMARY checkbook. (Remember, this account is linked using the *Cards>>Financial>>Checkbook* menu.) The Default Summary View defaults the views used in the Vendor Summary Inquiry window. The check format determines output for checks based on check stock.

Passwords Section: This section sets specific authorization controls. We looked at specific authorization in the setup topic of Chapter 5. These controls function similarly.

Options Section: Options that activate additional features. Most are self-explanatory. Here is where we find the option to track of purchase discounts available and the option that prints historical aged trial balance reports. Of course, S&S only has the ability to print historical reports when vendor cards and Purchase Order setup retain transaction history.

Options Button: This button opens the Payables Setup Options window (*F6:59*) that stores document control numbers.

Payables Setup Options				
Type	**Description**	**Code**	**Next Voucher Number**	00000000000000276
Invoice	Invoice	INV	**Next Payment Number**	00000000000000486
Finance Charge	Finance Charge	FIN	Next Schedule Number	SCHED00000000001
Misc Charge	Misc Charge	MIS		
Return	Return	RET	Tax Schedule IDs:	
Credit Memo	Credit Memo	CRM	Purchase	
Payment	Payment	PMT	Freight	
Schedule	Schedule	SCH	Miscellaneous	
			User-Defined 1	User-Defined 1
Next Temp. Vendor ID	TEMP00000000001		User-Defined 2	User-Defined 2

F6:59 Payables Setup Options

Close the Payables Setup Options window and open the Purchase Order Processing Setup window (*F6:60*). This window control activities performed under the Inventory Purchasing Tier. The following discussion focuses on items that may not be self-explanatory.

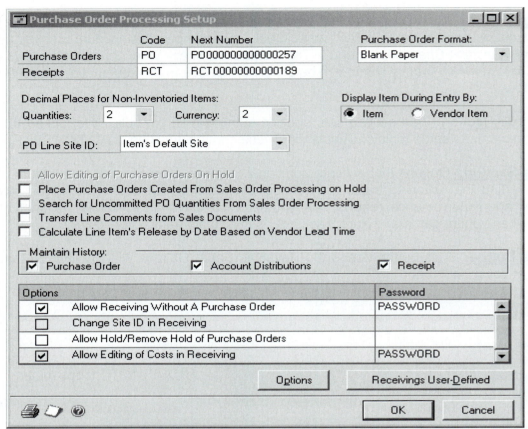

F6:60 Purchase Order Processing Setup

<u>Display Item During Entry:</u> When entering transactions, the Item option displays all items during lookups to the Inventory table, whereas Vendor Item displays only items linked to vendors in the Inventory Control Series. Thus, the Item option permits users to enter line items for inventory not sold by the vendor. Great Plains warns the user when making this selection; however, the user can override this warning by clicking Yes (**F6:61**) unless permission to access the vendor maintenance window has been denied. (Note: This is an example of adding inventory items "on-the-fly", which can only be controlled using the security features discussed in Chapter 3.)

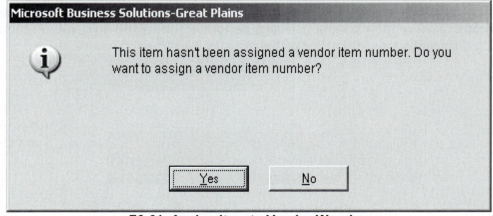

F6:61 Assign Item to Vendor Warning

1. Why would S&S want to password protect the Remove Vendor Hold option?

2. Explain why S&S activated the Allow Duplicate Invoices Per Vendors option.

3. Explain why S&S activated the Allow Receiving Without a Purchase Order option.

E6:8 Payables Management Controls

PURCHASE REPORTING AS A CONTROL TOOL

Level One highlighted several reports that assisted in controlling expenditure cycle activities. These reports, and others, are available under the *Reports>>Purchasing* menu. As with Sales Series reporting, we find reporting divided into categories. The History category prints detailed reports on posted transactions. These are useful when tracking posting errors. The Analysis category prints reports that help detect problems with purchasing activities. In addition, this category contains the Cash Requirements report used to project future cash flow requirements for the expenditure cycle. Finally, setup reports document internal controls for the Series.

PURCHASING SERIES: MONTH-END AND YEAR-END CLOSING PROCEDURES

Chapter 5 discussed the importance of performing month-end and year-end closings of the Sales Series and that importance remains for this Series. Recall that when period ending a Series, accountants are concerned with three areas: verifying transactions recorded to the proper period, verifying all valid transactions posted, and reconciling the Series to the Financial Series.

Verify Transactions Record to Proper Period
The procedures that verify posting to the proper period again focus on controls over batch processing. Like in the revenue cycle, period-end posting procedures are implemented by setting a month-end or year-end cutoff date. After this date, transactions for the period are entered to the Financial Series using journal entries.

Verify Valid Transactions Posted
The procedures followed to verify posting are similar to those performed in the revenue cycle. First, purchasing cycle activity reports are reviewed for delays in posting vendor invoices for inventory received. Outstanding POs are also reviewed and warehouse records checked for unposted receipts. In addition, the *Series Post* window is reviewed for suspended transactions.

However, unlike the revenue cycle, vendor invoices affecting the period are not always received before the cut-off date. For inventory receipts, this timing is not an issue because posting the receipt booked the liability and asset entry. However, for expenses like utilities and insurance, the accounting department must estimate and accrue expenses.   This accrual entry is discussed in Chapter 8.

Purchasing Series Reconciles with Financial Series

As with the Sales Series, the Purchasing Series trial balance report must equal the total for the control accounts in the Financial Series.   For S&S, these control accounts are 2100-00 and 2105-00.

Closing the Purchasing Series

The process for closing the month is the same as used to month-end the Sales Series. Remember, the path is *Tools>>Setup>>Company>>Fiscal Periods*. Year-ending the Series is performed by selecting the *Tools>>Routines>>Purchasing>>Year End Close* menu.

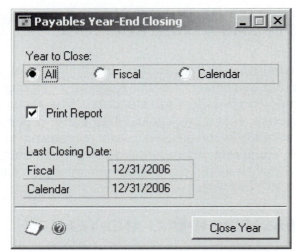

F6:62 Payables Year-End Closing Window

Once again, this process significantly alters data files; therefore, backed ups are performed prior to year-ending. In addition, vendor 1099s must be printed before year-ending because this process zeros out all vendor balances for the current year, transferring balances to history. Finally, transactions for the next year are saved to batches, but not posted until year-ending the Series.

LEVEL ONE QUESTIONS

1. Use Excel to analyze inventory sales for the past two months and to review current inventory levels. Based on your analysis, pinpoint items with on-hand levels insufficient to meet sales trends.

2. Select two inventory items from the above analysis indicating insufficient on-hand supply. Issue POs for the items, then complete all activities to process these POs from inventory receipt to vendor invoice posting. Turn in a copy of the POs and all control reports that printed during posting. Record all transactions in March of 2007.

3. Post Invoice 76P876, dated March 28, received from Office Rex for a desk costing $1,250.00. Review the posting reports and explain the accounts used for posting.

4. Reconcile the Purchasing Series with the Financial Series. Turn in documentation supporting your reconciliation.

5. As the purchasing manager, how would you analyze vendor performance?

6. As the accountant, explain how you would analyze the receiving department's performance and the accounts payable department's performance?

LEVEL TWO QUESTIONS

1. Review the threats and controls in the Purchasing Series Activities Diagram and describe, by department, Great Plains' role in controlling these threats.

2. As the accountant, how would verify that completed transactions have posted to the Financial Series before period-ending the Purchasing Series?

3. Explain the significance of monitoring orders received but not invoiced.

4. Describe specific instances where Purchasing Series transaction processing complies with GAAP.

CHAPTER 7: PAYROLL CYCLE AND GREAT PLAINS PAYROLL SERIES

CHAPTER OVERVIEW

The biggest expense for many companies is payroll. Payroll expenses include wages, salaries, commissions, and related payroll taxes and benefits. This chapter explains activities performed in the payroll cycle using Great Plains Payroll Series. Along the way, we will illustrate payroll cards, payroll transactions, payroll reporting, and activity controls. The Human Resource Series is included with the Student Edition, but not covered in this text.

> ➤ Level One focuses on using Great Plains to process employee paychecks. After an overview of payroll cycle activities, payroll cards are discussed. Data is then entered to produce employee wage, commission, and expense checks. More importantly, internal controls over payroll processing and external reporting requirements are explained.

> ➤ Level Two focuses on setting pervasive controls over payroll activities by using Payroll Series and Payroll Posting setup. In addition, month-end, quarter-end, and year-end procedures are discussed.

Level One covers:
> ➤ Routine payroll processing activities, including time entry and paycheck printing
> ➤ Employee, tax withholding, benefit, and deduction creation
> ➤ Reporting as a control tool and activity trigger

Level Two covers:
> ➤ Implementing internal controls through Payroll Series setup
> ➤ Month-end, quarter-end, and year-end closing procedures

LEVEL ONE

The activities for payroll processing [1] appear in *F7:1*. Payroll triggering events originate from both inside and outside the company. Government agencies, such as the IRS, and state or local taxing authorities, make changes in tax law that affect employer tax and employee withholding rates. S&S subscribes to Great Plains' online payroll update service to download federal and state employee withholding rates; however, local (city) tax, state unemployment, and worker compensation rates are entered manually.

The payroll cycle activity diagram shows that changes to employee and benefit master records originate through the HR department. For S&S, this department consists of the owners. The owners perform background checks on potential hires, process employee terminations, and negotiate employee benefit plans. Any changes affecting an employee's pay-period status, pay rate, deductions, withholdings, or benefits must be input prior to processing employee checks.

Unlike other cycles, the majority of payroll activities trigger by the due date for employee pay periods, tax withholding remittances, and employee benefit liabilities. In addition, there are due dates for tax report filings. The diagram shows that all departments submit authorized employee time data. The Sales Department also submits sales commission and expense reports. The time data is submitted at the end of each week, while the commission and expense information are submitted a few days before month-end.

Upon receipt of departmental time cards, payroll inputs time data to batches that await processing on the employee's pay date. S&S pays hourly employees biweekly, salaried employees semimonthly, and expense and commission checks monthly. Batched payroll data is validated after entry and the timeliness of HR and master tax file updates is confirmed prior to processing employee paychecks.

Payroll processing generates a variety of control reports. Payroll employees send summary reports to accounts payable, listing payment amounts for employer tax liabilities, employee tax withholdings, benefits liabilities, and payroll checking account deposits. Accounts payable processes these payments per the activities explained in Chapter 6.

For the payroll department, processing stops at the pre-check register. This register is then sent to the cashier for use when printing paychecks. These procedures segregate duties into recording and custody. After cutting checks, the cashier sends paychecks to department supervisors for distribution. In addition, the cashier makes the deposit of payroll checking account funds and prints the tax and benefit checks by the mandatory filing dates.

---

[1] For an in-depth discussion on activities performed in the payroll/human resources cycle, refer to Chapter 13 of Marshall Romney and Paul Steinbart, *Accounting Information Systems* (10th ed., Prentice Hall 2006).

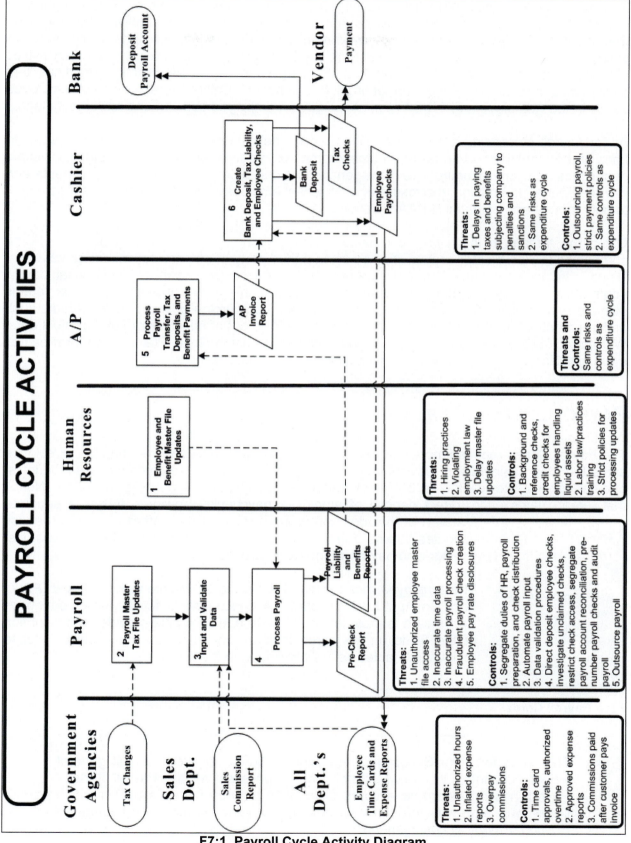

F7:1 Payroll Cycle Activity Diagram

The overview of payroll cycle activities appears simple. However, this cycle is fraught with potential errors and confidentiality disclosures. As we go through each activity, keep in mind that this cycle is heavily regulated by government agencies that impose fines or sanctions for violations. While we do not cover HR activities, it is important to be aware that these activities face heaviest regulation. State and federal government agencies sanction practices that discriminate in employee hiring, promotion, and termination. OSHA regulations cover employee safety in the workplace and ERISA regulations govern employee pension and retirement plans.

As for payroll processing activities, inefficient and/or delinquent activities subject companies to fines and/or sanctions when failing to timely remit tax liabilities, employee withholdings, benefit deductions, and tax reporting. Taxing agencies set due dates for remitting tax payments and payroll reports. In addition, disclosure of confidential employee information subjects a company to poor morale and potential HIPAA violations.

Given the threats in this cycle, companies often outsource payroll to third parties. Some companies realize greater cost savings by using a third party to prepare payroll and government filings. In addition, outsourcing companies may enhance protection of confidential payroll information. However, outsourcing does not remove all threats because the employer retains ultimate responsibility for payroll compliance. In fact, outsourcing poses different threats such as the potential threat that the outsource company will go out of business or fail to protect data. With payroll cycle threats in mind, turn your attention to using Great Plains to perform payroll cycle activities. Once again, we begin with the Series' master records.

PAYROLL SERIES CARDS

The Payroll Series requires more work with cards than other Series covered thus far. Employee cards form the basic master records for payroll. In addition, there are cards for taxes, benefits, and deductions. Review the list of Payroll Series cards using the _Cards>>Payroll_ menu. Notice that Great Plains offers direct deposit of employee paychecks, however, this is a separate feature not included with your version of the software. Direct deposit mitigates threats from paycheck issuance to fraudulent employees, lost checks, and payroll information disclosure.

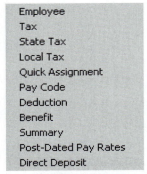

The _Employee_ menu opens the Employee Maintenance window (**F7:3**), Look up April Levine's card. A description of the fields appearing on April's card is provided in **T7:1**. In addition, **T7:2** provides a description of the fields on tax cards that are linked to employee card. Please review both tables before moving on to the next topic.

F7:2 Payroll Cards

The cards for other Series had an Accounts button for store default general ledger accounts. Where are distribution defaults set for the Payroll Series? Payroll has an extensive account distribution setup. Setup is performed in Level Two, however, you can view defaults by selecting the _Tools>>Setup>> Posting>Payroll Accounts_ menu.

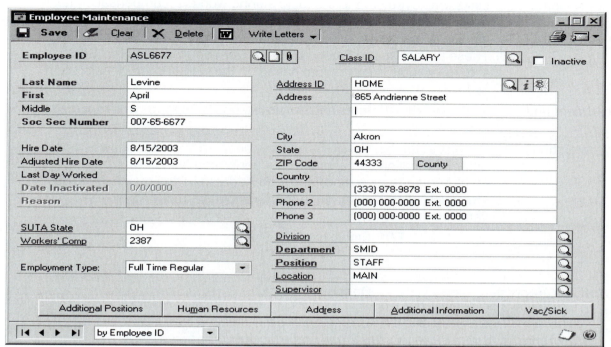

F7:3 Employee Maintenance Window

Field(s)	Description
Employee ID	Primary key for employee record. S&S uses the employee's initials and last four digits of the social security number.
Name and Soc. Sec. Number	Employee's name appears in three fields, complying with database normalization rules. The Soc. Sec. Number field is self-explanatory.
Class ID	S&S uses the SALARY and HOURLY classes to group employees by pay type.
Inactive	Status field used to terminate payroll for an employee since cards cannot be deleted until history is removed.
Address ID	Link to employee addresses.
Date Fields	The employee card contains four date fields used to track hire, adjusted hire, last day, and inactivate dates. Adjusted hire date used when an employee takes an extended leave of absence. The inactivate date tracks employee retirement and termination dates.
SUTA State	Links employee card to the table storing state unemployment tax rates. In most states, SUTA taxes are paid by the employer and taxes are assessed as a percentage of gross payroll up to an annual limit per employee. Percentages are based on an employer's layoff history. For S&S, the rate is 1.9% of the first $9,000 paid annually to each employee.

Workers' Comp	Links employee card to the table storing workers' compensation tax rates. Many states provide workers' compensation funds covering medical expenses and lost wages for employees injured on the job. These payments are funded by employer contributions. For S&S, state premiums are premium based on the worker's job classification code.
Department and Position	S&S uses departments and employee positions for payroll reporting and analysis.
Window Buttons	Buttons at the bottom of the window open additional windows used to enter information on items such as performance reviews, training, and other human resource activity. The Address button maintains multiple employee addresses and the Vac/Sick button tracks employee vacation and sick time.

T7:1 Employee Card Fields

Payroll Tax Records	Description
Federal, State, and Local Income Tax	Tax rate tables for employee federal, state, and local income tax withholdings.
Social Security and Medicare Tax	Social Security and Medicare taxes applicable to both employee and employer. The Social Security tax rate is 6.2% of gross pay subject to an annual cap on earnings. The Medicare rate is 1.45% of gross pay with no cap. Employers pay an amount equal to the employee's tax.
Federal and State Unemployment Tax	Federal unemployment tax rate is .08% of the first $8,000 of an employee's annual salary. State unemployment tax rates vary by employer and most carry similar annual pay limits. These taxes are paid by the employer.
State Workers' Compensation Tax	For states requiring employer contributions to an insurance fund paying employee medical expenses and lost wages when injured on the job. The tax rates vary by an employee's job responsibilities.

T7:2 Payroll Tax Descriptions

Close April's employee card. If you accidentally changed a field's data, press the Clear button to move on without saving. We now review April's links to tax, benefit, and deduction cards. This process is complex and omitting any of the steps produces erroneous paychecks. As we go through each step, refer back to the Cards menu (*F7:2*) and notice these steps move through menu items in order of appearance.

We begin at the Federal Tax window (*F7:4*). Open this window by clicking the *Tax* menu and look up April's tax record. The filing statuses and tax tables for the window were downloaded from the online payroll service discussed previously. We see that April's Federal Filing Status is Single and she takes zero Number of Exemptions. S&S used April's IRS Form W-4 to determine her federal filing status and exemptions.[2]   The Retirement Plan option is checked because April participates in S&S' 401-K plan. This option signals Great Plains to print April's annual plan contributions on her W-2.

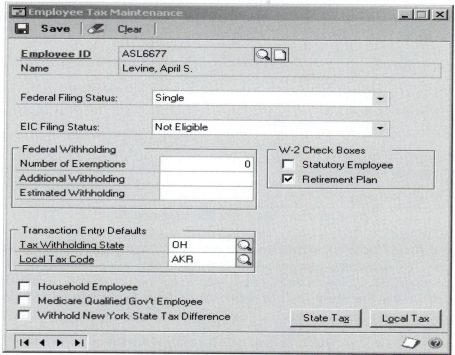

F7:4 Federal Tax Window

Thus far, we have determined April's federal tax withholdings. We now review her link to state tax records. Once again, these rates were downloaded from the online payroll service. To open April's state tax record, you can use either the State Tax button on the Employee Tax Maintenance window or the *State Tax* menu (**F7:5**). Notice April is linked to the OH tax rates (**F7:5**), thus paying state taxes to Ohio. Ohio has a withholding form similar to the federal W-4 that determines April's Personal Exemptions. Use the x icon and close this window.

---

[2] Form W-4 is available on the IRS' website at www.irs.gov. In addition, employees should complete a Department of Immigrations Form I-9, verifying authorization to work in the United States.

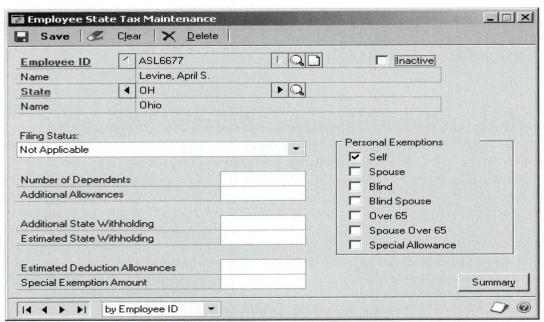

F7:5 Employee State Tax Maintenance Window

Let's now look at April's local tax record.   Once again, you can use either the Local Tax button on the Employee Tax Maintenance window or the *Local Tax* menu. The Employee Local Tax Maintenance window (*F7:6*) shows April pays Akron city income taxes, which deducts 2% of April's gross pay. Local tax rates are not downloaded from the online payroll service. These records are created by employers and discussed in Level Two. Use the x icon and close April's local tax record.

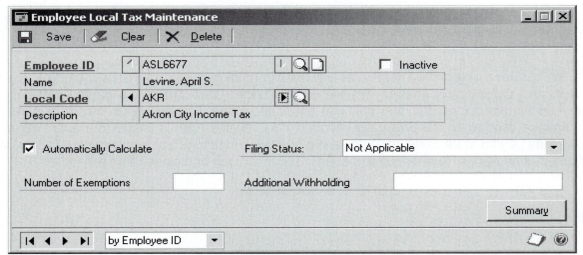

F7:6 Local Tax Link Window

After reviewing links to tax records, we review her links to pay rate, benefits, and deductions records. These links are reviewed by selecting the *Pay Code*, *Deduction*, and *Benefit* menus individually or by clicking on the *Quick Assignment* menu.

The Payroll Quick Employee Assignment window (*F7:7*) provides an efficient method for linking employee cards to company benefits, employee voluntary deductions, and employee pay rates. The Code Type and Display options determine the list that displays at the bottom of the window.

Select the All Company Codes option and then take a few minutes to review April's links for the Benefits, Deductions, and Pay Codes types. Remember, code setup is discussed in Level Two.

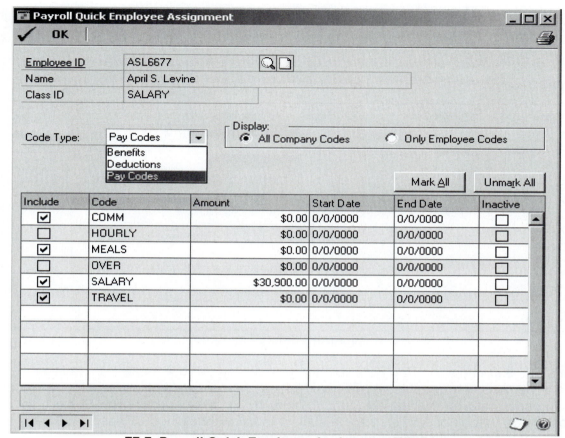

F7:7 Payroll Quick Employee Assignment Window

The Payroll Quick Employee Assignment window shows April's card is linked to the <u>COMM</u>, <u>MEALS</u>, <u>SALARY</u>, and <u>TRAVEL</u> pay codes. In addition, the <u>SALARY</u> code displays April's annual pay. This pay amount is entered by using the *Pay Code* menu item. Click on this menu and then look up April's record and her SALARY Pay Code (*F7:8*).

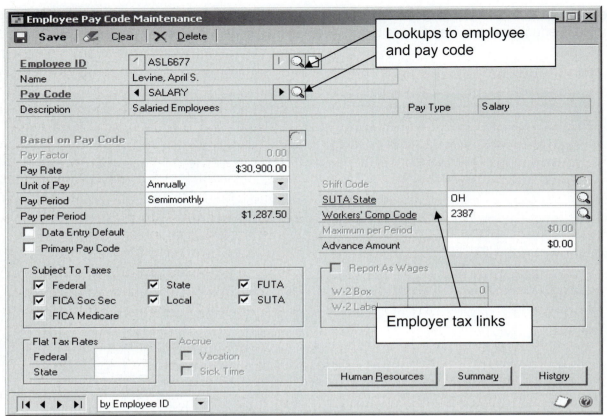

F7:8 April's Salary Pay Code

We find $30,900 under the Pay Rate with the Unit of Pay set to Annually. In addition, her Pay Period is Semimonthly, meaning April is paid $1,287.50 twice a month. Great Plains calculated the pay period rate by dividing the annual figure by 24 pay-periods. The Subject To Taxes section shows that all of April's salary is subject to tax withholdings. Finally, S&S pays SUTA and workers' compensation taxes on salary payments to April.

Change the Pay Code to <u>COMM</u> and view April's commission record (**F7:9**). This record shows zero as the Unit of Pay and the Pay Period as Monthly. The rate is empty because commissions are based on customer sales. We look at entering commission payments later in the chapter. Close the Employee Pay Code Maintenance window.

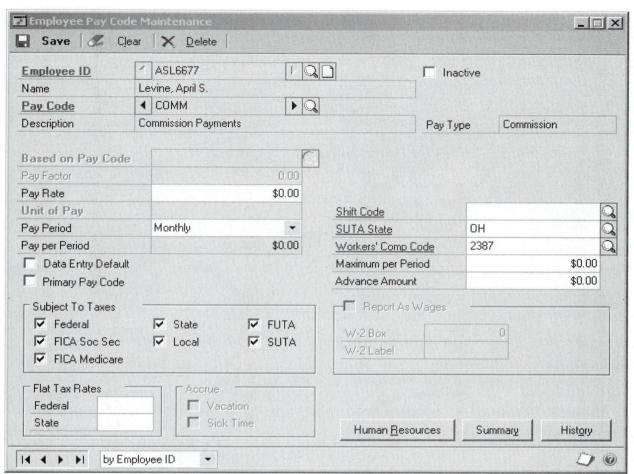

F7:9 April's Commission Pay Code

Let's look at Deduction codes. Click on the *Deduction* menu, look up April's card, and then use the right scroll button for the Deduction Code field to open one of her deductions. Your screen should now look like the Employee Deduction Maintenance window in *F7:10*. Deductions are *voluntary* amounts withheld from an employee's pay for items such as contributions to not-for-profits agencies, 401-K retirement plans, and health insurance cost-shares.   Deductions can be taken as fixed amounts or percentages of pay. Notice April's 401K code deducts 2.5% of her gross wages and this deduction occurs semimonthly, concurring with April's pay period. In addition, the deduction occurs before calculating her federal and state tax liabilities (TSA Sheltered From). Finally, April's annual deduction to her 401-K plan is limited to $13,000 as set by the Internal Revenue Service.

New links are created by looking up other deduction code and selecting the code. Look up the code HFAMI code and Great Plains prompts to assign default information for April's link to this code (*F7:11*). Click Default and the Employee Deduction Maintenance window now appears as shown in (*F7:12*).

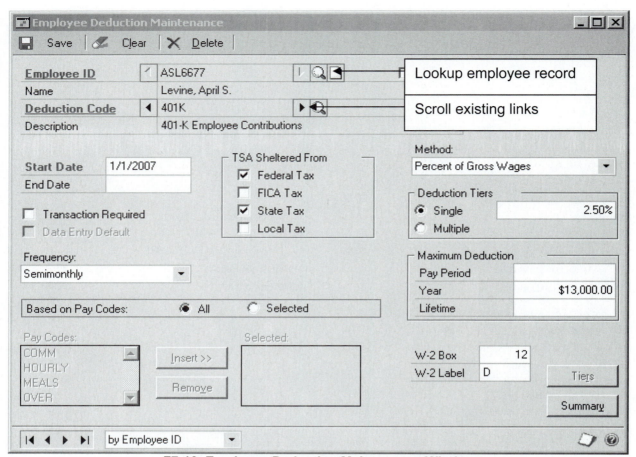

F7:10 Employee Deduction Maintenance Window

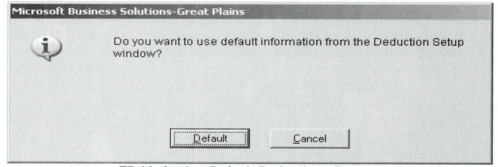

F7:11 Assign Default Deductions Prompt

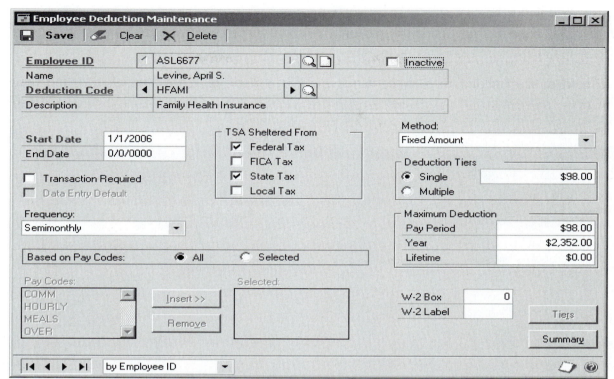

F7:12 April's Card Linked to HFAMI Deduction Code

The HFAMI code will deduct $98.00 from April's check each pay period starting on January 1, 2006 for family health insurance. Of course, this date would need to be changed to the actual start date. In addition, this deduction will be taken before calculating April's federal and state income tax liabilities.

Click the Save button to store the link and you receive a message warning that Human Resource is installed and therefore deduction links should be created in that Series and transferred to the Payroll Series (*F7:13*). However, S&S is not using the HR Series, so click Yes to continue.

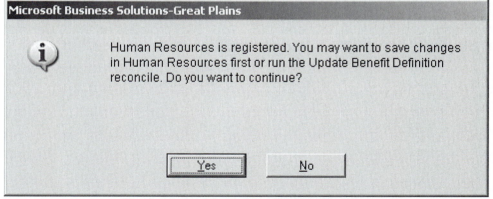

F7:13 Human Resource Series Warning

After saving, scroll through April's links. You find two deduction codes for health insurance, one for family coverage and one for single coverage. April would not be happy paying twice for health coverage, so let's remove the HFAMI code we just added.

To remove the link, display the code in the April's Employee Deduction Maintenance window and then click Delete. This action clears April's record from the window. Look up her employee card again and scroll through her deductions to verify the code was deleted.

The Employee Deduction Maintenance window in *F7:14* displays Adam Whitfield's United Way deductions. Look up Adam's employee card and <u>CONTR</u> link. This code deducts $10 (Fixed Amount) from Adam's check each pay period after calculating Adam's tax liabilities.

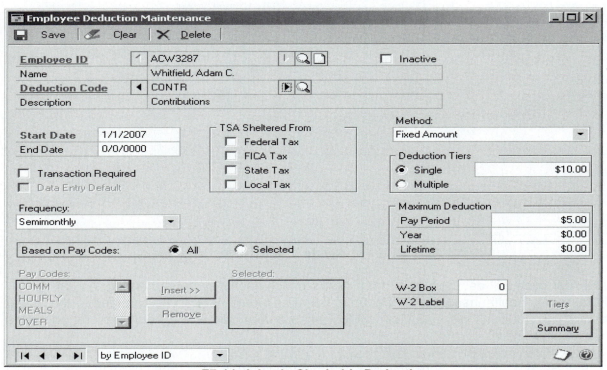

F7:14 Adam's Charitable Deduction

Close the Employee Deduction Maintenance window and click on the *Benefit* menu. Benefits are *employer* contributions made on behalf of employees for items such as pension and retirement plans. S&S matches employee contributions to the 401-K plan. Look up April's employee card and scroll to her 401K benefit (*F7:15*). S&S provides an employer match of 50% of April's contributions, up to $5,000. In addition, this match is non-taxable to April.

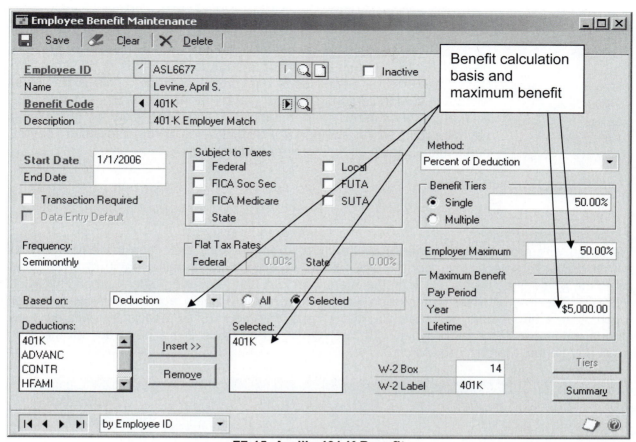

F7:15 April's 401-K Benefit

This topic illustrates that the Payroll Series requires more work with master records (cards) than any of the Series previously covered. Changes to employee wages, taxes, benefits, and deductions must be entered prior to processing payroll, which is the focus of the next topic.

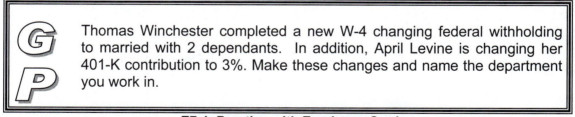

Thomas Winchester completed a new W-4 changing federal withholding to married with 2 dependants. In addition, April Levine is changing her 401-K contribution to 3%. Make these changes and name the department you work in.

E7:1 Practice with Employee Cards

PAYROLL SERIES TRANSACTIONS

As stated in the chapter's introduction, S&S prepares hourly payroll biweekly and salaried payroll semimonthly. The next date for preparing both pay types happens to occur on March 30. In addition, at the end of every month, S&S pays sales commission and expense checks. Therefore, we will prepare hourly and salary paychecks along with commission and expense checks for March 30th.

Transaction Entry
Mass Entry
Build Checks
Calculate Checks
Print Checks
Manual Checks
Batches
Void Checks
Activate Post-Dated

Click on *Transactions>>Payroll* to open the window used to process payroll (**F7:16**). Unlike transaction menus for the Sales and Purchasing Series, the Payroll Series uses one processing tier. This is because, without the Manufacturing Series, payroll transactions do not interface with any Series other than Financial. The complexity of processing payroll occurs when setting up Payroll Series cards; thereafter, payroll processing is fairly straightforward and repetitive.

F7:16 Payroll Transaction Menu

Process Hourly Payroll

We begin with processing paychecks for hourly paid employees. Selecting the employees to pay is similar to selecting vendors to pay. First, we will create an initial batch of employees using the *Mass Entry* menu. Click on this menu and look up the existing batch named HOURLY (**F7:17**). The Payroll Mass Transaction Entry window runs a query against employee master records, selecting employees matching the criteria entered. **F7:17** shows the window with criteria entered to select employees with the HOURLY Pay Code due a paycheck for the two-week pay period, March 17 to March 30.

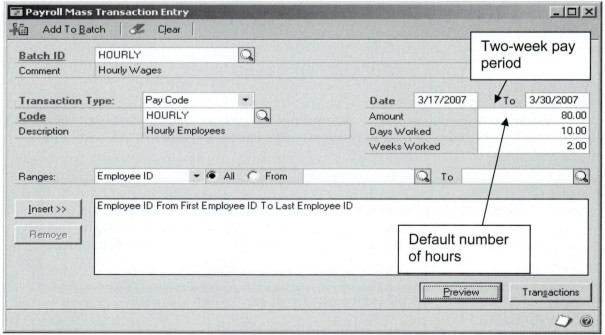

F7:17 Payroll Mass Transaction Entry Window

Click the Preview button to see the employee records selected for paychecks (**F7:18**). Additional employees can be added to this batch by entering the employee's ID and clicking the Add to Batch button. Use the x icon and close the Preview Mass Entry Transaction window.

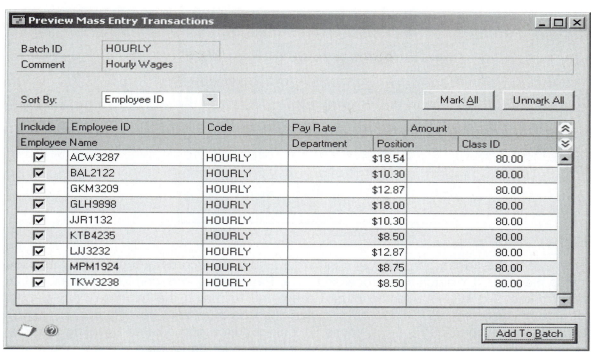

F7:18 Preview of Hourly Employee Records Selected

In addition, other pay codes can be added to the HOURLY batch by reentering selection criteria in the Payroll Mass Transaction Entry window and clicking the Add to Batch button, for instance, to add overtime pay records. This batch contains the correct pay code and employees, so close the window with the x icon without making changes.

Now click on the *Batches* menu and look up the HOURLY batch. Aston set this batch to recur biweekly (*F7:19*). Notice that Ashton set the Recurring Posting field to zero so the batch never expires.

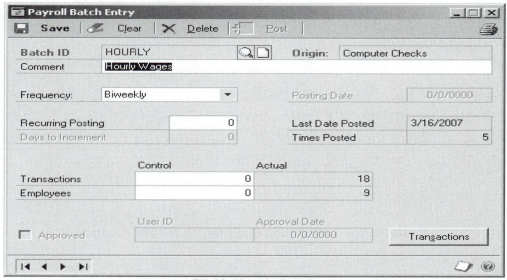

F7:19 Hourly Batch

Click the Transactions button and select Payroll Transaction Entry (*F7:20*), then click the Go to button.

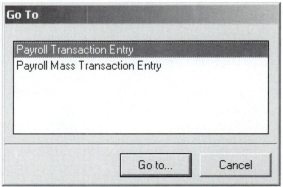

F7:20 Transaction Go To Window

This action opens the transaction window containing employee records and pay amounts used the last time the <u>HOURLY</u> batch was processed. The Pay Period From and To dates as well as the Days Worked and Weeks Worked must be entered to match the two-week pay period. Changes to employee records for new hires or terminations must also be entered. Employee records can be added by using the Employee ID lookup button and deleted by using the Row Delete icon. Finally, the Amount field for each employee must be entered. The Amount field represents an employee's regular (<u>HOURLY</u>) and overtime (<u>OVER</u>) hours.

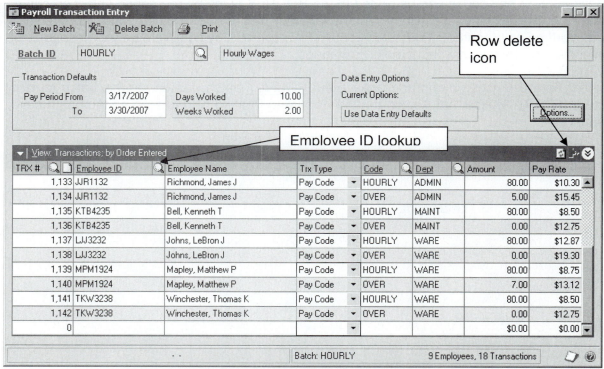

F7:21 Payroll Transaction Entry for the HOURLY Batch

Let's change the existing overtime hours for Richmond and Mapley to zero, since they did not work overtime during the pay period. When entering a zero amount, the informational message in *F7:22* appears. This message warns that records marked with zero do not calculate a pay amount. For our situation, this status is appropriate, so click Continue.

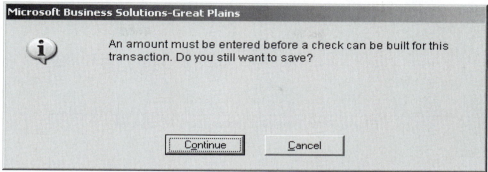

F7:22 Warning for Zero Amount

The Print button produces a Payroll Transaction Edit List (**F7:23**). This report is then compared to each employee's time card hours and to total hours to control data entry.

```
System:      5/23/2005  3:32:53 PM                  S&S, Incorporated                    Page:       1
User Date:   3/30/2007                        PAYROLL TRANSACTION EDIT LIST              User ID:   sa
                                                     U.S. Payroll
Ranges:
     Batch:      HOURLY              Hourly Wages
Trx Total Actual:      18      Trx Total Control:      0
Employee Total Actual: 9       Employee Total Control: 0
Approved: No          Approved By:              Approval Date: 0/0/0000


TRX Type
------------------------------------------------------------------------------------------------------

                                               Begin        End
TRX No.  Employee ID    Employee Name    Code  Date         Date          Pay Rate       Premium      Amount
------------------------------------------------------------------------------------------------------
                                         Dept  Position     Shift         Receipts
------------------------------------------------------------------------------------------------------
Pay Code
   1,125 ACW3287        Whitfield, Adam C  HOURLY 3/17/2007  3/30/2007     $18.54                      80.00
                                         TRANS  TRUCK        FIRST         $0.00
   1,126 ACW3287        Whitfield, Adam C  OVER   3/17/2007  3/30/2007     $27.81                       0.00
                                         TRANS  TRUCK        FIRST         $0.00
                                                                                             ---------------
                                                               Total Hours for Employee:              80.00

   1,127 BAL2122        Lane, Betsy A      HOURLY 3/17/2007  3/30/2007     $10.30                      80.00
                                         ADMIN  APCLER       FIRST         $0.00
   1,128 BAL2122        Lane, Betsy A      OVER   3/17/2007  3/30/2007     $15.45                       0.00
                                         ADMIN  APCLER       FIRST         $0.00
                                                                                             ---------------
                                                               Total Hours for Employee:              80.00

   1,129 GKM3209        McMahon, George K  HOURLY 3/17/2007  3/30/2007     $12.87                      80.00
                                         MAINT  SUPR         FIRST         $0.00
   1,130 GKM3209        McMahon, George K  OVER   3/17/2007  3/30/2007     $19.30                       0.00
                                         MAINT  SUPR         FIRST         $0.00
```

F7:23 Payroll Transaction Edit List for HOURLY Batch

After verifying hours, the Payroll Transaction Entry window is closed. Great Plains prompts to print the Payroll Transaction Audit List (**F7:24**), click Print and the report appears (**F7:25**). Printing this report is optional, however, S&S requires payroll supervisor to initial approval on the report before cutting paychecks.

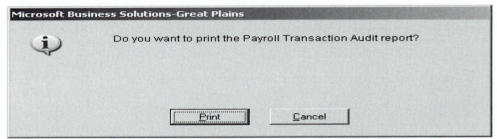

F7:24 Print Payroll Transaction Audit List

```
System:     5/23/2005  3:34:23 PM                    S&S, Incorporated                    Page:     1
User Date:  3/30/2007                          PAYROLL TRANSACTION AUDIT LIST             User ID:  sa
                                                      U.S. Payroll


A = New Transaction O = Modified Old Transaction N = Modified New Transaction
D = Deleted Transaction Z = Zero Units
X = No transaction created; vacation/sick time exceeded. Need password.
M = No transaction created; employee maximum for pay code per period exceeded.

                                          Date
TRX   Employee ID    Batch Number   Code   Begin       End            Pay Rate       Premium        Amount
---------------------------------------------------------------------------------------------------------
 O    JJR1132        HOURLY         OVER   3/17/2007   3/30/2007       $15.45                          0.00
 N    JJR1132        HOURLY         OVER   3/17/2007   3/30/2007       $15.45                          5.00
 O    MPM1924        HOURLY         OVER   3/17/2007   3/30/2007       $13.12                          0.00
 N    MPM1924        HOURLY         OVER   3/17/2007   3/30/2007       $13.12                          7.00

Total Transactions:          4
```

F7:25 Payroll Transaction Audit List

Process Sales Commission and Expenses

Next, we gather the information required to pay sales commission. Remember from Chapter 5, commission amounts due employees do not automatically transfer to payroll. Therefore, payroll uses the monthly sales commission report to enter commission payments. S&S pays commissions after the customer remits payment. This option was selected in Sales setup and reduces commission overpayments due to nonpaying customers.

Payroll employees enter commission amounts at the end of the month using a report approved by the sales manager. Let's generate the manager's report using *Tools>>Routines>> Sales>>Transfer Commissions* menu. Verify your system date is March 30 because Great Plains uses this date as the Last Transfer Date. (Note: The Last Transfer Date field in *F7:26* shows commissions were last transferred on February 28.) Select the Detail option and click the Process button to post commission liabilities, printing a report for amount posted (*F7:27*). A copy of this report is also sent to Ashton for use in entering an adjusting journal entry, discussed in Chapter 8.

F7:26 Transfer Commissions Window

(Remember, your numbers may differ from those shown in *F7:27* because commission liabilities are based on customer payments recorded in March.) The Commission Amount column shows the payments due to sales employees.

```
System:    5/23/2005   5:17:25 PM            S&S, Incorporated                        Page:    1
User Date: 3/30/2007          TRANSFERRED COMMISSIONS POSTING JOURNAL DETAIL      User ID: sa
                                     Receivables Management

Ranges:
   Audit Trail Code:   RMCOM00000018           Batch ID:       sa
   Posting Date:       3/30/2007               Batch Origin: Transfer Commission
Sorted: by Salesperson ID

Batch ID:      sa           Audit Trail Code: RMCOM00000018 Batch Frequency: Single Use   Number of TRX:      4
Transfer Date: 3/30/2007    Batch Comment:   Receivables Transfer Commissions

Salesperson ID Name (Last, First Middle)          Territory ID   Employee ID
-------------------------------------------------------------------------------------------------------
   Type Document Number   Customer ID       Sales Amount  % Sale  Comm %   Commission Amount Non-Commissioned Amount
-------------------------------------------------------------------------------------------------------
ASL6677       Levine, April S               MID               ASL6677
   SLS  INV000000194      GGHREGGS001      $189,000.00 100.00%   0.30%          $567.00              $0.00
                                          -------------                    ----------------   ----------------
                 Sub totals:               $189,000.00                          $567.00              $0.00

CJW7872       Warner, Curtis J              EAST              CJW7872
   SLS  INV000000196      LAUFMANS001      $147,551.00 100.00%   0.30%          $442.65              $0.00
                                          -------------                    ----------------   ----------------
                 Sub totals:               $147,551.00                          $442.65              $0.00

MTM3987       Murphy, Mary T                WEST              MTM3987
   SLS  INV000000195      DISCOUNTE001     $108,240.00 100.00%   0.30%          $324.72              $0.00
   SLS  INV000000197      SIXTHAV001        $77,935.00 100.00%   0.30%          $233.81              $0.00
                                          -------------                    ----------------   ----------------
                 Sub totals:               $186,175.00                          $558.53              $0.00

                                          -------------                    ----------------   ----------------
                 Totals:                   $522,726.00                        $1,568.18              $0.00
                                          =============                    ================   ================
```

F7:27 Transferred Commissions Report

The payroll clerk enters the commissions due employees using the existing <u>COMMISSIONS</u> batch (*F7:28*). Instead of hours, this time the Amount field stores the dollars due each salesperson. Amounts shown upon opening the batch are the commissions paid last month. You will use the Transferred Commission Report to enter payments for this month in the exercise that follows.

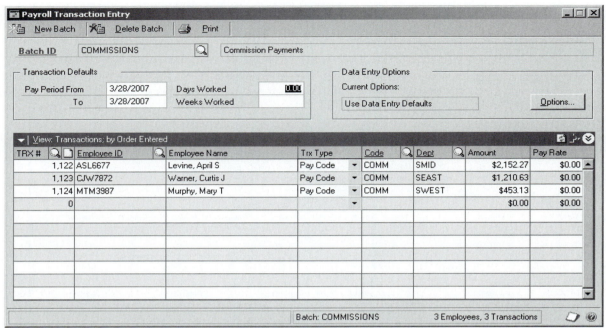

F7:28 Commissions Batch

Since S&S also cuts employee expense reimbursements at the end of the month, look up the <u>EXPENSES</u> batch. Again, the amounts show in *F7:29* are expenses paid last month. Expense reimbursements are entered from departmental approved expense reports. You will enter this month's reimbursements in the exercise that follows. Notice that expenses are broken into meals and travel so that amounts post to the correct general ledger account.

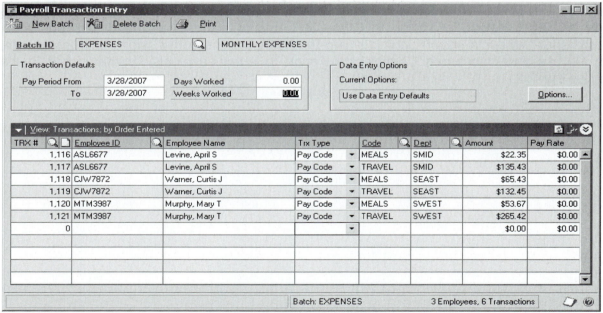

F7:29 Expenses Batch

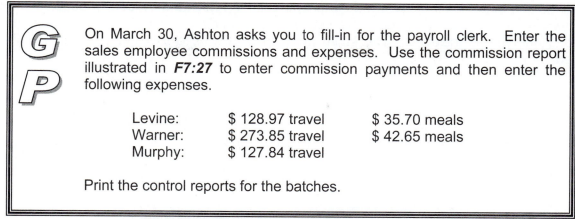

On March 30, Ashton asks you to fill-in for the payroll clerk. Enter the sales employee commissions and expenses. Use the commission report illustrated in *F7:27* to enter commission payments and then enter the following expenses.

Levine:	$ 128.97 travel	$ 35.70 meals
Warner:	$ 273.85 travel	$ 42.65 meals
Murphy:	$ 127.84 travel	

Print the control reports for the batches.

E7:2 Enter Commission and Expense Payments

Process Salary Payroll

Salaried employees are paid the same wages each pay period, regardless of hours worked. Therefore, we do not enter hours using the Payroll Transaction Entry window. Instead, we use the *Build Checks* menu, opening the Build Payroll Checks window, and enter employee selection criteria. The Build Payroll Checks window contains an existing SALARYPAY batch. Open this batch and review the fields in *F7:30*.

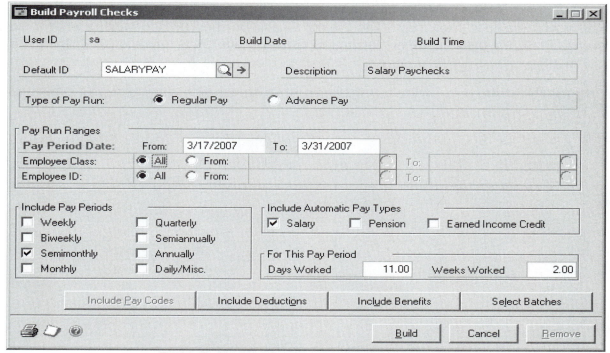

F7:30 Build Checks Window for Salary Pay Codes

We see that the SALARYPAY batch selects employee cards linked to the Salary pay type. In addition, employees with this pay type are paid semimonthly, so the Include Pay Periods is set to this option.

The Pay Period Date must be changed each time the batch is used. In addition, payroll deductions and benefits for these checks must be verified. Click the Include Deductions button that opens the Payroll Check Deductions window shown in *F7:31*. The Selected option shows all deductions will be included. The same procedures are used to verify all benefits will be included.

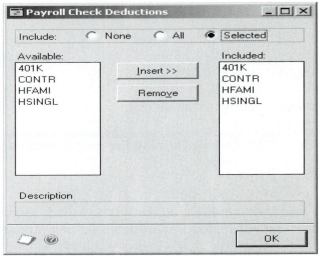

F7:31 Include Deductions Window

The Select Batches button adds additional batches to this pay run for salaried employees. Since it is the end of the month, we will add the <u>EXPENSES</u> and <u>COMMISSIONS</u> batches you updated in the previous exercises. The Payroll Check Batches (*F7:32*) window shows the selection of these two batches. After marking the batches, click OK to return to the Build Payroll Checks window.

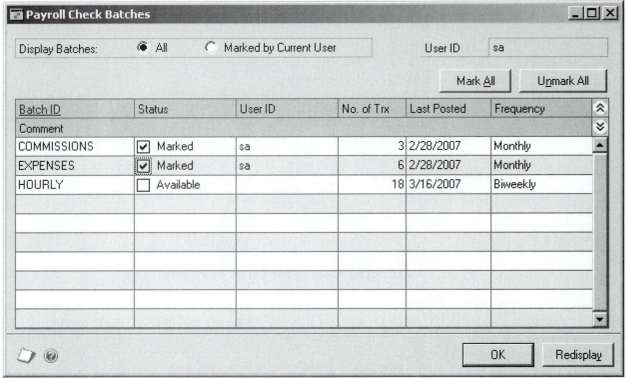

F7:32 Payroll Check Batches Window

The <u>SALARYPAY</u> batch is now ready to build employee paychecks. Click the Build button and save the batch when prompted. Give the system time to build the batch. When finished, print the payroll Check File Report and verify that the batch includes salary, commission, and expense entries.

```
System:    5/23/2005  7:27:17 PM                 S&S, Incorporated              Page:    1
User Date: 3/30/2007                             CHECK FILE REPORT             User ID: sa
                                                   U.S. Payroll

Employee ID    Name
-----------------------------------------------------------------------------------------------
            Code    Description      Dept    Position  Shift      Pay Rate       Premium      Amount/Units
-----------------------------------------------------------------------------------------------
            State   Local            W/Comp  SUTA      Weeks  Days              Receipts      Batch ID
-----------------------------------------------------------------------------------------------
APF3232        Fleming, Ashton P
   Pay:     SALARY  Salary           ADMIN   ACCT                 $2,358.33                    $2,358.33
            OH      AKR              2387    OH       2.00   11.00
   Benefit: 401K    401-K Employer Match                              50.00% of Deduction
   Deduction: 401K  401-K Employee Contributions                       4.00% of Gross Wages
            HSINGL  Single Health Insurance                           $60.00
   State Tax: OH    Ohio
   Local Tax: AKR   Akron City Income Tax

ASL6677        Levine, April S
   Pay:     SALARY  Salary           SMID    STAFF                $1,287.50                    $1,287.50
            OH      AKR              2387    OH       2.00   11.00
            COMM    Commission       SMID    STAFF                                              $567.00
            OH      AKR              2387    OH       0.00   0.00                 COMMISSIONS
            MEALS   Bus Expense      SMID    STAFF                                               $35.70
                                     2387             0.00   0.00                 EXPENSES
            TRAVEL  Bus Expense      SMID    STAFF                                              $128.97
                                     2387             0.00   0.00                 EXPENSES
   Benefit: 401K    401-K Employer Match                              50.00% of Deduction
   Deduction: 401K  401-K Employee Contributions                       3.00% of Gross Wages
            HSINGL  Single Health Insurance                           $60.00
   State Tax: OH    Ohio
   Local Tax: AKR   Akron City Income Tax

CJW7872        Warner, Curtis J
   Pay:     SALARY  Salary           SEAST   STAFF                $1,244.58                    $1,244.58
            OH      AKR              2387    OH       2.00   11.00
            COMM    Commission       SEAST   STAFF                                              $442.65
```

F7:33 Payroll Check File Report

With the build process complete, paychecks are ready for calculation. Click the *Calculate Checks* menu to open the window in ***F7:34***. Calculation determines the net pay by applying tax rates, deductions, and benefits against gross pay. Click OK to calculate paychecks for the batch.

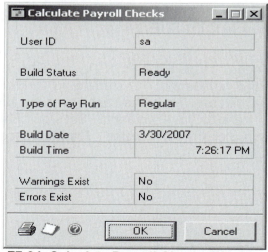

F7:34 Calculate Payroll Checks Window

Be patient while the system calculates checks and print the Calculate Check Report when finished. Review the report (**F7:35**) for errors or warnings. Checks containing errors must be corrected before Great Plains will print employee paychecks. Checks containing a warning will print; however, paycheck integrity is compromised.

```
System:     5/23/2005  8:06:50 PM           S&S, Incorporated                    Page:    1
User Date:  3/30/2007                     CALCULATE CHECKS REPORT                 User ID: sa
                                               U.S. Payroll

Employee ID    Name                        Soc Sec Number
-------------------------------------------------------------------------------------------------
    Code   Pay Type      Dept   Position      Pay Rate    Amount/Units    Gross Wages    Ben/Ded/Tax      Net Wages
-------------------------------------------------------------------------------------------------
APF3232        Fleming, Ashton P            083-25-3232
    SALARY Salary        ADMIN  ACCT         $2,358.33                      $2,358.33
                                                                          ----------------
                                                                           $2,358.33

                                Benefits:     401K   401-K Employer Match                   $47.17
                                                                                          ----------------
                                                                                           $47.17

                                Deductions:   401K   401-K Employee Contributions          $94.33
                                              HSINGL Single Health Insurance                $54.00
                                                                                          ----------------
                                                                                           $148.33

                                Taxes On Wages: FICA Soc Sec Withheld                       $146.22
                                                FICA Medicare Withheld                      $34.19
                                                Federal Withheld                           $389.79
                                                OH   State Withheld                         $89.75
                                                AKR    Local Withheld                       $47.17
                                                                                          ----------------
                                                                                           $707.12

                                                                                          ----------------
                                                                                                       $1,502.88
                                                                                          ================

ASL6677        Levine, April S             007-65-6677
    SALARY Salary        SMID   STAFF        $1,287.50                      $1,287.50
    COMM   Commission    SMID   STAFF                      $567.00            $567.00
```

F7:35 Calculate Checks Report

Errors most commonly occur when a general ledger account is missing under payroll setup (discussed in Level Two.) Warnings usually occur because the pay period set on the batch is incorrect. S&S' internal control policies require printing paychecks by the cashier. Therefore, the payroll department confidentially sends this report to the cashier to trigger the final step in paying employees.

CASHIER DEPARTMENT ACTIVITIES

Click on the _Print Checks_ menu to open the Print Payroll Checks window (**F7:36**). Before printing the checks, the cashier verifies that the starting number on check stock matches the Starting Check Number in the window. Next, the cashier makes sure the Print option is set to Checks because this option defaults to Alignment. Set your Print Payroll Checks window options as show in **F7:36**, then click the Print button. Print the checks to the screen and close the report after reviewing output.

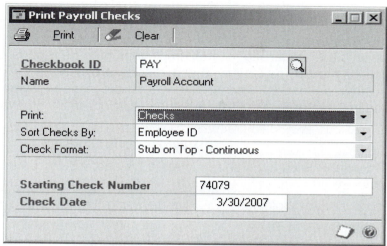

F7:36 Print Payroll Checks Window

After printing, the Post Payroll Checks window appears (*F7:37*). This window contains several Process options such as voiding printed checks and then reprinting checks. Before setting the option to Post checks, the cashier verifies checks print correctly.

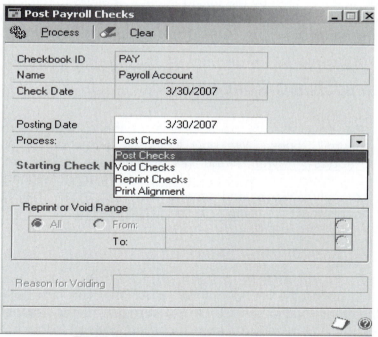

F7:37 Post Payroll Checks Window

Set the Process option to Post Checks and click the Process button. The Check Register report prints to the screen (not illustrated). A copy of this register is filed in the cashier department and a copy is sent to the payroll department as confirmation of check printing.

ACCOUNTS PAYABLE DEPARTMENT ACTIVITIES

Every time payroll checks are processed, payroll employees prepare reports showing the taxes, benefits, and deductions for the pay run. These reports are sent to the accounts payable department for remitting payments. Accounts payable processes payments following the procedures discussed in Chapter 6. **T7:3** lists the due dates for remitting payroll liabilities.

Payroll Liability	Payment Due Dates
Federal Income, Social Security, and Medicare Tax Withholdings	Three days after issuing payroll checks
State and Local Income Tax Withholdings	Five days after month-end
Federal and State Unemployment Taxes	Five days after quarter-end
State Workers' Compensation Tax	Fifteen days after June 30 and after December 31
401-K and Other Voluntary Deductions	Five days after month-end

T7:3 Payroll Liability Due Dates

The tax payment due dates are set by the taxing agency. Failure to remit payments by the due date results in agency imposed penalties and interest; therefore, monitoring compliance is critical to company performance.

PAYROLL SERIES: BASIC REPORTING

Employee Lists
Wage and Hour
History
Reprint Journals
Setup
Groups
Period-End
Quarter-End
Cross-Company

We have already used several of the control reports produced by the Payroll Series. We now focus on a few of the other reports.[3] The *Reports>>Payroll* menu (**F7:38**) groups reports into categories. The *Employee Lists*, *Wage and Hour*, and *History* categories print reports used to analyze wages and general ledger postings. The categories focused on in this topic are *Period-End* and *Quarter-End*.

F7:38 Payroll Report Menu

The *Period-End* menu opens the window shown in **F7:39**. The Month Type is used to print payroll reports for the month and to post FUTA, SUTA and Workers' Compensation taxes. Until these Post Liabilities options are selected and processed, general ledger entries for these taxes are not posted. The Period Type functions the same as the Month Type, however, it permits the entry of a date range for reporting and processing.

S&S sends reports appearing on the left of the window to accounts payable instead of reports printed during payroll processing because data is summarized, thus keeping sensitive data confidential.

---

[3] For an in-depth discussion on payroll reporting, refer to pages 509 through 511 in Marshall Romney and Paul Steinbart, *Accounting Information Systems* (10th ed., Prentice Hall 2006).

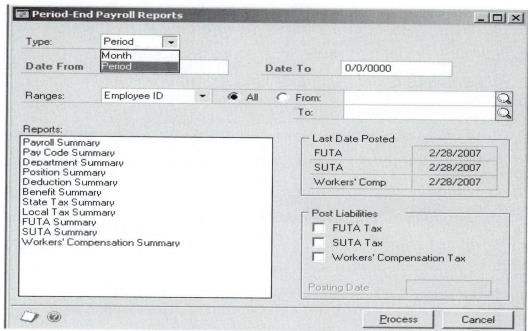

F7:39 Period-End Reporting Window

The Payroll Summary report tells accounts payable the transfer requirements for the payroll checking account. It also provides liability amounts due to the IRS for employee withholdings and employer taxes. The State Tax Summary and Local Tax Summary tell accounts payable the liability amounts due for employee tax withholdings to those agencies. The Deduction Summary and Benefit Summary list amounts due to vendors receiving 401-K contributions and charitable contributions.

As illustrated in Chapter 6, the health insurance vendor remits a monthly bill for medical insurance; therefore, insurance deductions listed on the Deduction Summary report are not used to pay the health insurer. Instead, this amounts shows employee deductions that reduce health insurance costs.

This brings us to the Post Liabilities option. Select the FUTA, SUTA, and Workers' Compensation options, select the reports shown on the left, and click the Process button (**F7:40**). Review the reports and notice that the summary reports for these items lists employee wage information. Therefore, payroll sends the last report that prints (General Posting Journal) to accounts payable for use in paying these tax liabilities.

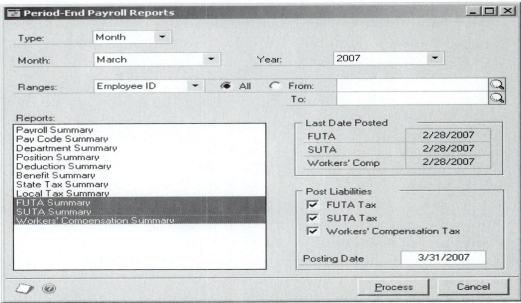

F7:40 Process FUTA, SUTA, and Workers' Compensation Taxes

March triggers end of quarter processing. Therefore, in addition to processing monthly reports, quarterly reporting is also printed. Click on the *Quarter-End* menu to open the Quarter-End Payroll Reports window shown in *F7:41*. The IRS requires companies file Federal Form 941 at the end of every quarter. This report reconciles company tax deposits made over the quarter to the liabilities incurred for federal income, social security, and medicare taxes. Mark the preparation report option shown in the window, then click the Process button. The report shows S&S' tax remittances over the quarter. The balance due should reflect zero when S&S has remitted all payments prior to printing the report.

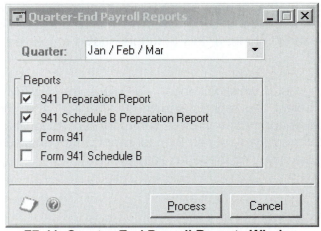

F7:41 Quarter-End Payroll Reports Window

At year-end, the payroll department adds W-2 printing to its list of reports. W-2s are printed by clicking the *Tools>>Routines>>Payroll>>Print W-2s* menu to open the Print W-2 Forms window show in *F7:42*. W-2s are sent to employees by January 31st of each year and copies are sent to the Social Security Administration, along with a W-3 transmittal form, by the end of February. In addition, many states and local taxing authorities require copies of W-2s.

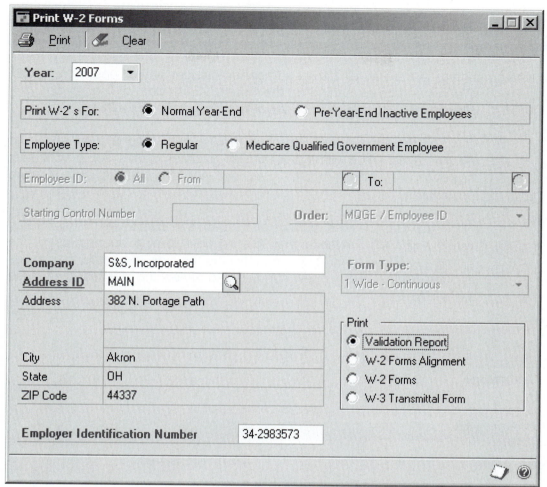

F7:42 Print W-2 Forms Window

The Print options for this window prints a Validation Report to review information before printing W-2s. This report should be reconciled to total wages, taxes, and benefits on payroll reports prior to printing W-2s. Should there be an error on one of the W-2s, the *Tools>>Routines>> Payroll>>Edit W-2s* opens a window to adjust information.

1. Print the Payroll Summary report for the March 17th to March 30th pay period. Does the report list all the information accounts payable needs to pay tax liabilities for the pay period? If not, name additional reports that should be sent?

2. Print the Pay Code Summary report for the same time-period. What additional information does this report provide accounts payable that is not available on the Payroll Summary report?

E7:3 Payroll Reporting

Level Two focuses on setting up the Payroll Series and general ledger payroll posting options.[4] We will first cover setting up the Series. Click on the *Tools>>Setup>> Payroll* menu to see a list of items requiring setup (*F7:43*).

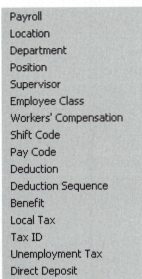

Click on the *Payroll* menu to open the Payroll Setup window shown in *F7:44*. This setup window is similar to other Series setup windows; however, Payroll's window does not contain specific authorization passwords.

Click on the Classes button and open the Employee Class Setup window (*F7:45*). (Notice that this window is also opened using the *Employee Class* menu.) Payroll classes function the same as classes in other Series. Take a few minutes and review the classes, then close the window.

F7:43 Payroll Setup Menu

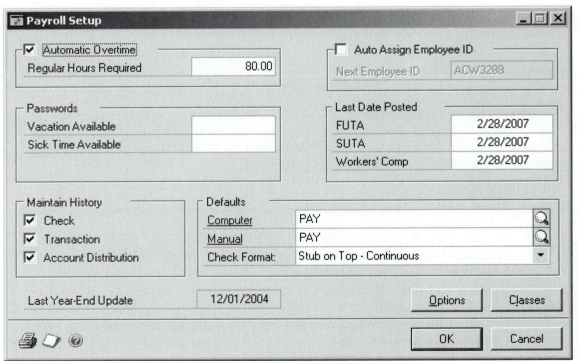

F7:44 Payroll Setup

---

[4] Before reading this section, students are benefited by referring to payroll and human resources internal control topics covered on pages 504 through 509 of Marshall Romney and Paul Steinbart, *Accounting Information Systems* (10th ed., Prentice Hall 2006).

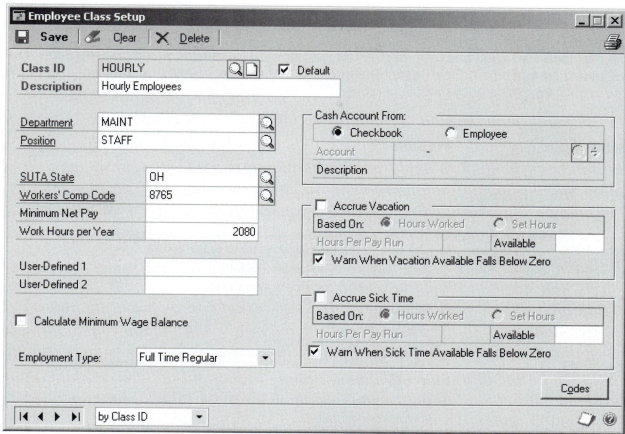

F7:45 Employee Class Setup Window

Now click the Options button to open the Payroll Setup Options window (*F7:46*). Once again, we find audit trail document codes and other settings that control the Payroll Series.

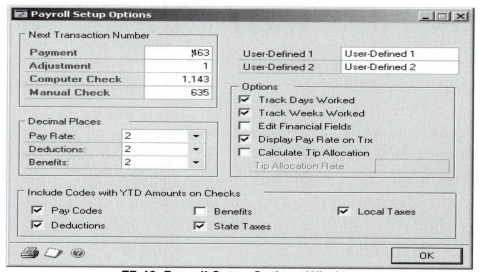

F7:46 Payroll Setup Options Window

These windows covered the basic setup of the Payroll Series; however, the menu shows that many other items require setup. These items are discussed in the next topic.

Setup of Pay Type, Tax, Deduction, and Benefit Codes

In Level One, we linked pay type, tax, benefit, and deduction codes to an employee's card. The remaining menu items on the Payroll Setup menu are used for creating and maintaining these codes. *T7:4* explains each menu's purpose.

Setup Menu Item	Purpose
Location	Codes for processing employee payroll by company sites.
Department	Department codes that facilitate reporting.
Position	Position codes classifying employees by job responsibilities for reporting.
Supervisor	Codes use to assign employees to supervisors
Workers' Compensation	Codes containing worker classifications and rates used to calculate workers' compensation tax.
Shift Code	Codes establishing shift differentials. Some companies increase base pay rates when working second or third shift. When applicable, these codes are linked to Pay Codes.
Pay Code	Codes for the hourly, salary, commission, travel expense, and meal expense pay types.
Deduction	Codes for health insurance, employee 401-K contributions, and charitable contributions.
Deduction Sequence	Sequence determines the priorities used to take deductions. For instance, if an employee has wage attachments or child support liabilities, these should be deducted before charitable contributions.
Benefit	Code for the employer's matching 401-K contribution.
Local Tax	Codes for local taxing agencies and related tax rates.
Unemployment Tax	Codes for FUTA and SUTA taxes. The FED code stores the FUTA tax rate. This rate automatically updates with the online payroll service. SUTA rates are entered manually. S&S uses the OH code to calculate SUTA taxes.

T7:4 Payroll Setup Codes

After reviewing the table, let's look at a few of these codes. Click on the *Pay Code* menu to open the Pay Code Setup window (*F7:47*), then look up the HOURLY code. This window contains defaults assigned to hourly paid employees. Notice the Pay Period frequency of Biweekly and the Hourly Unit of Pay. These fields correspond to how S&S pays hourly employees. A base pay rate is not stored to avoid automatically assigning default pay rates to employees. Instead, pay rates are entered through the employee's card, as illustrated in Level One. Take the time to review other pay codes.

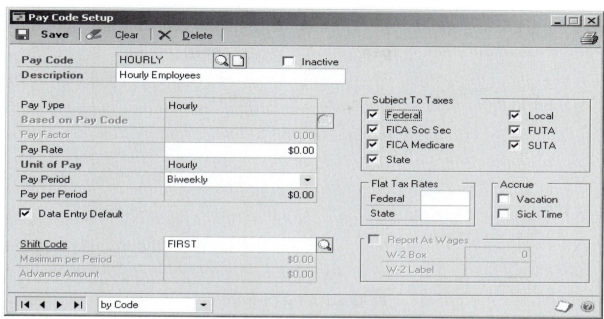

F7:47 Pay Code Setup Window

Now click on the _Local Tax_ menu and look up the AKR code show in **_F7:48_**. This code stores the tax rate used to withhold Akron city tax. Notice that Akron City Income Tax is deducted as 2% of gross pay. Remember that local taxes are not downloaded through the online payroll service, thus all rates must be created and stored using this window.

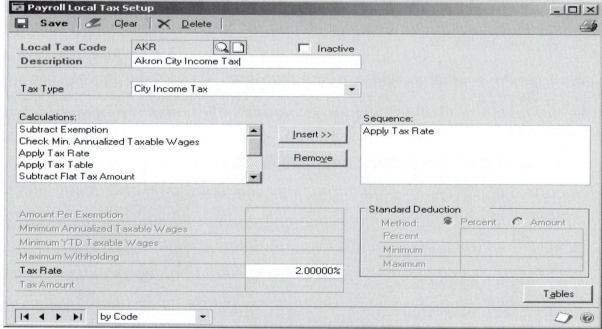

F7:48 Local Tax Code

Finally, click on the _Unemployment Tax_ menu to open the Unemployment Tax Setup window shown in **_F7:49_**. Look up the OH code that shows S&S pays SUTA at a rate of 1.9% on the first $9,000 paid annually to each employee. Like local taxes, unemployment tax codes and rates are manually entered.

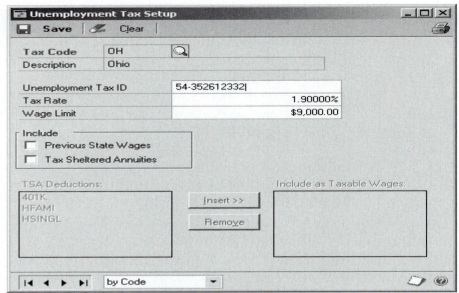

F7:49 SUTA Tax Code

PAYROLL POSTING ACCOUNTS

The most significant difference between the Payroll Series and other Series is found in the assignment of default general ledger accounts. In Chapter 6, we illustrated that default general ledger account for the Sales and Purchasing Series are assigned using customer, vendor, or inventory cards.   In the Payroll Series, defaults are assigned using the *Tools>>Setup>> Posting>>Payroll Accounts* menu. Click on this menu and open the Payroll Posting Accounts Setup window shown in *F7:50*.

With payroll, general ledger accounts are assigned by Payroll Account Type. These types are viewed using the dropdown list. Each type is assigned its own default posting accounts. These accounts are pervasive, meaning there is no opportunity to change the account during transaction processing

F7:50 Payroll Posting Accounts Setup Window

Take a few minutes to look through default accounts assigned to each type. Notice that some of the types record entries to allocation accounts. Remember, allocation accounts distribute entries using fixed amounts or percentages stored on the account's Financial Series card.

PAYROLL SERIES: MONTH-END AND YEAR-END CLOSING PROCEDURES

Our last topic focused on closing the Payroll Series. Like other Series, a month is closed using the *Tools>>Setup>>Company>>Fiscal Periods* window after posting all transactions for the period and printing payroll reports. For the Payroll Series, this would include posting FUTA, SUTA, and Workers' Compensation taxes as illustrated in Level One.

Reconciling the Payroll Series to the Financial Series is performed by running payroll reports and comparing balances in department expense accounts. Also, balances in payroll tax withholding, deduction, and benefit accounts should be reconciled to reports.

Year-ending payroll is critical and must be performed before processing payroll for the next year. Ending a year resets employee pay totals, which in turn resets tax withholding, social security, SUTA, FUTA, and workers' compensation calculations. In addition, W-2s and quarterly reports must be prepared before closing a year.

The Payroll Series is year-ended by clicking the *Tools>>Routines>>Payroll>>Year-End Closing* menu (**F7:51**). Clicking the Process button archives the year-end report. This report is then accessed from the *Tools>>Routines>>Payroll>>Year-End Wage Report* menu. DO NOT year-end S&S' Payroll Series.

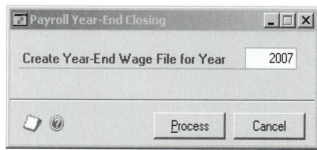

F7:51 Year-End Window

LEVEL ONE QUESTIONS

1. Adam Whitfield asked for an advance on payroll and the owners granted his request. How could you pay this advance and maintain control over the transaction?

2. Explain the difference between benefit and deduction codes.

3. Explain how Great Plains assists in validating the payroll hours entered during paycheck processing.

4. Explain the errors that would occur if you failed to link an employee's card to the Payroll Series codes affecting the employee. Provide specific examples.

5. Describe the difference between human resource activities and payroll activities. Include an explanation that analyzes the different threats faced by each activity.

LEVEL TWO QUESTIONS

1. Recommend how S&S could implement detective controls over overtime hours.

2. Analyze payroll cycle threats by explaining the controls S&S implemented to mitigate these threats.

3. Explain why it is important to monitor the timely payment of payroll liabilities and how S&S performs this activity.

4. Based on your review of payroll posting setup, what payroll entries are being allocated and why?

5. Explain the errors that would occur if January payroll were processed before closing the Payroll Series for the prior year.

CHAPTER 8: FINANCIAL REPORTING AND GREAT PLAINS FINANCIAL SERIES

CHAPTER OVERVIEW

The Financial Series controls general ledger accounts used to produce financial reports.[1] This Series integrates with other Series, but the integration runs one-way. All other Series link their transactions to general ledger accounts in the Financial Series. In addition, the Financial Series posts transactions directly to general ledger accounts.

Preceding chapters introduced a diagram explaining cycle activities by department and then used a Great Plains Series to perform those activities. However, financial reporting is not a cycle and the accounting department performs all activities in this Series. This department reviews postings for the period, ensuring validity and completeness, and then uses the Financial Series to make adjusting or correcting entries prior to issuing financial statements. After reporting, the accounting department closes the accounting period to prevent additional postings. With this background, we introduce accounting department activities as follows:

> ➤ Level One focuses on implementing an accounting period closing checklist. This checklist is the basis for learning Financials Series adjusting and correcting entries, bank reconciliation procedures, and financial reporting.

> ➤ Level Two focuses on advanced reporting and closing the Financial Series.

Level One covers:
> ➤ Using a closing checklist to monitor accounting period closing activities
> ➤ Using journal entries to record correcting, adjusting and reversing entries
> ➤ Bank reconciliation and financial reporting

Level Two covers:
> ➤ Creating basic financial statements and using advanced financials to customize statements
> ➤ Closing the accounting month and year to prevent additional postings

---

[1] Before reading this chapter, students are benefited by reading the topics on financial reporting in Chapter 14 of Marshall Romney and Paul Steinbart, *Accounting Information Systems* (10th ed., Prentice Hall 2006).

The March 30th accounting period has ended. On April 4, Ashton, reviews the expenditure cycle closing checklists shown in **F8:1**. This checklist shows that the Purchasing Manager completed his activities and made notes for adjusting and correcting entries. Aston is responsible for performing activities for the controller's office and for posting the purchasing manager's entries. Although not illustrated, each cycle has a similar closing checklist for which Ashton is also responsible.

S&S, Incorporated				
Expenditure Cycle Closing Checklist				
For Period Ended March 30, 2007				
Cutoff Date: 4/3/2007				
Activity	**Due Date**	**Status**	**Date**	**Notes**
Purchasing Manager				
Finalized Vendor Postings	4/3/2007	Completed	4/3/2007	
Adjusting and Correcting Entries	4/3/2007	Correcting	3/15/2007	Reclass $1,250 for desk on Office Rex invoice number 17650 dated 3/01/2007
		Adjusting		Accrue water bill
Controller's Office				
Finalized Purchase Series Postings	4/4/2007			
Posted Purchasing Adjusting and Correcting Entries	4/4/2007			
Reconciled Series	4/5/2007			
Prepared Purchasing Reports	4/5/2007			
Closed Purchasing Series	4/5/2007			

F8:1 **Expenditure Cycle Closing Checklist**

In addition to finalizing checklists for each cycle, Ashton completes an accounting department closing checklist (**F8:2**). These checklists form the basis for discussions in Level One. Please take a few moments to review them.

S&S, Incorporated
Accounting Department Closing Checklist
For Period Ended March 30, 2007

Cutoff Date: **4/6/2007**

Activity	Due Date	Status	Date	Notes
Correcting/Adjusting Entries				
Reclassed Commission Transfer	4/5/2007			Total commission transfer for March 30 was $1,568.18
Posted Depreciation	4/5/2007			Add accounting department desk from Office Rex for $1,250 purchased 3/01/2007
Accrued Wages	4/5/2007			Accrue 7 days of average monthly wages for hourly employees
Posted Savings Account Interest	4/5/2007			Statement arrives on the 3rd
Adjusted Prepaid Insurance	4/5/2007			
Accrued Bank Note Interest	4/5/2007			
Accrued Income Taxes	4/6/2007			
Review Activities				
Reviewed Detail General Ledger Report	4/4/2007			
Confirmed Owners Reconciled Bank Statements	4/5/2007			
Reporting Activities				
Preliminary review of Financial Statements	4/6/2007			
Finalized Financial Statements	4/7/2007			
Printed Management Reports	4/7/2007			
Closed Financial Series	4/7/2007			

F8:2 Accounting Department Closing Checklist

FINANCIAL CARDS

As with previous chapters, we begin with the Financial Series cards menu (**F8:3**). Cards are the Series' master records. In Chapter 2, we discussed the _Account_, _Unit Account_, _Variable Allocation_, and _Fixed Allocation_ menus. In addition, we have worked with Financial Series cards throughout the text.

Account
Checkbook

Account Currencies
Unit Account
Variable Allocation
Fixed Allocation
Account History
Budgets
Mass Modify

Currency Account Update
Analysis Groups
Analysis Defaults

Click on the _Account_ menu and look up the cash card shown in **F8:4**. The Summary button displays transactions for the current period, while the History button shows prior year transactions. In addition, the Budget button views budget data on the account. Great Plains offers Excel Based Budgeting for importing data to Great Plains from Excel.

F8:3 Financial Cards Menu

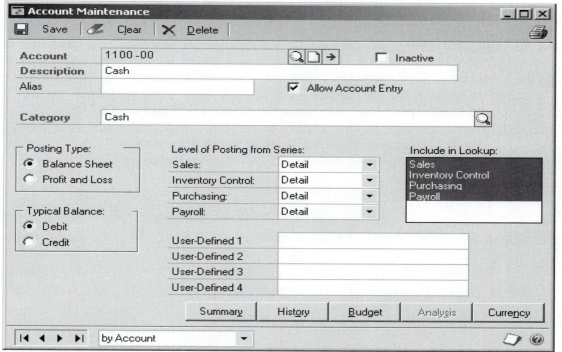

F8:4 Cash Financial Card

Return to the cards menu and notice the _Mass Modify_ item. Click on this item to open the Mass Modify Chart of Accounts window shown in **F8:5**. This window assists companies in creating the chart of accounts. For instance, the Copy option can be used to create all the departmental meals and entertainment accounts instead of creating them individually using the _Account_ menu. The _Analysis Groups_ and _Analysis Defaults_ menus work together to group accounts used in analyzing segments of revenues and expenses.

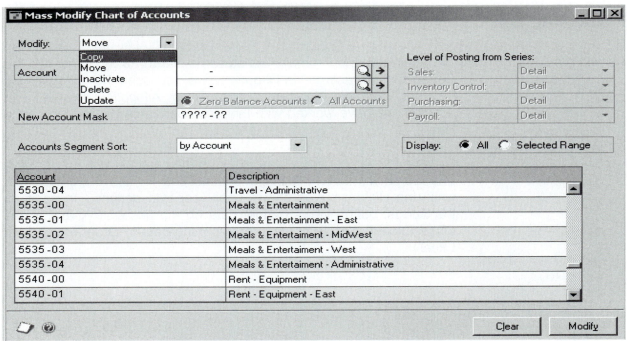

F8:5 Mass Modify Chart of Accounts Window

Click on the *Checkbook* menu, opening the Checkbook Maintenance window used to establish a link between the cash account and the bank reconciliation feature of Great Plains (*F8:6*). Look up the Checkbook ID of <u>PRIMARY</u>. We find a control password that limits the maximum check expenditure without authorization.   This window also assigns default general ledger accounts for posting cash receipts and disbursements when not assigned by other Series cards and other information relevant to this checking account.   Did you notice that the Current Checkbook Balance field does not equal the Cash Account Balance field? This out-of-balance condition is corrected after reconciling the checkbook later in the chapter.

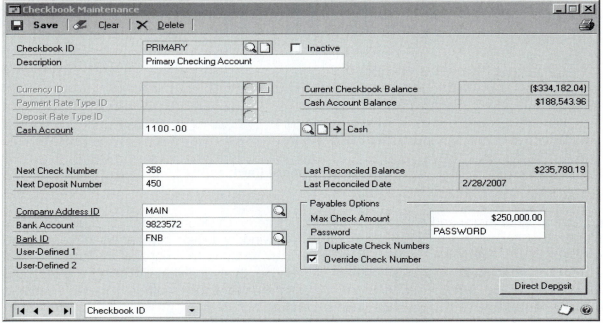

F8:6 Checkbook Maintenance Window

The topics that follow take us through completing the activities on Ashton's accounting period closing checklist for March 30, 2007.

FINANCIAL SERIES TRANSACTIONS

Closing procedures listed on the Expenditure Cycle Checklist were discussed in Chapter 6. Therefore, we know that finalizing postings in the Purchase Series means checking the Series Post window for suspended transactions. We also know how to reconcile the Purchasing Series, to prepare purchasing reports, and to close the Series.

Notice that purchasing signaled Ashton to make two general journal entries for the month. Let's make these entries. First, click on the *Transaction>>Financial>>General* menu and open the Transaction Entry window (*F8:7*). Before recording the entries, review *T8:1* to understand the fields in this window.

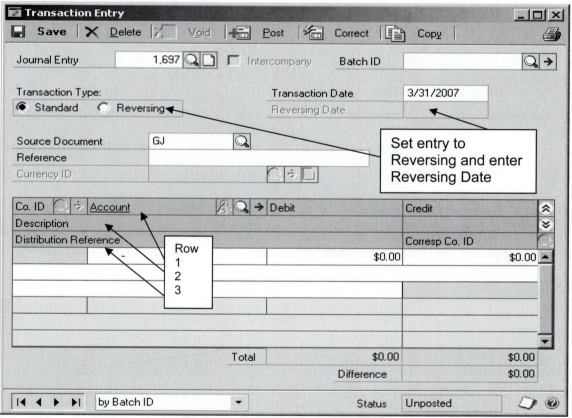

F8:7 Transaction Entry Window

Transaction Field	Description
Journal Entry	Sequential number used by the audit trail.
Batch ID	Batch folder created using the _Transactions>>Financial>> Batches_ menu.
Transaction Type	Option to set entry as standard or reversing. The Reversing option records an entry to one accounting period and then records an entry to reverse in the next accounting period. When selected, the Reversing Date field activates.
Transaction Date	Transaction date appearing in the general ledger accounts.
Source Document	Document type used by the audit trial. Source document types were discussed in Chapter 2.
Reference	Text typed into this field appears with the audit trail and under account inquiries; therefore, use concise descriptions to quickly identify adjustments.
Transaction Row 1	The Account field stores the general ledger account number affected by transactions and the Debit or Credit fields store the amount. The Co ID field is used with the Intercompany Series and is not covered in this text.
Transaction Row 2	Description row auto-fills to show the general ledger account name and number.
Transaction Row 3	Distribution Reference row that permits entering additional details about the transaction. The Distribution Reference field appears on general ledger detail reports and in the detail transaction inquiry window.

T8:1 Financial Transaction Entry Fields

We are now ready to enter our first Financial Series transaction. We begin with recording correcting entries and then move to adjusting entries.

Correcting Entries
Correcting entries are used to fix posting errors. Often these entries reclassify a debit or credit from one account to a different account. For example, the Expenditure Cycle Closing Checklist notes that the Office Rex invoice requires a correcting entry to reclassify the cost of a desk from the office expense account to a fixed asset account. The purchasing manager forwarded Ashton the transaction posting report showing that the invoice posted to 5580-04 Supplies Expenses-Administrative. Refer to **_F8:8_** and enter the correcting entry. Notice the transaction date coincides with the original posting date and the Reference and Distribution Reference fields supply descriptions documenting the reason for correcting. Whenever correcting a transaction posted in the current account period, always use the original posting transaction date. This simplifies tracing corrections on detailed general ledger reports.

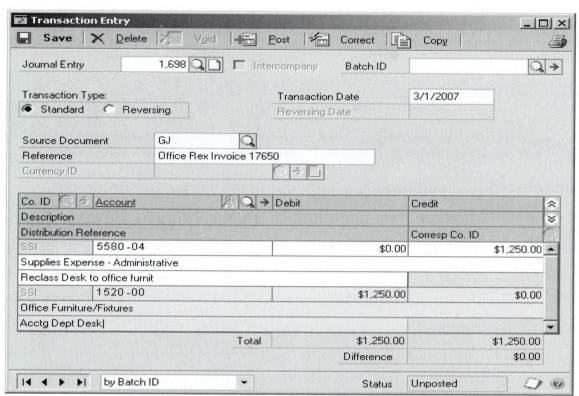

F8:8 Reclass Entry for Office Rex Invoice

Click on the Post button, close the window, and the posting journal prints. Whether batched or individual, Financial Series transactions always post immediately to the general ledger. In other words, these transactions never suspend. To review your posting, click on the *Inquiry>>Financial>>Detail* menu and look up the two accounts affected by this transaction. Notice the location of your Reference and Distribution Reference descriptions. This review helps in understanding entry documentation.

There is one last point to make about correcting entries. When using a journal entry to correct a transaction posted backwards, always post a transaction to reverse the original transaction and then post a transaction for the correct entry. For example, Ashton recorded the savings account interest income as a debit to interest income and a credit to the savings account. To correct this, he posts one entry reversing the original debit and credit and then posts a separate entry recording the interest correctly. Again, this simplifies tracing entries on detailed general ledger reports.

Adjusting Entries

Adjusting entries are posted the same way as correcting entries. However, accountants often use the word "adjusting" because these entries do not record as part of a cycle's activities. For instance, adjusting entries are used to post accrued wages, deferred revenue, depreciation expense, and the expired portions of prepaid insurance. Adjusting entries occur every accounting period, thus Ashton stores many of these entries in recurring batches.

Click on the *Transactions>>Financial>>Batches* and look up the list of existing batches (*F8:9*). Recurring batches use the Monthly Frequency. (Note: When you have suspended transactions, you will have batches other than those illustrated. These batches are identified with the Single Frequency.)

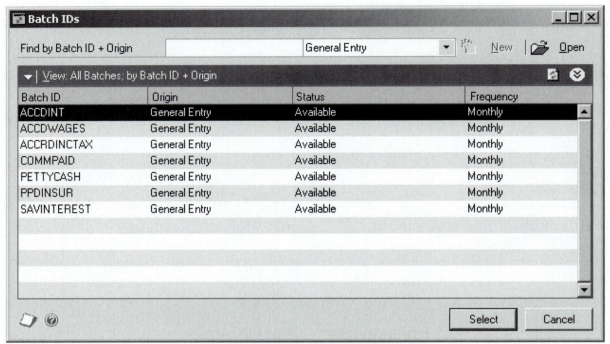

F8:9 Recurring Batches

Select the commission batch. This is a rare example of a correcting entry stored in a recurring batch. Every month, this entry reclassifies the entry posted by transferring commissions in the Sales Series.   The Sales Series posts commission expense as a credit to 2230-00 Commissions Payable and a debit to 5200-00 Commissions Expense.   However, S&S pays commissions using the Payroll Series and payroll is setup to debit a department's commission expense account (instead of Commissions Payable) and then credit the payroll cash account. This setup is used to record expense by department.   However, commission expense is now double booked, so Ashton reverses the amount posted during Sales Series transfer. So why didn't Ashton make the 5200-00 Commission Expense account an allocation account and avoid this entry? Unfortunately, commissions cannot be allocated by a fixed amount or a variable percentage because commission expense corresponds to cash payments made by the customers linked to the salesperson.

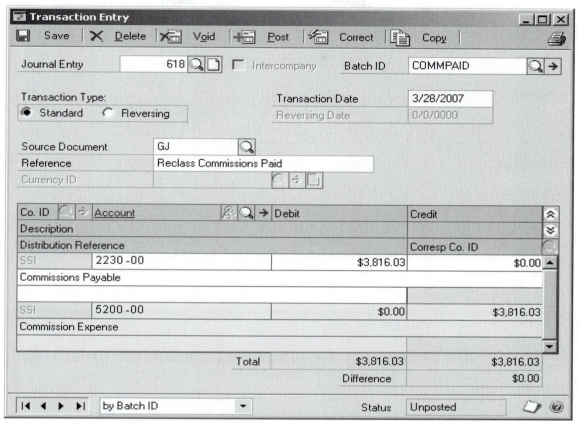

F8:10 Commission Reclass Entry

The amounts appearing in *F8:10* are those from last month's posting; therefore, adjust the debit and credit amounts to equal $1,568.18, since this is the transfer amount shown on Ashton's Accounting Department Closing Checklist. Also, set the transaction date to 3/30/2007. Save the transaction when finished because Ashton wants to use the Series Post window to finalize the transaction.   Click on the *Transactions>>Financial>>Series Post* menu.   Select the commission batch and post the entry. Close the window and move on to recording depreciation.

Depreciation Entries
Ashton uses an Excel spreadsheet to calculate the monthly entry for depreciation. (Note: The Fixed Asset Series is included with your software but is not covered in this text. This Series integrates fixed asset transactions and depreciation with the Financial Series.) *F8:11* is the summary sheet used to record depreciation. This spreadsheet also tracks detailed asset information on separate worksheets that are not illustrated.

S&S Straight Line Depreciation   FYE 12/31/2007

Asset Class	Estimated Useful Life (Years)	Prior Year Cost	Deletion Cost	Acquisition Cost	Current Year Cost	Monthly Depreciation
Buildings	50	$765,000			$ 765,000	$ 1,275.00
Office Furniture and Fixtures	7	$165,000			$ 165,000	$ 1,964.29
Vehicles	5	$367,876			$ 367,876	$ 6,131.27
Computer Hardware	4	$165,000			$ 165,000	$ 3,437.50
Computer Software	3	$ 67,000			$ 67,000	$ 1,861.11
Total						$ 14,669.17

F8:11   Excel Depreciation Worksheet

Using the Excel worksheet and information on the closing checklist, create a recurring depreciation batch for Ashton. Post this batch for March.

E8:1   Practice with Adjusting Entries

REVIEW ACTIVITIES

Ashton's review of general ledger postings occurs at the same time he records entries. He continues to review postings until the Financial Series is closed. Ashton prints a general ledger detail report for the month to assist him with reviewing entries. This report was discussed in Chapter 2. Ashton looks for suspicious entries or entries requiring reclassification. In addition, he looks for entries that have not been recorded for the month.

Upon review, Ashton notices that the owners' have not reconciled the bank statement because the monthly entries for interest income and bank charges are missing. Let's reconcile the primary checking account for the owners.

First, bank transfers from the primary account to the payroll account for March 30 are recorded because the owners transferred funds to payroll instead of cutting a check for deposit. Click on the *Transactions>>Financial>>Bank Transfers* menu and enter the information shown in **F8:12**. When finished, click the Post button and close the window. The posting report shows an entry recorded between the two checking accounts.

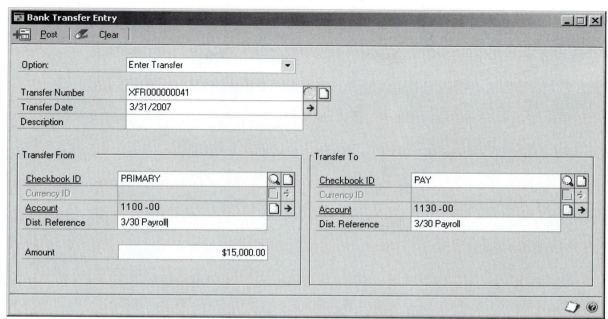

F8:12 Bank Transfer Entry Window

Next, we review the bank statement for additional charges, other than service charges. These charges could include items such as an automatic bank withdrawal for loan payments. This month's statement does not contain additional charges; however; when charges are present, they are posted by clicking on the *Transactions>>Financial>>Bank Transactions* menu to open the window shown in *F8:13.*

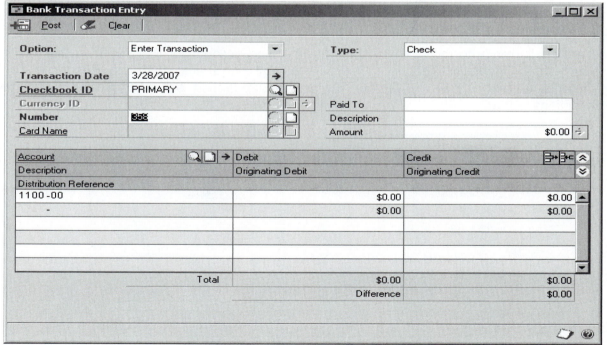

F8:13 Bank Transaction Entry Window

Now click on the *Transactions>>Financial>>Bank Deposits* menu. This opens the Bank Deposit Entry window shown in *F8:14*. The deposits selected in this window are those deposits appearing on the bank statement. Mark the deposits shown and click Post. Post does not affect financial accounts; instead, it transfers the deposits made during the month to the window used for reconciling the bank statement. Review the reports that print after posting.

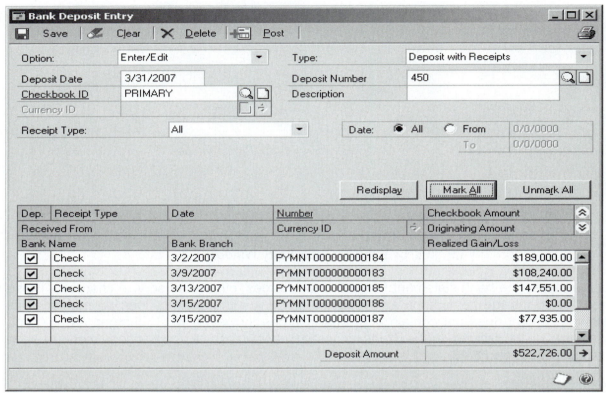

F8:14 Bank Deposit Entry Window

You are finally ready to reconcile the primary checking account for March 30th. Click on the *Transactions>>Financial>>Reconcile Bank Statement* menu and open the Reconcile Bank Statements window shown in *F8:15*. Enter the information as illustrated and click the Transactions button.

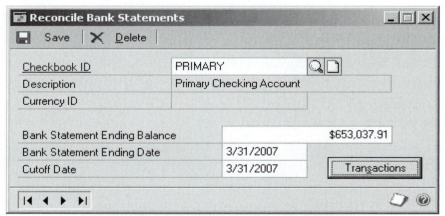

F8:15 Reconcile Bank Statements Window

The Select Bank Transactions window shows the bank deposits (DEP) previously transferred are already selected; therefore, all that remains is selecting the checks cleared during the month and entering the monthly service charges.

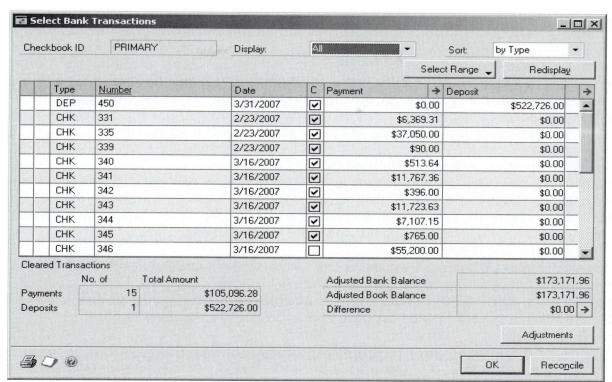

F8:16 Select Bank Transactions Window

Mark the cleared checks (CHK) shown in **F8:16**. Now click the Adjustments button and enter March's bank charges as shown in **F8:17** and then click OK.   The Difference field at the bottom of the Select Bank Transactions window should now equal zero. If not, look over the window for selection mistakes because the statement does not reconcile until the difference is zero. Click the Reconcile button and print the reconciliation report. This also posts the bank charges.

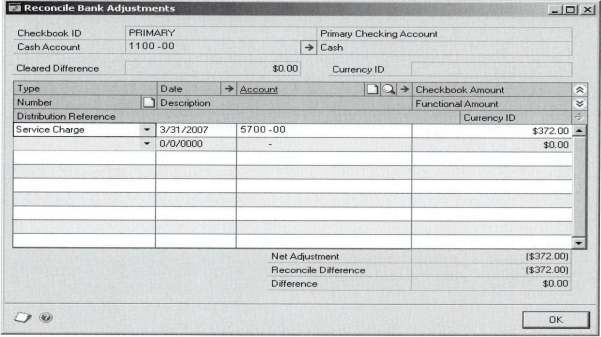

F8:17 Service Charge Entry Window

REPORT ACTIVITIES

We are now ready to print financial statements. Ashton previously prepared preliminary financials and recorded the accrued tax entry. He is now ready to print financial statements for the owners and the bank. Click on the *Reports>>Financial>>Financial Statements* menu. Ashton designed every report listed in this window's lookup (***F8:18***). He has two income statements, one for consolidated income and the other for departmental income.

Select S&S' Income Statement, Balance Sheet, and Statement of Cash Flow to print. Remember you can insert all three reports to the Print window to print simultaneously. These statements use Great Plains' system date as the report date. As long as reports relate to the current year, changing the system date will print reports for a prior month. Level Two discusses printing historical year reports by using the *Advanced Financial* menu.

Ashton also prepares other management reports for the owners, including a performance report that compares actual results to budget projections. (Note: The sample data does not include budget numbers; therefore, these reports are not illustrated.) After preparing all reports, Ashton closes the March accounting period using the instructions provided in Level Two.

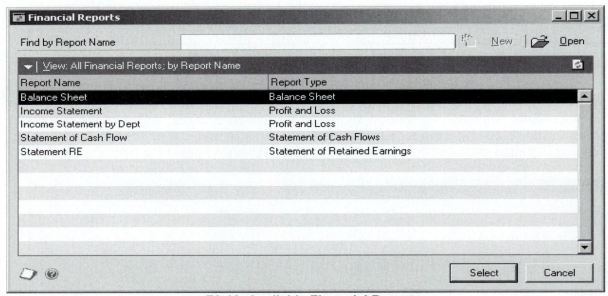

F8:18 Available Financial Reports

LEVEL TWO

Level Two covers financial statement account categories, advanced reporting features, and month-ending and year-ending the Series. We begin with account categories since these items impact account groups appearing on financial statements.

ACCOUNT CATEGORIES

The Account Category Setup window is accessed using the *Tools>>Setup>>Financial>> Category* menu. As illustrated in Chapter 2, category numbers are entered on general ledger account cards, instructing Great Plains during reporting. This window permits changes to the Category Description field but not to the Number field.

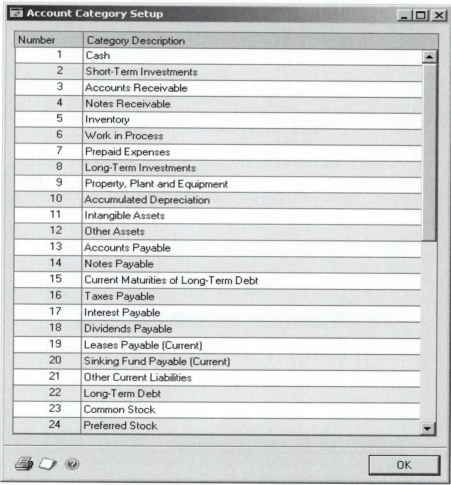

Number	Category Description
1	Cash
2	Short-Term Investments
3	Accounts Receivable
4	Notes Receivable
5	Inventory
6	Work in Process
7	Prepaid Expenses
8	Long-Term Investments
9	Property, Plant and Equipment
10	Accumulated Depreciation
11	Intangible Assets
12	Other Assets
13	Accounts Payable
14	Notes Payable
15	Current Maturities of Long-Term Debt
16	Taxes Payable
17	Interest Payable
18	Dividends Payable
19	Leases Payable (Current)
20	Sinking Fund Payable (Current)
21	Other Current Liabilities
22	Long-Term Debt
23	Common Stock
24	Preferred Stock

F8:19 Account Category Setup Window

ADVANCED FINANCIALS

Financial statements are initially created in the Quick Financial Setup window (**F8:20**). Click on the *Reports>>Financial>>Quick Financial* menu and open this window. The income statement is created first because the balance sheet requires this statement's name as the value for the Net Income/Loss Source field (**F8:20**). After creating the basic reports, the statements are printed using the *Reports>>Financial>>Financial Statements* as illustrated in Level One.

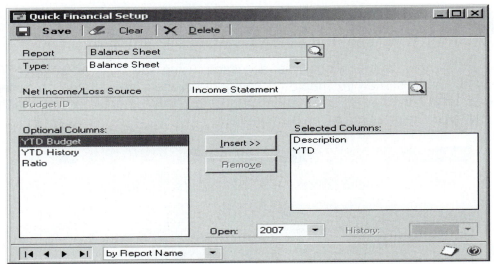

F8:20 Quick Financial Window

Ashton was not satisfied with the layout of the basic income statement, so he customized the report. Click on the *Reports>>Financial>>Advanced Financial* menu to open the Advanced Financial Reports window illustrated in **F8:21**. Highlight the Income Statement report and then click Open.

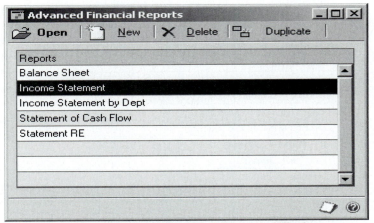

F8:21 Advanced Financial Reports Window

This opens the Advanced Financial Report Definition window shown in **F8:22**. Click the Layout button to open the Advanced Financial Report Layout window shown in **F8:23**.

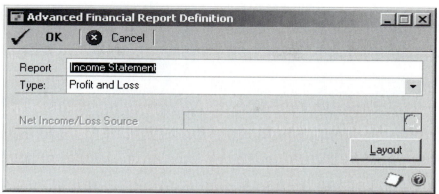

F8:22 Advanced Financial Report Definition Window

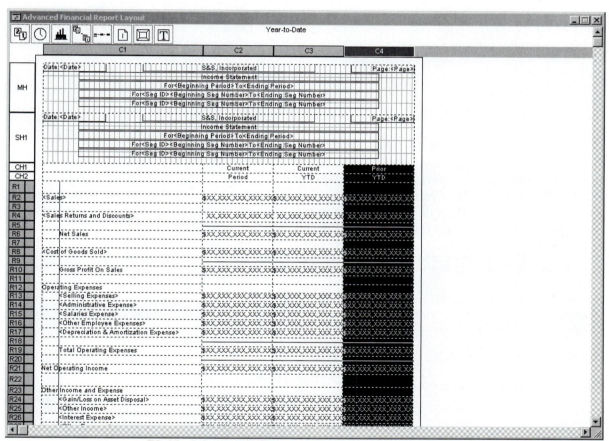

F8:23 Advanced Financial Report Layout Window

The report's layout is manipulated by double-clicking row numbers and column labels. Double-click on the column labeled C2 to open the Financial Column Definition window (*F8:24*).

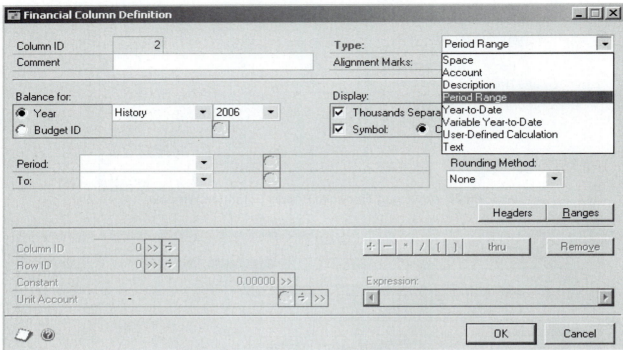

F8:24 Financial Column Definition Window

This window illustrates printing an income statement for a prior year by changing the Open field to History and selecting the year. Since this column prints results for one month, the Type is set to Period Range. C3's type is Year-to-Date to print results for the year. Close this window and double-click on Row 4 to open the Financial Row Definition window shown in *F8:25*.

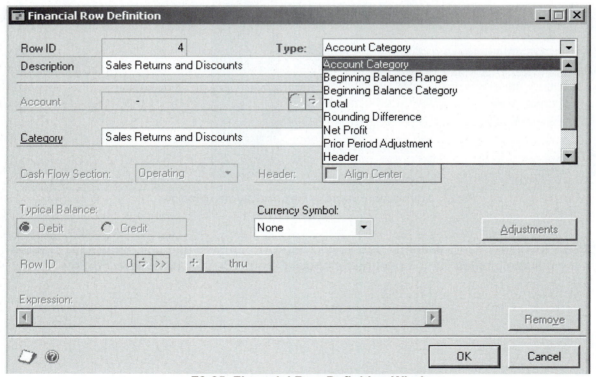

F8:25 Financial Row Definition Window

This row's Type is Account Category and is used to display the balance in general ledger accounts assigned to the category of Sales Returns and Discounts. Now look at the Type for Row 19. Double-click this row and find the account type is Total (**F8:26**) and sums rows R13 through R17 to calculate total operating expenses.

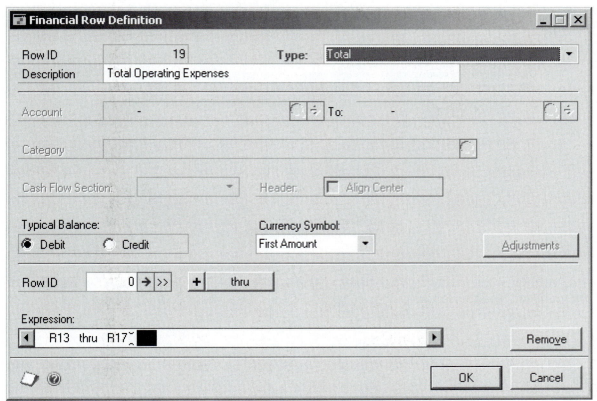

F8:26 Total Type

Take the time to look through some of the other rows on the report. Rows and columns are deleted and added to a report by clicking on the *File>>Delete* or *Insert* menus.

Click on the x icon to close the layout window, discarding any changes made to the report. This returns you to the report definition window. Click OK to return to the Advanced Financials Report window. Notice that this window also contains buttons for deleting and duplicating existing reports. Click the x icon to close this window.

FINANCIAL SERIES: MONTH-END AND YEAR-END CLOSING PROCEDURES

As in other Series, the Financial Series is month-ended by clicking on the *Tools>> Setup>>Company>>Fiscal Periods* menu and selecting the month. Ashton performs a month-end closing after finalizing the closing checklists and printing financial statements and management reports.

Every January, Ashton closes the month and year-ends the Financial Series. Click on the *Tools>>Routines>>Financial>>Year-End Closing* menu to open the window shown in **F8:27**. Before year-ending, Ashton prints additional reports for external auditors. Ashton keeps the Financial Series open until mid-January to record adjusting entries. However, Great Plains does not generate beginning balances in general ledger accounts until the Financial Series is year-ended. Therefore, it would be impossible to run financial statements for January without year-ending.

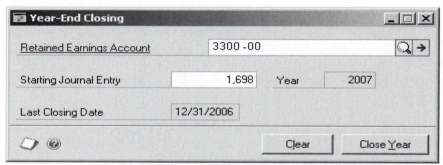

F8:27 Year-End Closing Window

Of course, we give the usual advice before year-ending, BACK UP THE DATA FILES. In addition, many companies archive these backup files. Use the x icon to close this window without year-ending the Financial Series.

Congratulations on completing this text! You now have a solid background in using Great Plains. You know how to post transactions for the Sales, Inventory, Purchasing, Payroll, and Financial Series. But your skills go beyond posting transactions. You also understand the importance of implementing strong internal controls over accounting activities. You know how to implement preventative controls in Great Plains and to use reporting as a detective tool. You also know the reports Great Plains provides for analyzing company performance and for evaluating accounting cycle efficiencies.

LEVEL ONE QUESTIONS

1. Return to Ashton's Accounting Period Closing checklist and post the accrued wages entry for March. You will need to prepare a payroll report to assist you in this task.

2. Run a detailed general ledger report for February and March. Search for missing March adjusting entries by comparing entries on the reports. List the entries that are missing.

3. Explain the internal control reason for setting the recurring depreciation entry to expire on December 31.

4. Explain the difference between adjusting and correcting entries.

5. Why does S&S record a monthly reclassification entry for the commission amounts paid in the Payroll Series?

6. Explain why Ashton closes other Series before closing the Financial Series.

LEVEL TWO QUESTIONS

1. Analyze the threats posed by activities in the Financial Series. Describe controls that will mitigate these threats. Did S&S implement any of your controls?

2. How would you use a cross-reference report to reduce threats to financial data?

3. The external auditors arrive next week. What reports will you prepare prior to their arrival?

4. Explain the significance of the account appearing in the year-end closing window.

APPENDIX A: DATA BACKUP AND RESTORE PROCEDURES AND GREAT PLAINS ERRORS

BACKUP AND RESTORE OF GREAT PLAINS DYNAMICS AND COMPANY DATABASES

After using Great Plains, perform a backup of the files by selecting the Great Plains menu commands *File>>Backup*. Great Plains prompts for a system password and this password is *sa*. The figure below illustrates the Database Backup Window and the files for backup. Backup procedures encompass companies worked on during the Great Plains session and the System Database.

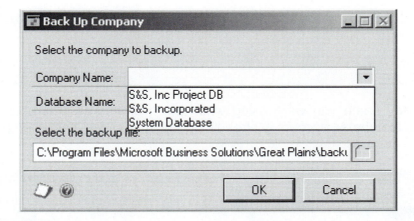

Click OK to write back up files to the location shown in the pathname. You may select the folder icon to rename the path and to change the backup name; however, remember this location and name for future use. When not changing the backup name, Great Plains attaches a backup date to the filename each time the procedure is performed.

To Restore data files, return to the Great Plains File menu and select *Restore*. The window appears the same as above. Selecting a company database activates the folder icon for browsing folders and selecting the backup file to restore. When restoring, Great Plains exits the software. The restore process may take time; therefore, be patient and do not close any windows.

IF YOU HAVE NOT PERFORMED A BACKUP, database files cannot be restored; therefore, you must return to the original CD and follow the data file copy procedures discussed in Chapter 1.

GREAT PLAINS ERROR MESSAGES

User Already Logged In Message

When your system crashes or Great Plains abruptly closes, your user ID remains logged in Great Plains. Thus, upon returning, the Current Users and Users Allowed fields shown below are the same.

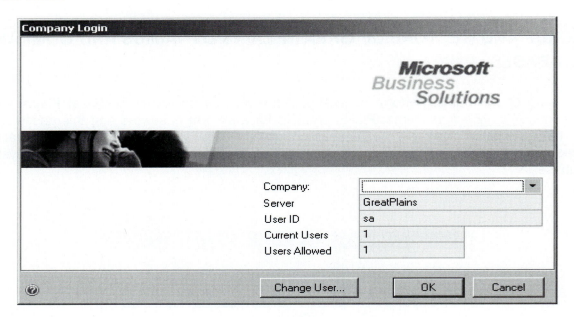

Select the company name you were using when the system was interrupted. Great Plains sends a message that the _sa_ account is already logged in. Answer Yes when prompted to view the current login.

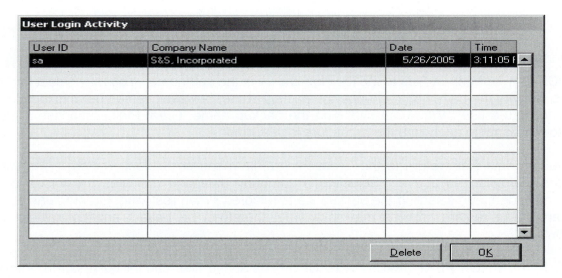

Highlight the _sa_ account, then click Delete. This action returns you to the Great Plains login screen where the Current Users field contains a zero. You can now select any company for login.

OLE Pathname Error

When porting a database, the path for storing notes is not stored with the database files. If you receive the message below, then select a location on your computer to use for storing OLE files. Click the folder icon to select a path and then click OK.

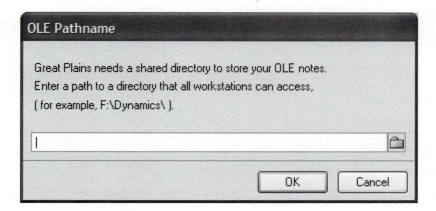

APPENDIX B: COMPANY SPECIFICS

S&S, INC. CHART OF ACCOUNTS

Account Number	Account Description	Posting Type	Account Category
0000-01	Square Feet – East	Unit Account	
0000-02	Square Feet – MidWest	Unit Account	
0000-03	Square Feet – West	Unit Account	
0000-04	Square Feet - Administrative	Unit Account	
1100-00	Cash	Balance Sheet	Cash
1110-00	Cash-Savings	Balance Sheet	Cash
1120-00	Petty Cash	Balance Sheet	Cash
1130-00	Checking - Payroll	Balance Sheet	Cash
1200-00	Accounts Receivable	Balance Sheet	Accounts Receivable
1205-00	Sales Discounts Available	Balance Sheet	Accounts Receivable
1210-00	Allowance for Doubtful Accounts	Balance Sheet	Accounts Receivable
1270-00	Marketable Securities	Balance Sheet	Short-Term Investments
1310-00	Inventory	Balance Sheet	Inventory
1410-00	Prepaid Insurance	Balance Sheet	Prepaid Expenses
1430-00	Prepaid - Other	Balance Sheet	Prepaid Expenses
1500-00	Land	Balance Sheet	Property, Plant and Equipment
1510-00	Buildings	Balance Sheet	Property, Plant and Equipment
1515-00	Accum Depr - Buildings	Balance Sheet	Accumulated Depreciation
1520-00	Office Furniture/Fixtures	Balance Sheet	Property, Plant and Equipment
1525-00	Accum Depr - Office Furn/Fixtures	Balance Sheet	Accumulated Depreciation
1530-00	Vehicles	Balance Sheet	Property, Plant and Equipment
1535-00	Accum Depr - Vehicles	Balance Sheet	Accumulated Depreciation
1540-00	Computer Hardware	Balance Sheet	Property, Plant and Equipment
1545-00	Accum Depr - Computer Hardware	Balance Sheet	Accumulated Depreciation
1550-00	Computer Software	Balance Sheet	Property, Plant and Equipment
1555-00	Amortization - Computer Software	Balance Sheet	Accumulated Depreciation
2100-00	Accounts Payable	Balance Sheet	Accounts Payable
2105-00	Purchase Discounts Available	Balance Sheet	Accounts Payable

Account Number	Account Description	Posting Type	Account Category
2120-00	Accrued Payables	Balance Sheet	Accounts Payable
2150-00	Notes Payable	Balance Sheet	Notes Payable
2160-00	Current Maturities Long Term Debt	Balance Sheet	Current Maturities of Long-Term Debt
2170-00	Interest Payable	Balance Sheet	Interest Payable
2210-00	Wages Payable	Balance Sheet	Other Current Liabilities
2230-00	Commissions Payable	Balance Sheet	Other Current Liabilities
2260-00	FUTA Taxes Payable	Balance Sheet	Taxes Payable
2265-00	SUTA Taxes Payable	Balance Sheet	Taxes Payable
2270-00	FICA Taxes Payable	Balance Sheet	Taxes Payable
2275-00	Federal Withholding Taxes Payable	Balance Sheet	Taxes Payable
2280-00	State Withholding Taxes Payable	Balance Sheet	Taxes Payable
2285-00	City Withholding Taxes Payable	Balance Sheet	Taxes Payable
2290-00	Sales Taxes Payable	Balance Sheet	Taxes Payable
2295-00	Worker's Comp Payable	Balance Sheet	Taxes Payable
2310-00	Deductions Payable	Balance Sheet	Other Current Liabilities
2320-00	401-K Payable	Balance Sheet	Other Current Liabilities
2330-00	Unearned Revenue	Balance Sheet	Other Current Liabilities
2340-00	Dividends Payable	Balance Sheet	Other Current Liabilities
2350-00	Accrued Income Taxes	Balance Sheet	Taxes Payable
2410-00	Notes Payable - Long Term	Balance Sheet	Long-Term Debt
2420-00	Mortgage Payable	Balance Sheet	Long-Term Debt
3000-00	Common Stock	Balance Sheet	Common Stock
3100-00	Additional Paid In Capital	Balance Sheet	Additional Paid-in Capital - Common
3300-00	Retained Earnings	Balance Sheet	Retained Earnings
4100-00	Sales	Profit and Loss	Sales
4100-01	Sales - East	Profit and Loss	Sales
4100-02	Sales - MidWest	Profit and Loss	Sales
4100-03	Sales - West	Profit and Loss	Sales
4300-00	Sales Returns	Profit and Loss	Sales Returns and Discounts
4300-01	Sales Returns - East	Profit and Loss	Sales Returns and Discounts
4300-02	Sales Returns - MidWest	Profit and Loss	Sales Returns and Discounts
4300-03	Sales Returns - West	Profit and Loss	Sales Returns and Discounts
4400-00	Sales Discounts	Profit and Loss	Sales Returns and Discounts
4400-01	Sales Discounts - East	Profit and Loss	Sales Returns and Discounts

Account Number	Account Description	Posting Type	Account Category
4400-02	Sales Discounts - MidWest	Profit and Loss	Sales Returns and Discounts
4400-03	Sales Discounts - West	Profit and Loss	Sales Returns and Discounts
4500-00	Cost of Goods Sold	Profit and Loss	Cost of Goods Sold
4500-01	Cost of Goods Sold - East	Profit and Loss	Cost of Goods Sold
4500-02	Cost of Goods Sold - MidWest	Profit and Loss	Cost of Goods Sold
4500-03	Cost of Goods Sold - West	Profit and Loss	Cost of Goods Sold
4510-00	Purchases Variance	Profit and Loss	Cost of Goods Sold
4520-00	Freight Charges	Profit and Loss	Cost of Goods Sold
4530-00	Shrinkage & Waste	Profit and Loss	Cost of Goods Sold
4540-00	Transportation Expense	Profit and Loss	Cost of Goods Sold
4600-00	Purchase Discounts Taken	Profit and Loss	Cost of Goods Sold
5100-00	Wages/Salaries Expense	Profit and Loss	Salaries Expense
5100-01	Wages/Salaries - East	Profit and Loss	Salaries Expense
5100-02	Wages/Salaries - MidWest	Profit and Loss	Salaries Expense
5100-03	Wages/Salaries - West	Profit and Loss	Salaries Expense
5100-04	Wages/Salaries - Administration	Profit and Loss	Salaries Expense
5100-05	Wages - Warehouse/Truckers	Allocation	
5200-00	Commission Expense	Profit and Loss	Salaries Expense
5200-01	Commission Expense - East	Profit and Loss	Salaries Expense
5200-02	Commission Expense - MidWest	Profit and Loss	Salaries Expense
5200-03	Commission Expense - West	Profit and Loss	Salaries Expense
5300-00	Payroll Tax Expense	Profit and Loss	Salaries Expense
5310-01	FICA Tax Expense - East	Profit and Loss	Salaries Expense
5310-02	FICA Tax Expense - MidWest	Profit and Loss	Salaries Expense
5310-03	FICA Tax Expense - West	Profit and Loss	Salaries Expense
5310-04	FICA Tax Expense - Administration	Profit and Loss	Salaries Expense
5310-05	FICA - Warehouse/Truckers	Allocation	
5320-01	FUTA Tax Expense - East	Profit and Loss	Salaries Expense
5320-02	FUTA Tax Expense - MidWest	Profit and Loss	Salaries Expense
5320-03	FUTA Tax Expense - West	Profit and Loss	Salaries Expense
5320-04	FUTA Tax Expense - Administration	Profit and Loss	Salaries Expense
5320-05	FUTA - Warehouse/Truckers	Allocation	
5330-01	SUTA Tax Expense - East	Profit and Loss	Salaries Expense
5330-02	SUTA Tax Expense - MidWest	Profit and Loss	Salaries Expense
5330-03	SUTA Tax Expense - West	Profit and Loss	Salaries Expense

Account Number	Account Description	Posting Type	Account Category
5330-04	SUTA Tax Expense - Adminstration	Profit and Loss	Salaries Expense
5330-05	SUTA - Warehouse/Truckers	Allocation	
5340-01	Workers Comp Expense - East	Profit and Loss	Salaries Expense
5340-02	Workers Comp Expense - MidWest	Profit and Loss	Salaries Expense
5340-03	Workers Comp Expense - West	Profit and Loss	Salaries Expense
5340-04	Workers Comp Expense - Administration	Profit and Loss	Salaries Expense
5340-05	Workers Comp - Warehouse/Truckers	Allocation	
5400-00	Employee Benefits	Profit and Loss	Other Employee Expenses
5410-01	Health Insurance Expense - East	Profit and Loss	Other Employee Expenses
5410-02	Health Insurance Expense - MidWest	Profit and Loss	Other Employee Expenses
5410-03	Health Insurance Expense - West	Profit and Loss	Other Employee Expenses
5410-04	Health Insurance Expense - Administration	Profit and Loss	Other Employee Expenses
5410-05	Health Insur - Warehouse/Truckers	Allocation	
5420-01	401-K Expense - East	Profit and Loss	Other Employee Expenses
5420-02	401-K Expense - MidWest	Profit and Loss	Other Employee Expenses
5420-03	401-K Expense - West	Profit and Loss	Other Employee Expenses
5420-04	401-K Expense - Admininstration	Profit and Loss	Other Employee Expenses
5420-05	401-K Expense - Warehouse/Truckers	Allocation	
5500-00	Advertising Expense	Profit and Loss	Selling Expense
5500-01	Advertising Expense - East	Profit and Loss	Selling Expense
5500-02	Advertising Expense - MidWest	Profit and Loss	Selling Expense
5500-03	Advertising Expense - West	Profit and Loss	Selling Expense
5510-00	Contracted Labor	Profit and Loss	Administrative Expense
5510-04	Contracted Labor - Administrative	Profit and Loss	Administrative Expense
5520-00	Repairs & Maintenance - Building	Profit and Loss	Administrative Expense
5520-01	Repairs & Maintentance - East	Profit and Loss	Selling Expense
5520-04	Repairs & Maintenance - Administrative	Profit and Loss	Administrative Expense
5530-00	Travel	Profit and Loss	Administrative Expense
5530-01	Travel - East	Profit and Loss	Selling Expense
5530-02	Travel - MidWest	Profit and Loss	Selling Expense
5530-03	Travel - West	Profit and Loss	Selling Expense
5530-04	Travel - Administrative	Profit and Loss	Selling Expense
5535-00	Meals & Entertainment	Profit and Loss	Selling Expense

Account Number	Account Description	Posting Type	Account Category
5535-01	Meals & Entertainment - East	Profit and Loss	Selling Expense
5535-02	Meals & Entertainment - MidWest	Profit and Loss	Selling Expense
5535-03	Meals & Entertainment - West	Profit and Loss	Selling Expense
5535-04	Meals & Entertainment - Administrative	Profit and Loss	Administrative Expense
5540-00	Rent - Equipment	Profit and Loss	Administrative Expense
5540-01	Rent - Equipment - East	Profit and Loss	Selling Expense
5540-02	Rent - Equipment - Mid	Profit and Loss	Selling Expense
5540-03	Rent - Equipment - West	Profit and Loss	Selling Expense
5540-04	Rent - Equipment - Administrative	Profit and Loss	Administrative Expense
5560-00	Postage & Freight	Profit and Loss	Administrative Expense
5560-04	Postage & Freight - Administrative	Profit and Loss	Administrative Expense
5580-00	Supplies Expense	Profit and Loss	Administrative Expense
5580-01	Supplies Expense - East	Profit and Loss	Selling Expense
5580-02	Supplies Expense - Mid	Profit and Loss	Selling Expense
5580-03	Supplies Expense - West	Profit and Loss	Selling Expense
5580-04	Supplies Expense - Administrative	Profit and Loss	Administrative Expense
5600-00	Telephone Expense	Profit and Loss	Selling Expense
5600-01	Telephone Expense - East	Profit and Loss	Selling Expense
5600-02	Telephone Expense - MidWest	Profit and Loss	Selling Expense
5600-03	Telephone Expense - West	Profit and Loss	Selling Expense
5600-04	Telephone Expense - Administration	Profit and Loss	Administrative Expense
5600-05	Telephone Fixed Allocation Account	Allocation	
5610-00	Utilities	Profit and Loss	Selling Expense
5610-01	Utilities - East	Profit and Loss	Selling Expense
5610-02	Utilities - MidWest	Profit and Loss	Selling Expense
5610-03	Utilities - West	Profit and Loss	Selling Expense
5610-04	Utilities - Administrative	Profit and Loss	Administrative Expense
5610-05	Utilities - Fixed Allocation Account	Allocation	
5620-00	Insurance Expense	Profit and Loss	Administrative Expense
5620-04	Insurance Expense - Administration	Profit and Loss	Administrative Expense
5700-00	Bank Charges & Fees	Profit and Loss	Administrative Expense
5710-00	Bad Debt Expense	Profit and Loss	Administrative Expense
5810-00	Depreciation Expense	Profit and Loss	Depreciation & Amortization Expense
5820-00	Amortization Expense	Profit and Loss	Depreciation & Amortization Expense

Account Number	Account Description	Posting Type	Account Category
7010-00	Finance Charge Income	Profit and Loss	Other Income
7020-00	Interest Income	Profit and Loss	Other Income
7030-00	Miscellaneous Income	Profit and Loss	Other Income
7040-00	Gain on Disposal of Assets	Profit and Loss	Gain/Loss on Asset Disposal
8010-00	Interest Expense	Profit and Loss	Interest Expense
8030-00	Miscellaneous Expense	Profit and Loss	Other Expenses
8040-00	Loss on Disposal of Assets	Profit and Loss	Gain/Loss on Asset Disposal
9010-00	Income Tax Expense	Profit and Loss	Income Tax Expense
9999-00	Suspense	Profit and Loss	Nonfinancial Accounts

S&S, INC. INVENTORY

Item Number	Item Description	Short Name	Current Cost
AUDJV50WMP3	Javix 50 Watt 4 Channel MP3	MP3	$150.00
AUDNPXM4CD	NeerPio XM Ready 4 Channel CD R/RW	SatRadio	$102.00
AUDOR256MPORT	ORI 256MG Portable Digital Audio Player	PortAud	$85.00
AUDSNCDMP3	Sunyung CD/MP3/ATRAC3	MP3	$36.00
AUDSNCDMP3AMFM	Sunyung Portable CD/MP3/AM/FM/TV	PortAud	$50.00
AUDWW52WCD	WAWA 52 Watt X4 Channel Car Stereo CD-R/RW	CarAud	$60.00
DCCN22XDZ	Canyon DigCamcord 22X Optical / 440X Digital Zoom	Camcord	$280.00
DCJV16XDZ	Javix DigCamcord 16X Optical / 700X Digital Zoom	Camcord	$245.00
DCNK4XDZ	Nikki DigiCamcord 8Mg Pixel 4X Digital Zoom	Camcord	$460.00
DCSM10XDZ	Sunyung DigCamcord 10X Optical/120X Digital Zoom	Camcord	$315.00
DCSM18XDZ	Sumsang DigCamcord 18X Optical / 900X Digital Zoom	Camcord	$191.67
DP0Y4MG3XD	Olympium 4Mg Pixel 3XOptical 4XDigital Camera	DigiCam	$127.00
DPCN32MG10XD	Canyon 3.2Mg Pixel 10X Optical/3.2X Digital Camera	DigiCam	$284.00
DPDS128MCARD	DiscSun 128MB Flash Memory Card	Memory	$26.00
DPDS128MGST	DiscSun 128MB Memory Stick	Memory	$30.00
DPFJ52MG32XDC	Fujiyama 5.2Mg Pixel 3.2X Optical/3.9X Digital Camera	DigiCam	$173.00
DPSN51MG3XDC	Sunyung 5.1Mg Pixel 3X Optical/2X Digital Camera	DigiCam	$200.00
DVDLPRW80G	Lipsphi Progressive Scan DVD R/RW 80G	DigiCam	$300.00
DVDNTPHFVCR	Nithze Progressive DVD HiFi VCR	DVDCombo	$150.00

Item Number	Item Description	Short Name	Current Cost
DVDNVPCD	Navox Progressive DVD/CD	DVDCombo	$25.00
DVDRD7PORT	Roidlop 7 Inch Portable DVD	DVD	$100.00
DVDSMCD	Sumsang DVD/CD Near HD	DVDCombo	$105.00
DVDVNVHS	Vania DVD/VHS	DVDCombo	$42.00
DVDVX8PORT	VoxAudi 8 Inch Portable DVD	DVD	$195.00
DVRVT40	Vito 40 HR DVR	DVR	$56.67
DVRVT80	Vito 80 HR DVR	DVR	$72.00
HEMY71C980W	MaYaha 7.1 Channel 980 watt	Stereo	$410.00
HESB51DVD	SEBO 38 DVD 5.1 Home Entertainment	HomeEnt	$1,350.00
HESB6SPKR	SEBO 6 Speaker System	Stereo	$360.00
HESN51DVDVCR	Sunyung 5.1 Home Entertainment Combo DVD/VCR	HomeEnt	$435.00
SERVAUDIO	AUDIO SERVICES	SERVICES	$0.00
SERVCAMERA	CAMERA SERVICES	SERVICES	$0.00
SERVVIDEO	VIDEO SERVICES	SERVICES	$0.00
TVBT46WPJ	Batoshi 46 Inch Widescreen Projection	HDWide	$690.00
TVLP42HD	Lipsphi 42 Inch HDTV	HDTV	$560.00
TVPS60HDTV	Pasanovic 60 Inch Widescreen HDTV	HDWide	$1,905.00
TVSB52W	Subishi 52 Inch Widescreen DLP	Widescreen	$1,860.00
TVSN34W	Sunyung 34 Inch Widescreen	Widescreen	$2,200.00
TVSN42W	Sunyung 42 Inch Widescreen Projection	Projection	$1,365.00
TVSN50W	Sunyung 50 Inch Widescreen Projection	Projection	$1,610.00
TVSP37P	SonicPan 37 Inch Plasma	Plasma	$1,070.00

S&S, INC. CUSTOMERS

Customer Number	Customer Name	Sales Territory	Payment Terms ID
APPLEDEM001	Apple Dempling, Inc	EAST	Net 30
BAMAZON001	Bamozon, Inc.	WEST	Net 30
BARTERBA001	Barter Bay, Inc.	WEST	Net 30
BETTERBU001	Better Buy, Inc.	MID	2% 10/Net 30
BOOKBUYE001	Book Buy Earnest, Inc.	EAST	Net 30
CANDYBOW001	Candy Bowl Catalog, Inc.	EAST	Net 30
DANMAYLO001	Dan Maylor, Inc.	WEST	Net 30

Customer Number	Customer Name	Sales Territory	Payment Terms ID
DISCOUNTE001	Discount Electronics,Inc.	WEST	Net 30
ELECTRON001	Electronic Town, Inc.	MID	Net 30
ETRADERS001	E-Traders Market, Inc	MID	Net 30
FILLARDS001	Fillards, Inc.	MID	Net 30
GGHREGGS001	GG HREGG Stores, Inc.	MID	Net 30
GIGGLEPL001	Giggle Place, Inc.	MID	Net 30
JANEDYAN001	Jane Dyant, Inc.	EAST	Net 30
KDPENNYS001	KD Penny's, Inc.	MID	Net 30
KOLLISTE001	Kollister's, Inc.	MID	Net 30
LAUFMANS001	Laufmans, Inc	EAST	Net 30
LERNEERS001	Lerneers & Lowers, Inc.	WEST	Net 30
MARKETPL001	Market Place, Inc.	MID	Net 30
PINKHOUS001	Pink House Electronics ,Inc.	WEST	Net 30
PRECISEM001	Precise Markets, Inc	MID	Net 30
RICKSSPO001	Rick's Specialty Goods, Inc.	EAST	Net 30
SIXTHAV001	Sixth Avenue, Inc.	WEST	Net 30
SMALLSCR001	Small Screen Sales, Inc.	EAST	Net 30
STEPHANI001	Stephanie's Discount, Inc.	MID	Net 30
TEDDIGO001	Teddi Gower, Inc.	WEST	Net 30
TELEVISI001	Television World, Inc.	EAST	Net 30
TIFFANYS001	Tiffany's Bargains, Inc.	EAST	Net 30
TRADERST001	Traders Table, Inc.	MID	Net 30
TRADESRU001	Trades R Us, Inc.	EAST	Net 30
TUBESTUR001	Tubes & Turners, Inc.	WEST	Net 30
TVTIMEST001	TV Time Stores, Inc	MID	Net 30
WORLDOFC001	World of Circuits, Inc.	MID	Net 30
ZEARSSTO001	Zears Stores, Inc.	EAST	2% 10/Net 30

S&S, INC. VENDORS

Vendor ID	Vendor Name	Payment Terms ID	Vendor Class ID
AKRONCIT001	Akron City Tax	IMMED	PAY/ADM
BANKAMER001	Bank Amerex	IMMED	PAY/ADM
BRIGHTEL001	Bright Electric, Inc.	Net 30	R&M
CANYONCA001	Canyon Cam, Inc.	2% 10/Net 30	SUPPLIERS
CBSPHONE001	CBS Phone Company, Inc.	Net 10	UTILITIES
CELLULAR001	Cellular America	Net 30	MARKETING
CHANNELO001	Channel Oxe, Inc.	Net 30	MARKETING
CHEXPAYI001	Chexpay, Inc.	Net 30	PAY/ADM

Vendor ID	Vendor Name	Payment Terms ID	Vendor Class ID
COOLEYSA001	Cooley's AC Repair, Inc	Net 30	R&M
CUPSNPAP001	Cups N Paper Stuff, Inc.	Net 30	OTHER
EMARKETI001	E-Marketing Company, Inc.	Net 30	MARKETING
FEDERALXP001	Federal Xpert	Net 30	PAY/ADM
FIRSTNAT001	First National Bank	IMMED	PAY/ADM
FLIPFLOP001	Flipflop Travel Agency, Inc	Net 30	PAY/ADM
INTERNAL001	Internal Revenue Services	IMMED	PAY/ADM
JAVIXCAM001	Javix Cam, Inc.	2% 10/Net 30	SUPPLIERS
LAWNGREE001	Lawn Green, Inc.	Net 30	R&M
LOAINTER001	LOA Internet, Inc.	Net 10	UTILITIES
MUTUALHE001	Mutual Health Insurance, Inc.	Net 10	PAY/ADM
NEERPIOI001	Neer Pio, Inc.	Net 30	OTHER
NIKKICAM001	Nikki Cam, Inc.	Net 30	SUPPLIERS
OFFICEREOO1	Office Rex, Inc.	Net 30	OTHER
OHIODEPT001	Ohio Department Unemployment	IMMED	PAY/ADM
OHIOREDI001	Ohio Redision, Inc.	Net 10	UTILITIES
OHIOTAXD001	Ohio Tax Department	IMMED	PAY/ADM
OHIOWORK001	Ohio Workers Comp	Check	PAY/ADM
OLYMPIUM001	Olympium Pic, Inc.	Net 30	SUPPLIERS
ORICORPO0001	Ori Corporation	Net 30	SUPPLIERS
OSCARDIS001	Oscar Disposal, Inc.	Net 10	R&M
PASANOVI001	Pasanovic, Inc.	Net 30	SUPPLIERS
PAYDAYPR001	Payday Processing, Inc.	Net 30	PAY/ADM
PBFUELCO001	PB Fuel Company	Net 30	OTHER
PETTYCAS001	Petty Cash	IMMED	PAY/ADM
RADIOWKR001	Radio WKRP, Inc.	Net 30	MARKETING
RETIREME001	Retirement Benefits	IMMED	PAY/ADM
RIGHTMAR001	Right Marketing, Inc.	Net 30	MARKETING
ROOTROTE001	Root Roter Plumbing, Inc.	Net 30	R&M
RYANDANG001	Ryan Dan Group, Inc.	Net 30	MARKETING
SHELLYST001	Shelly's Temp Service	Net 30	PAY/ADM
SOFTWARE001	Software People, Inc.	Net 30	PAY/ADM
SONICPAN001	Sonic Pan, Inc.	Net 30	SUPPLIERS
SUBISHII001	Subishi, Inc.	Net 30	SUPPLIERS
SUMSANGCO001	SumSang Corporation	Net 30	SUPPLIERS
SUNYUNGH001	Sunyung Home, Inc.	2% 10/Net 30	SUPPLIERS
TRAVELOR001	Travelor's Business	Net 30	PAY/ADM
TRUCKSUP001	Truck Supplies, Inc.	Net 30	R&M
UNITEDHE001	United Health Insurance	Net 10	PAY/ADM
UNITEDPA001	United Parcel Service	Net 30	PAY/ADM
UNITEDST001	United States Post Office	IMMED	PAY/ADM
UNITEDWA001	United Way	IMMED	PAY/ADM

Vendor ID	Vendor Name	Payment Terms ID	Vendor Class ID
WATERCLE001	Water Clear, Inc.	Net 10	UTILITIES
WAWACOMP001	WAWA Company	Net 30	SUPPLIERS
WENERTIM001	Wener Time Cable, Inc.	Net 10	UTILITIES
WESTDOMI001	West Dominion Gas, Inc.	Net 10	UTILITIES
ZEARSSTO001	Zears Stores, Inc.	Net 30	SUPPLIERS
ZELLCOMP001	Zell Computer Repair, Inc.	Net 30	R&M

S&S, INC. EMPLOYEES

Employee ID	Last Name	First Name	Employee Class	Department	Job Title
KTB4235	Bell	Kenneth	HOURLY	MAINT	STAFF
APF3232	Fleming	Ashton	SALARY	ADMIN	ACCT
SMG4255	Gonzalez	Susan	SALARY	ADMIN	OWNER
GLH9898	Hanratty	George	HOURLY	TRANS	TRUCK
LJJ3232	Johns	LeBron	HOURLY	WARE	SUPR
BAL2122	Lane	Betsy	HOURLY	ADMIN	APCLER
ASL6677	Levine	April	SALARY	SMID	STAFF
MPM1924	Mapley	Matthew	HOURLY	WARE	STAFF
GKM3209	McMahon	George	HOURLY	MAINT	SUPR
MTM3987	Murphy	Mary	SALARY	SWEST	STAFF
SJP5132	Parry	Scott	SALARY	ADMIN	OWNER
JJR1132	Richmond	James	HOURLY	ADMIN	ARCLER
CJW7872	Warner	Curtis	SALARY	SEAST	STAFF
ACW3287	Whitfield	Adam	HOURLY	TRANS	TRUCK
TKW3238	Winchester	Thomas	HOURLY	WARE	STAFF

APPENDIX C: CORRECTING POSTING ERRORS

COMMON ERRORS

Errors in Distribution Accounts or Posting to a Closed Period

Whenever a Series posts a transaction to the wrong distribution account, a Financial Series correcting entry solves the problem. See topic on recording correcting entries in Chapter 8.

Whenever a default account is not present on the transaction, then posting suspends and Great Plains issues the error below.

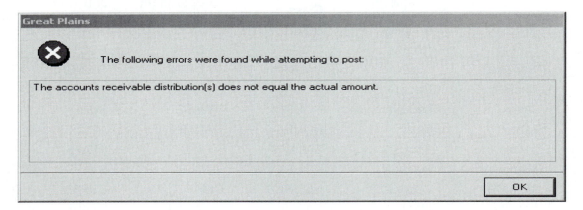

The transaction is released by using the *Tools>>Routines>>Batch Recovery* window illustrated below. Selecting Continue releases the batch. The batch is then opened within the originating Series and corrected. The entry can then be posted.

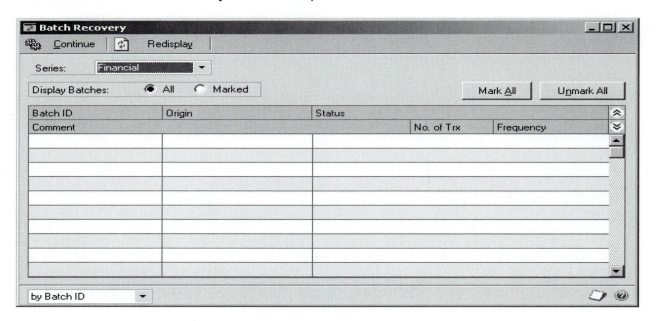

ERROR CORRECTION PROCEDURES

Implementing a computerized accounting solution involves more than just installation and data entry. Invariably, errors occur when processing transactions. Thus, proper error correction procedures are vital to maintaining data integrity. The procedures that correct posting errors in the Inventory Control Series are performed by making the adjusting entries explained in Chapter 4. Additionally, the procedures that correct posting transactions to the wrong general ledger account were discussed in Chapter 8. Below are the instructions for correcting errors in the Sales, Purchasing, and Payroll Series.

Sales Series Error Corrections

Sales Series posting errors come in several forms. For simplicity, let's categorize them as:

1. Errors prior to posting
2. Errors after posting: with and without inventory

1) Errors Prior to Posting

Errors occurring before posting are easy to correct. Simply open the transaction, correct, and then save. Depending on internal control settings, you may be required to delete or void the transaction and then reenter a new transaction. Nevertheless, the error is easily resolved because it has not interfaced with another Series.

2) Errors After Posting

Errors Involving Inventory

Errors involving inventory that occur after posting are trickier to correct. Once a transaction interfaces with inventory, corrections are made by entering one transaction that reverses the original entry and then a new transaction for the correct entry.

For example, where an invoice with inventory was posted to the wrong customer account. The correction procedures are: (Note be careful to use the original transaction's date):

- Issue a return to the incorrect customer account using the Invoice Processing Tier, noting the reason for the entry in the description field.
- Issue an Invoice to the correct customer

This will correct the customer's card and provide lookup details in the event the customer makes future inquiries.

Errors with no Inventory Involved

Posted transactions that do not involve inventory are simpler to correct. Assume that a credit memo to a customer posted in error. To correct this entry, use the *Posted Transactions* menu to open the window shown below, locate the customer and document, and then press Void. Close the window to post and print the posting reports.

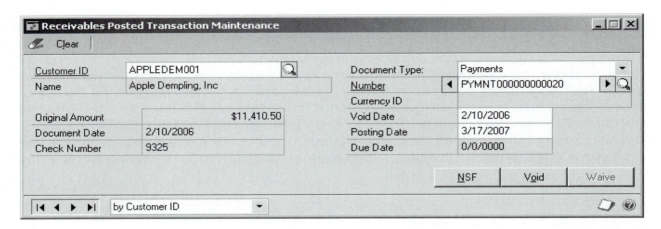

Minor Corrections

One last error correction tool needs discussed. The *Edit Transaction Information* menu opens a window allowing changes to miscellaneous information. The window permits changes to a transaction's dates, PO number, and description.

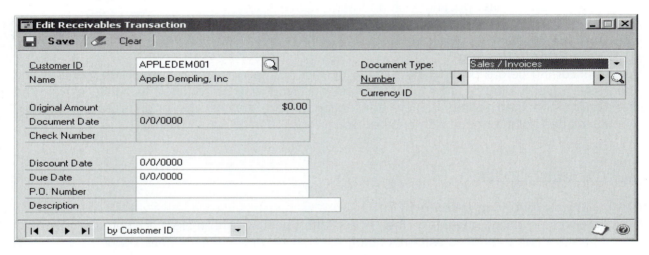

Purchasing Series Error Corrections

Error correction procedures for vendors are similar to the procedures discussed for Sales Series errors. Purchasing errors may include invoices posted to the wrong vendor or invoices posted to an incorrect inventory item. These errors are a normal part of doing business.

Again, the errors are categorized as:
1. Errors prior to posting
2. Errors after posting: with and without inventory

1) Errors Prior to Posting

Errors occurring before posting are corrected by performing the same steps as illustrated for Sales Series errors. For printed POs, use the *Edit Purchase Orders*. For PO receiving, vendor invoicing, or check payment batches, simply open the transaction record, correct the transaction, then save the record.

2) Errors After Posting

Transactions Involving Inventory

Once an inventory receipt has been applied against a PO and posted, errors are only corrected by using the following steps:

1. Ensure the PO is closed by going to the *Transactions>>Purchasing>>Edit Purchase Orders* menu. Select the original PO and check the status. If all items on the PO were fully received, then the status is closed, otherwise, select the Closed status and then click Process.

2. Using the *Routines>>Purchasing>>Remove PO* menu, select the PO for the document range then click Process to remove the PO.

3. Using the *Utilities>>Purchasing>>Remove Purch Hist* menu, select Purchase Order as the History Type and insert the PO in the To & From fields. Mark the Remove History then Process.

4. Return to the menu used in step 3, and select Receipt as the Type and mark Include Account Distribution. Insert the original receipt number in the To & From fields, mark Remove History then Process.

5. Using the *Utilities>>Purchasing>>Remove Trx History* menu, insert the Vendor ID and the Document numbers into the options field and the Removed Transaction and Remove Distribution Options.

6. Finally, in the Inventory module post a decrease adjustment to offset the original shipment receipt transaction as discussed in Chapter 4.

The PO can now be re-entered and received against. (Ouch – that hurt).

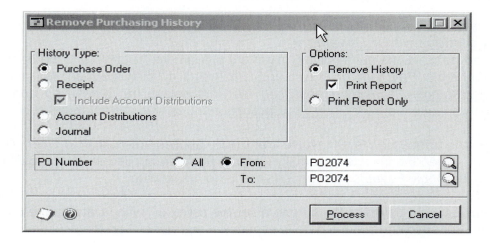

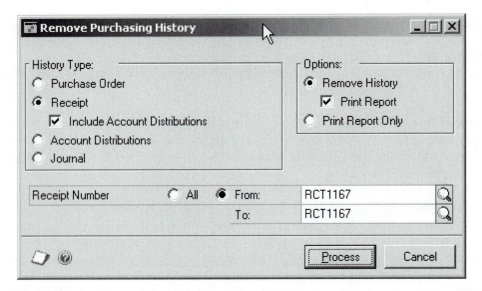

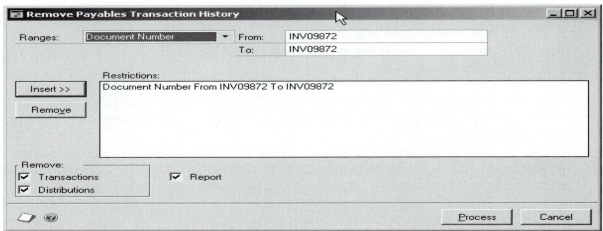

Transactions with no Inventory

Posted transactions not involving inventory are simpler to correct. If the transaction is a Credit Memo, Payment, or Return and is fully applied then it will be in History. Use the _Void Historical Payables Transaction_ menu to select the transaction and click Void. Otherwise, use the _Void Open Transactions_ menu to void current transactions.

When the transaction is an invoice that is fully applied, use the _Void Open Transactions_ menu. When the invoice is partially applied, then the applied amount must be removed using the _Apply Payables Documents_ menu before voiding.

When voiding a payment, be sure to enter the correct Posting Date before correcting the entry. For stale checks, the date is especially important when the accounting period has not been closed because the void will affect prior reconciled cash balances.

Minor Corrections

One last error correction tool remains. The _Edit Transaction Information_ menu opens a window that allows changes to miscellaneous information. The window permits changes to a transaction's dates, PO, and description.

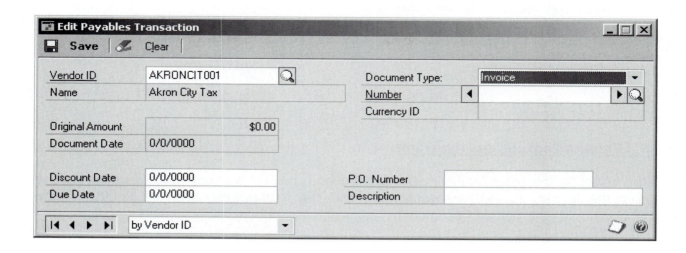

Payroll Series Error Correction Procedures

You have to be very careful when correcting payroll errors because these corrections affect employee W-2's and withholdings as well as company tax reporting. On the Transactions menu for Payroll, Great Plains provides the Void Check menu to corrected payroll checks.

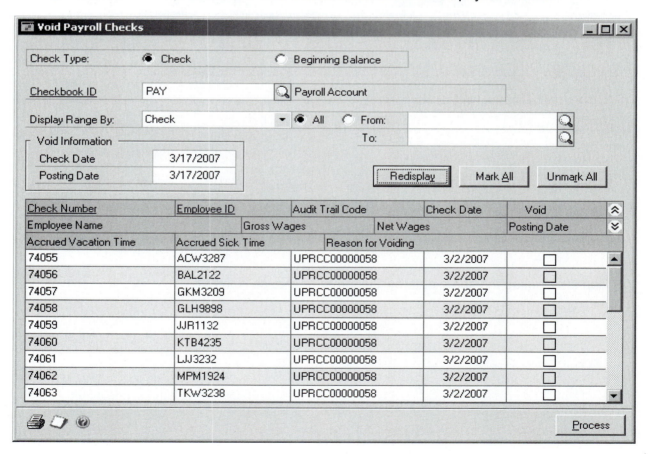

APPENDIX D: EXERCISE SOLUTIONS

CHAPTER 1 EXERCISES

E1:1 Practice Lookups and Hyperlinks

After selecting the *Inquiry>>Financial>>Detail* menu, pull up account 4100-01 Sales – East. Select the January 25, 2007 transaction and click the Journal Entry hyperlink. In the window that opens, click the Source Document hyperlink and the window below appears.

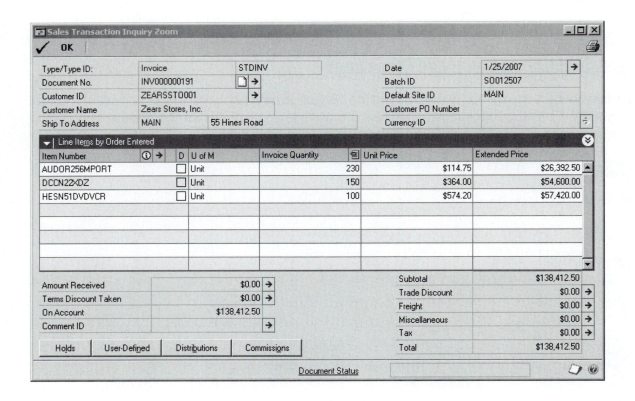

You can also lookup the same data by Customer or Invoice Number.

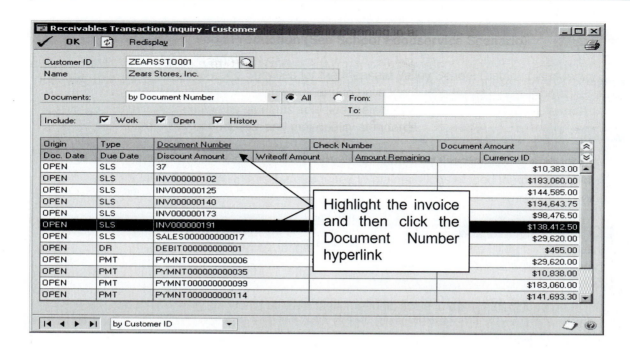

In addition, you can lookup By Document.

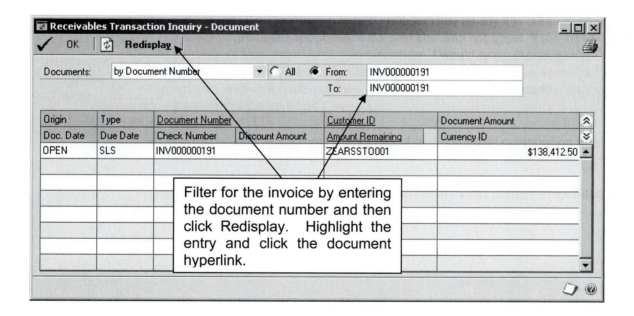

E1:2 Practice Printing Multiple Reports

Lookup the Income Statement category, highlight the report, and then click Insert. Then lookup the Balance Sheet category, highlight the report, and click insert. The report window print multiple reports is illustrated below.

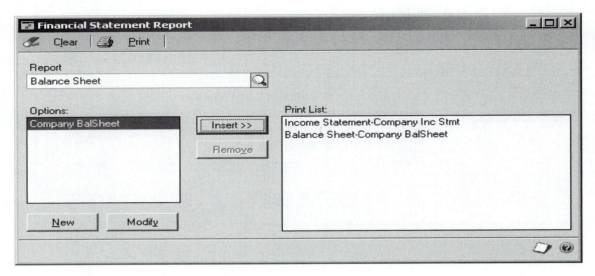

CHAPTER 2 EXERCISES

E2:1 Create and Delete General Ledger Posting Accounts

Use the *Cards>>Financial>>Account* menu to create the new building addition account illustrated below.

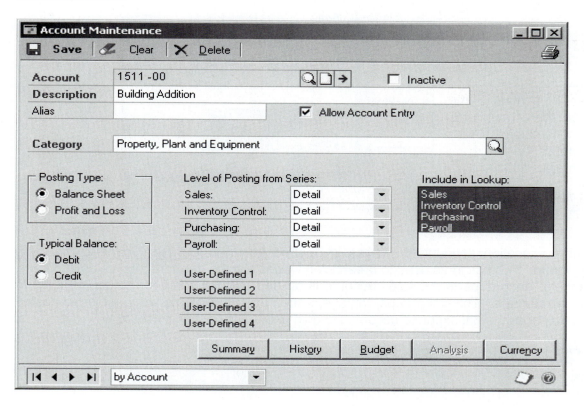

E2:2 Variable and Fixed Allocation Accounts

The fixed allocation account is reviewed by using the *Cards>>Financial>>Fixed Allocation* menu. The card that allocates utilities is illustrated below.

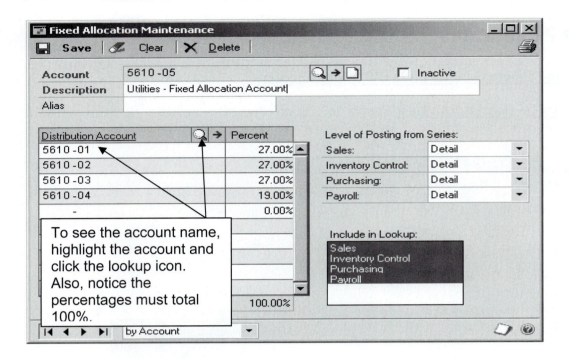

The variable allocation account for wages is opened from the *Cards>>Financial>>Variable Allocation* menu. The accounts used to breakdown wages are the departmental sales accounts. The balance in each department sales account is divided by total sales for all departments to obtain the percentage. This varying percentage is then used to allocate wage expense posted in 5100-05 to departmental expense accounts shown under Distribution Account.

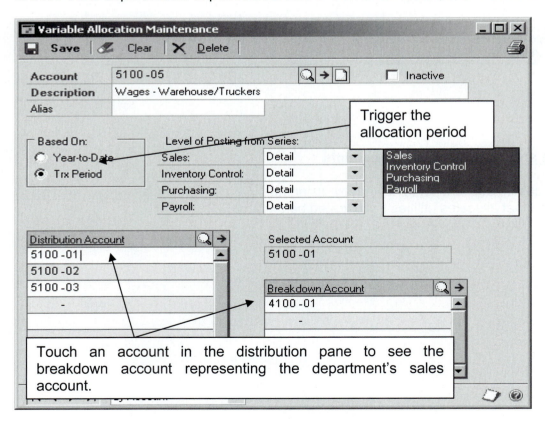

E2:3 Generate COA Report

The report is printed by using the Reports>>Financial>>Account menu. Select the Fixed Allocation report category and then click New. Assign a name to the Option field and check the Destination prints to the screen. You can click save to keep this report for future use.

```
System:      3/25/2005   12:47:26 PM                S&S Incorporated                      Page:    1
User Date:   3/25/2005                        FIXED ALLOCATION ACCOUNTS LIST              User ID: sa
                                                    General Ledger

Ranges:                      From:                                    To:
  Account                    First                                    Last
  Account Description         First                                    Last

Sorted By:   Main                                                     Include:

Allocation Account           Description                             Alias                Active
-----------------------------------------------------------------------------------------------------
                                                                     Distribution Account      Percentage
-----------------------------------------------------------------------------------------------------
5600-05                      Telephone Fixed Allocation Account                            Yes
                                                                     5600-01                     27.00%
                                                                     5600-02                     27.00%
                                                                     5600-03                     27.00%
                                                                     5600-04                     19.00%
                                                                                               ----------
                                                                     Total Distribution Percentage:  100.00%

5610-05                      Utilities - Fixed Allocation Account                          Yes
                                                                     5610-01                     27.00%
                                                                     5610-02                     27.00%
                                                                     5610-03                     27.00%
                                                                     5610-04                     19.00%
                                                                                               ----------
                                                                     Total Distribution Percentage:  100.00%

Total Fixed Allocation Accounts:          2
```

CHAPTER 4 EXERCISES

E4:1 Test an Item's Sales Price

The test transaction confirms the item's price as $195.

E4:2 Practice Assigning Vendors

To assign Nikki Cam as the preferred vendor for <u>DPD128MCARD</u>, open the Item Quantities Maintenance window, select the item, change the site to Main, and then change the link for preferred vendor's to Nikki's ID. Save the record when finished.

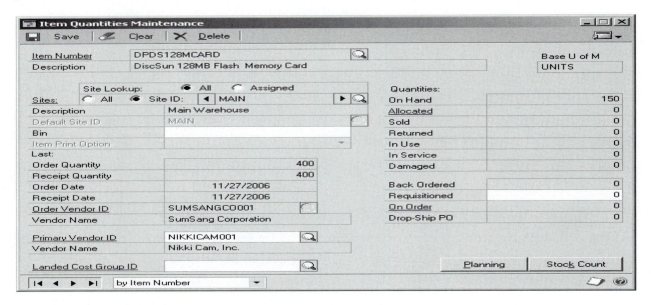

After selecting Nikki Cam as the Primary Vendor ID, the Item Vendors Maintenance window shown below opens to save the item link for this vendor.   Save the record with the added vendor ID.

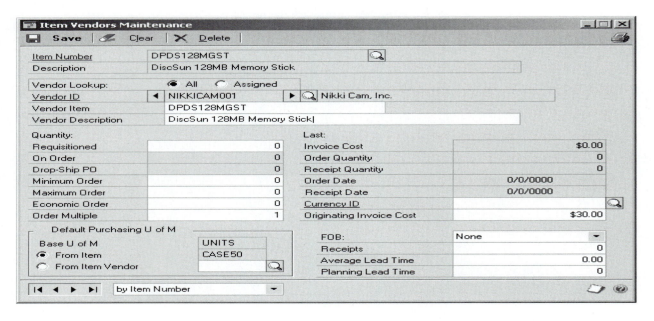

E4:3 Practice Recording Inventory Variance

Use the *Transactions>>Inventory>>Transactions Entry* menu to enter the transaction illustrated below. The unit cost is not entered because this defaults from the item's card. Click Post and the posting reports print.

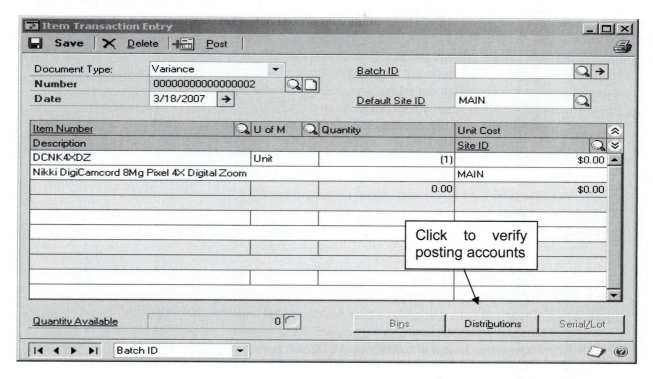

The posting reports that print were selected under the *Tools>>Setup>>Posting>>Posting* menu with the Inventory Series and Transaction Entry Origin. Remember, you posted a single transaction, therefore the transaction remains suspended in the Master Posting window. A review of the audit trial codes reveals this transaction is assigned the IVADJ prefix.

CHAPTER 5 EXERCISES

E5:1 Practice With Customer Cards

1. Using the *Cards>>Sales>>Customer* menu, lookup Giggle Place and then click the Address button. The new address is shown below. Notice the Address ID assigned is <u>SHIPPING</u>.

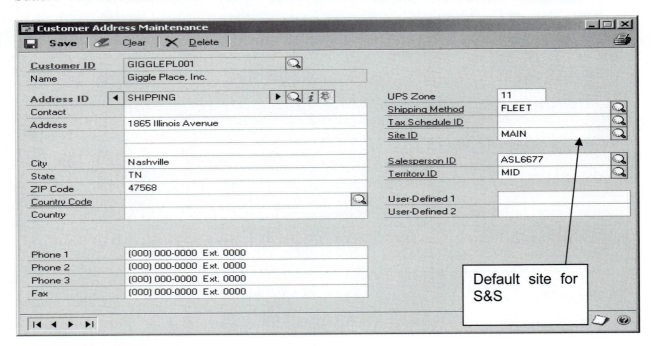

After saving the new address, the ID is linked to the field shown below.

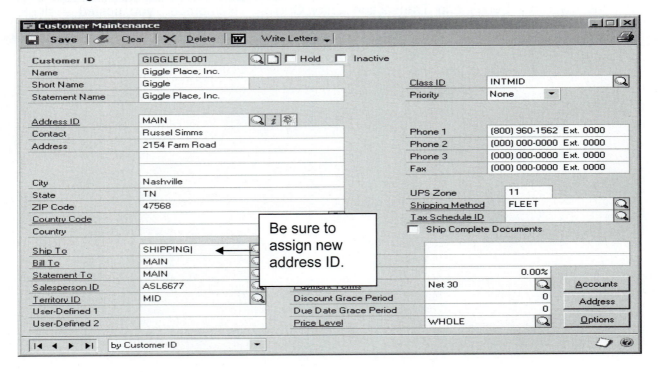

2. To increase Fillard's credit limit, lookup the customer card and click the Options button. The credit limit field is shown below.

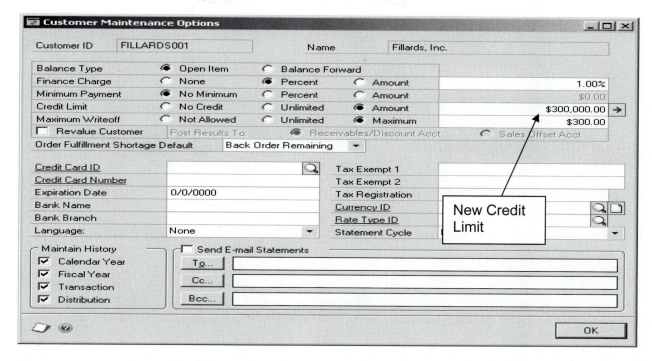

The changes to Fillards' payment terms are made to the Payment Terms field of the card as shown below.

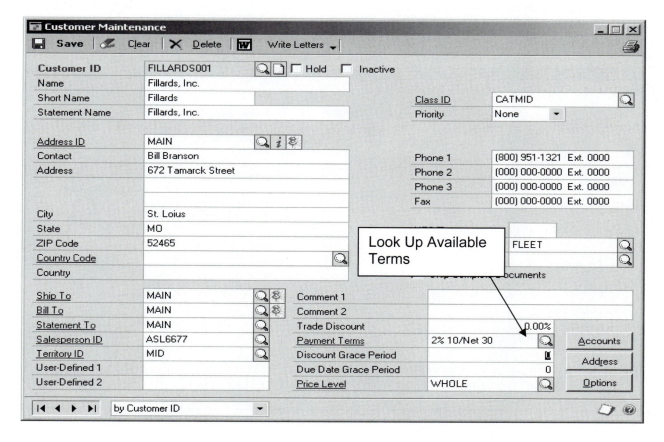

3. To see customers assigned to the Midwest territory, change the Customer Maintenance window's filtering options to by Sales Territory ID and then lookup the customers. The records are now sorted by territory in the lookup window as shown below.

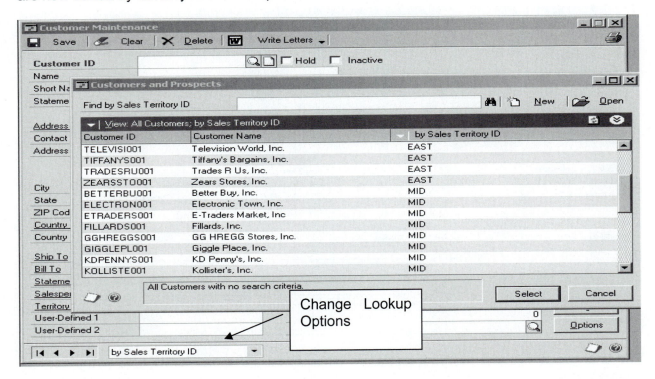

To see the salesperson for this territory, select a MID customer card and then click the hyperlink to the Salesperson ID. This pulls up the Salesperson Maintenance window for April Levine as illustrated below.

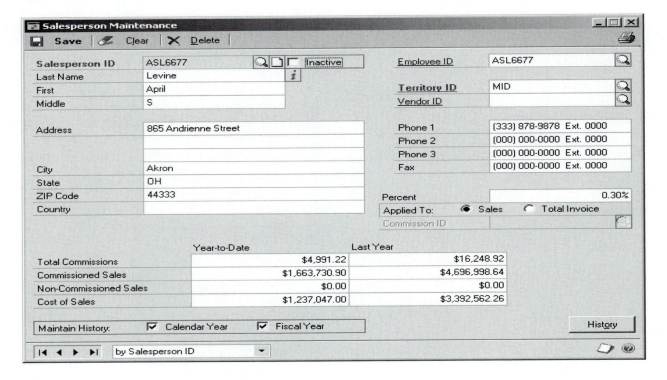

4. The credit department is authorized to create new customers and establish other critical controls such as credit limits and payment terms. At smaller companies, like S&S, where there is not a credit department, this responsibility normally falls to the owners, Susan and Scott.

5. Sales and Accounts Receivable department employees may have permission to change noncritical customer information. Great Plains provides a separate menu command to change address information under *Cards>>Sales>>Addresses*. Thus, security to the Cards menu can be restricted but permitted to the addresses menu to implement these permissions. Chapter 3 discussed setting security in Great Plains.

E5:2 Add a New Customer

New customers are added using the Cards>>Sales>>Customer menu. The Customer ID for Electronic is ELECTRON002 using Ashton's primary key scheme.

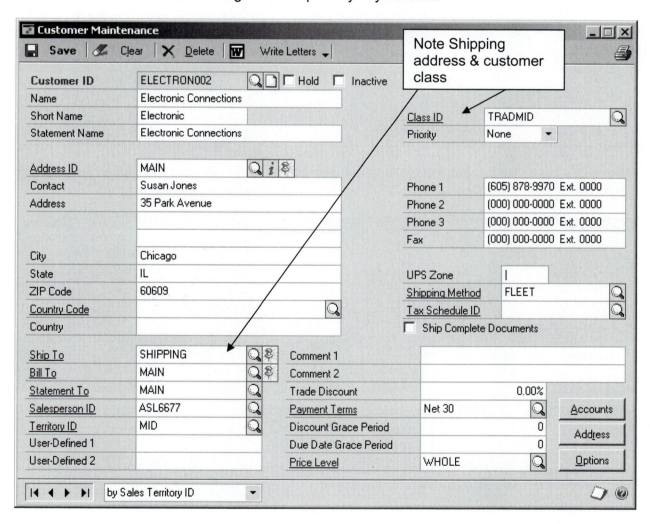

The shipping address card for Electronic is illustrated below.

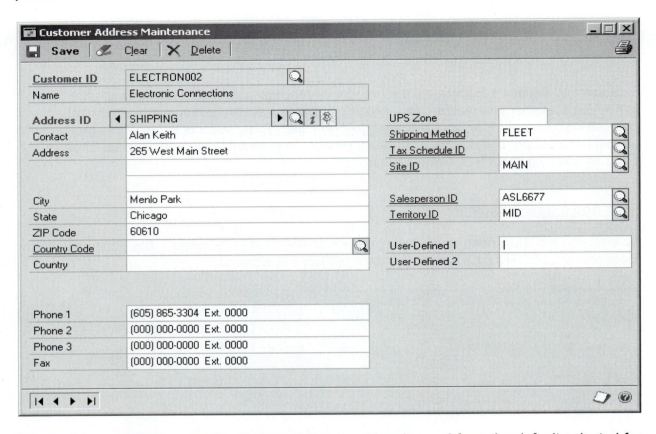

Electronic's credit limit under the Options button must be changed from the default selected for the customer class, see below.

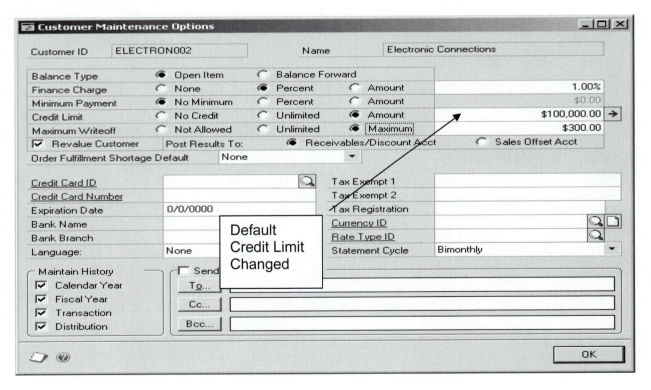

The general ledger accounts are assigned from the customer class, thus already present on Electronic's card.

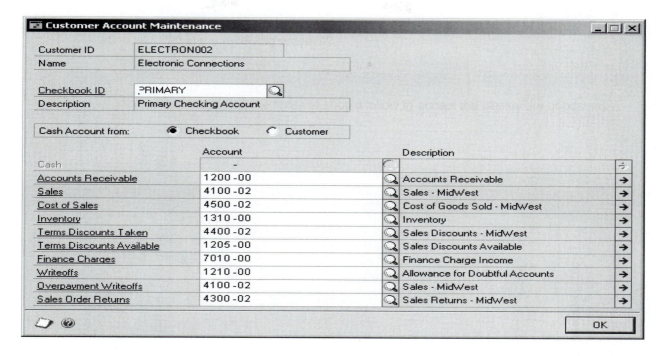

E5:3 Capturing Sales Orders

First create the batch shown below and then the transaction shown next. Ensure the date for both windows is March 19, 2007.

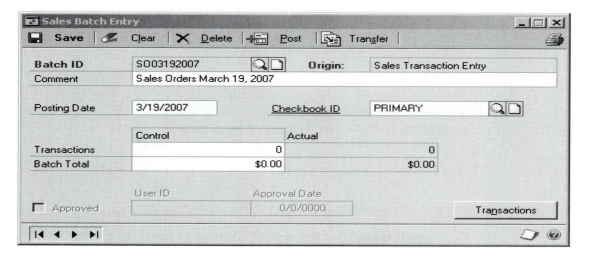

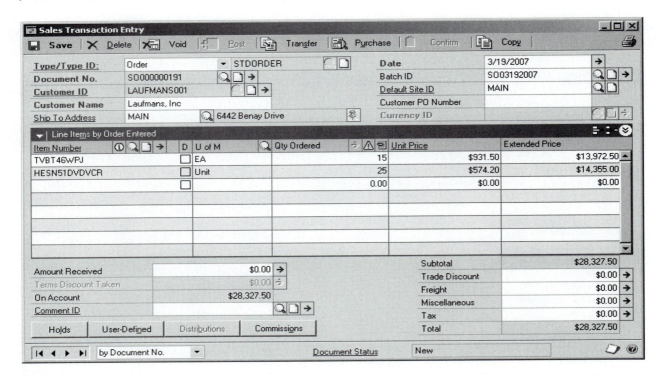

The next step is printing the sales documentation, including the invoice and picking ticket. This can be performed by clicking the printer icon on the tope of the window. Remember, an invoice is sent to the customer, to accounts receivable, and to shipping. The picking ticket is sent to the warehouse. The picking ticket is shown below. Note the areas reserved for warehouse employees to enter quantities filled. Save the order when finished.

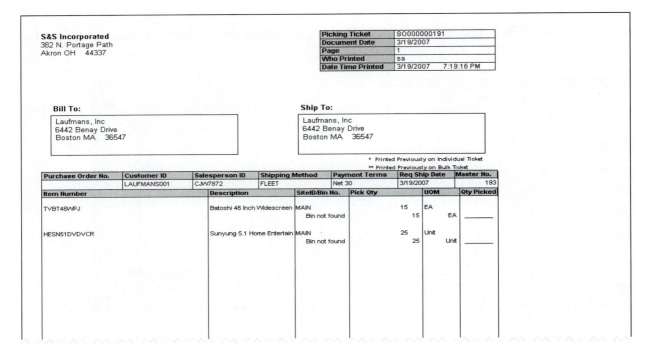

E5:4 Control Reporting

The batch list prints all transactions in a batch (see below). An edit list prints only transactions ready to post, such as invoices. For Laufmans' transaction, you will need to print a batch list since the transaction is still an order. This report is critical control to ensure the integrity of data entered for the sales order. It permits a visual review of transactions prior to printing picking tickets and sales orders.

To illustrate the importance of control reports we will discuss the types of errors that can occur during data entry. First, you could select the wrong customer account. Thus, should the order ship today, it arrives at the wrong customer. This results in added costs of contacting the receiving company to return the items (besides the embarrassment). Moreover, customer "bad will" results since the ordering customer doesn't receive items when expected. Second, you could enter the wrong inventory or quantity to the order. Again, the company bears added costs and risks losing customer good will. A review of batch lists prior to producing documentation mitigates the risk of data entry errors.

```
Batch ID:       S003192007
Batch Comment: Sales Orders March 19, 2007

Approved:                     Batch Total Actual:      $28,327.50   Batch Total Control:        $0.00
Approved By:                  Trx Total Actual:                 1   Trx Total Control:              0
Approval Date:     0/0/0000


* Allocation Attempted     ^ Repeating Document

Type   Document Number   Doc Date   Post Date   Customer ID     Name                    Salesperson
----------------------------------------------------------------------------------------------------
         Subtotal     Trade Discount    Freight Amount     Misc Amount      Tax Amount     Document Total   Discount Avail
----------------------------------------------------------------------------------------------------
ORD    S0000000191     3/19/2007  0/0/0000    LAUFMANS001     Laufmans, Inc           CJW7872
        $28,327.50          $0.00            $0.00             $0.00           $0.00       $28,327.50          $0.00

Item Number                         Description                                      Markdown
                                    U of M    Site                   Quantity        Unit Price       Extended Price
--------------------------------    ----------   ----------    --------------------   -------------    ------------------
TVBT46WPJ                           Batoshi 46 Inch Widescreen Projection               $0.00
                                    EA     MAIN                      15               $931.50           $13,972.50
HESN51DVDVCR                        Sunyung 5.1 Home Entertainment Combo DVD/VCR        $0.00
                                    Unit   MAIN                      25               $574.20           $14,355.00
                                                                                                       ------------------
                                                                                                       $28,327.50

Salesperson Name                    Sales Territory ID        Comm %    % of Sale     Sales Amount     Commission Amount
--------------------------------    --------------------   -----------  -----------   --------------   ------------------
Warner, Curtis                      EAST                       0.30%    100.00%         28,327.50              84.99
                                                                                     ------------------   ------------------
                                                                                       $28,327.50             $84.99


        Subtotal     Trade Discount    Freight Amount     Misc Amount      Tax Amount     Document Total   Discount Avail
----------------   ----------------   -----------------   ----------------   -------------   ----------------   ----------------
        $28,327.50          $0.00            $0.00             $0.00           $0.00       $28,327.50          $0.00
----------------   ----------------   -----------------   ----------------   -------------   ----------------   ----------------
```

E5:5 Transfer Laufmans' Order to Invoice

Using the batch menu, lookup the sales order batch and transaction from *E5:3*. Click the document details arrow to bring up the Sales Document Detail Entry window.

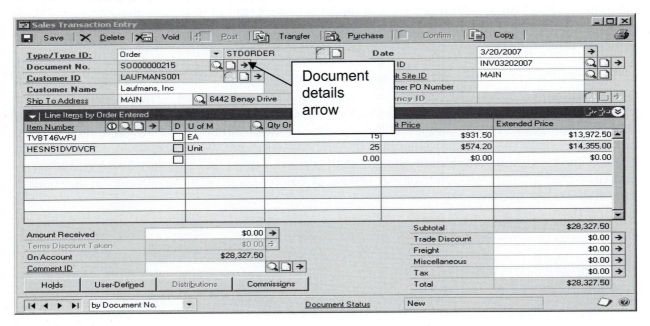

In the window below, enter the Batch ID to store the transferred invoice. Click OK then transfer the invoice while in the transaction window and the SOP Transfer log prints. This log must not contain errors.

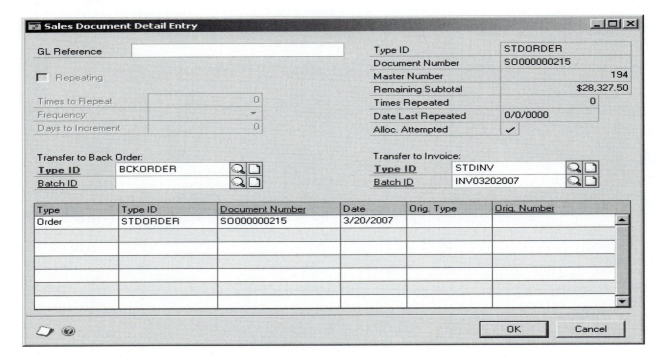

The transferred invoice illustrated below is now stored in the INV03202007 batch. Change the date for the invoice to 3/20/2007 and then click the Distributions button to verify the general ledger accounts that will be used when the invoice posts.

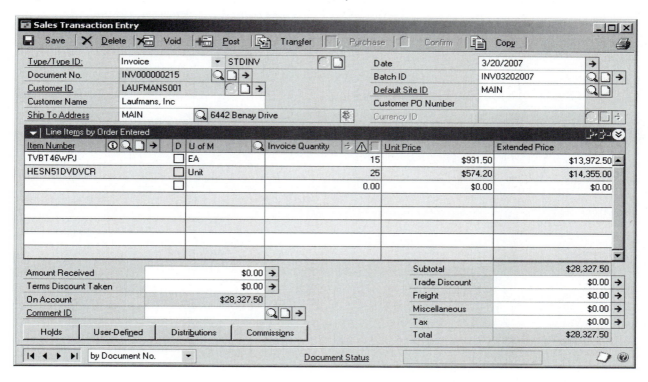

This window shows the general ledger accounts that will be used when the invoice posts. Accounts can be changed in this window when necessary. Close this window and save the invoice.

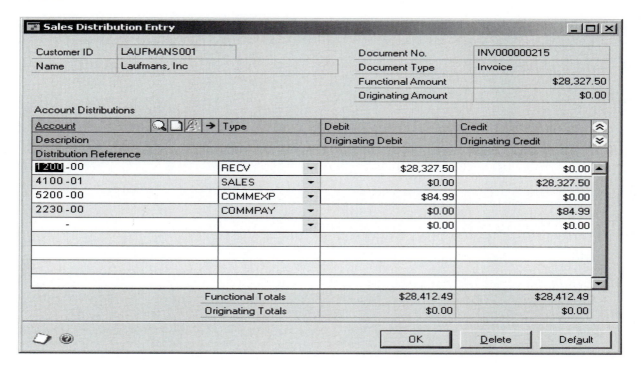

Return to the batch window and pull up the batch storing the invoice and click Post. Below are the control reports that print after posting.

```
Batch ID:      INV03202007                    Audit Trail Code:    SLSTE00000083
Batch Comment: SO Trnf to Invoice

Approved:                      Batch Total Actual:    $28,327.50   Batch Total Control:      $0.00
Approved By:                   Trx Total Actual:              1    Trx Total Control:            0
Approval Date:    0/0/0000



Type  Document Number   Doc Date   Post Date   Customer ID    Name                    Salesperson
----------------------------------------------------------------------------------------------------
         Subtotal     Trade Discount   Freight Amount     Misc Amount      Tax Amount    Document Total   Discount Avail
----------------------------------------------------------------------------------------------------
INV   INV000000215    3/20/2007  3/20/2007   LAUFMANS001   Laufmans, Inc            CJW7872
         $28,327.50         $0.00          $0.00           $0.00          $0.00       $28,327.50         $0.00


                                                                          Markdown
Item Number                Description                                    Unit Price        Extended Price
                           U of M    Site                  Quantity
----------------------------------------------------------------------------------------------------
TVBT46WPJ                  Batoshi 46 Inch Widescreen Projection             $0.00
                           EA        MAIN                      15          $931.50            $13,972.50
HESN51DVDVCR               Sunyung 5.1 Home Entertainment Combo DVD/VCR      $0.00
                           Unit      MAIN                      25          $574.20            $14,355.00
                                                                                        -----------------
                                                                                            $28,327.50


Account Number             Account Description           Account Type     Debit Amount       Credit Amount
----------------------------------------------------------------------------------------------------
1200-00                    Accounts Receivable           RECV             $28,327.50              $0.00
4100-01                    Sales - East                  SALES                 $0.00         $28,327.50
5200-00                    Commission Expense            COMMEXP             $84.99              $0.00
2230-00                    Commissions Payable           COMMPAY              $0.00             $84.99
1310-00                    Inventory                     INV                  $0.00         $21,225.00
4500-01                    Cost of Goods Sold - East     COGS             $21,225.00              $0.00
                                                                          --------------     --------------
                                                                          $49,637.49         $49,637.49


Salesperson Name           Sales Territory ID      Comm %    % of Sale     Sales Amount      Commission Amount
----------------------------------------------------------------------------------------------------
Warner, Curtis             EAST                     0.30%    100.00%         28,327.50              84.99
                                                                          --------------     --------------
                                                                            $28,327.50             $84.99
```

```
System:     5/16/2005   6:38:56 PM              S&S, Inc Project DB              Page:    1
User Date:  3/20/2007                          INVENTORY SALES REGISTER         User ID: sa
                                                Sales Order Processing

Audit Trail Code: SLSTE00000083

Item Number               Item Description
----------------------------------------------------------------------------------------------------
Document Number   Date        Customer ID   Customer Name        Unit    Qty Invoiced  Unit Price  Markdown   Ext Price
----------------------------------------------------------------------------------------------------
HESN51DVDVCR              Sunyung 5.1 Home Entertainment Combo DVD/VCR
   INV000000215   3/20/2007  LAUFMANS001   Laufmans, Inc        Unit          25       $574.20     $0.00    $14,355.00
                                                                        --------------                    ----------------
                                                        Item Totals:      25.00000                          $14,355.00
TVBT46WPJ                 Batoshi 46 Inch Widescreen Projection
   INV000000215   3/20/2007  LAUFMANS001   Laufmans, Inc        EA            15       $931.50     $0.00    $13,972.50
                                                                        --------------                    ----------------
                                                        Item Totals:      15.00000                          $13,972.50
                                                                        --------------                    ----------------
                                                      Report Totals:      40.00000                          $28,327.50
                                                                        ==============                    ================
```

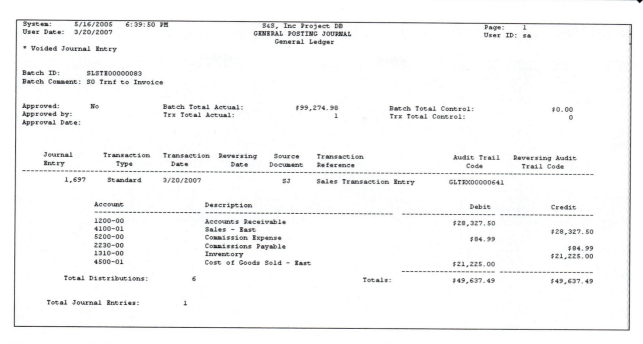

```
System:     5/16/2005   6:39:50 PM                    S&S, Inc Project DB              Page:      1
User Date:  3/20/2007                               GENERAL POSTING JOURNAL           User ID: sa
                                                        General Ledger

* Voided Journal Entry


Batch ID:      SLSTE00000083
Batch Comment: SO Trnf to Invoice


Approved:      No              Batch Total Actual:        $99,274.98    Batch Total Control:      $0.00
Approved by:                   Trx Total Actual:                   1    Trx Total Control:           0
Approval Date:


   Journal      Transaction   Transaction  Reversing   Source     Transaction              Audit Trail    Reversing Audit
   Entry        Type          Date         Date        Document   Reference                 Code           Trail Code
   -------------------------------------------------------------------------------------------------------------------
      1,697     Standard      3/20/2007                SJ         Sales Transaction Entry   GLTRX00000641

              Account                  Description                              Debit          Credit
              --------------------     --------------------------------     -------------    ------------
              1200-00                  Accounts Receivable                   $28,327.50
              4100-01                  Sales - East                                          $28,327.50
              5200-00                  Commission Expense                        $84.99
              2230-00                  Commissions Payable                                       $84.99
              1310-00                  Inventory                                             $21,225.00
              4500-01                  Cost of Goods Sold - East             $21,225.00
                                                                           -------------    ------------
              Total Distributions:        6                      Totals:    $49,637.49       $49,637.49


       Total Journal Entries:            1
```

These reports, in order, are the Sales Order Posting Journal, Inventory Sales Register, Cost Variance Journal, and General Posting Journal. The Sales Order Posting Journal is not shown in its entirety and the Cost Variance Journal is not shown because there was no inventory cost variance. The last report to print shows this transaction posted to the general ledger. The three preceding reports show the transactions effect on the Sales and Inventory Control Series. These reports should be stored for later reference. In addition, an edit list should have been printed and reviewed prior to posting the invoice.

E5:6 Laufmans' Cash Receipt

The batch (not illustrated) is created using the *Receivables Batches* menu. The cash receipts transaction is illustrated below.

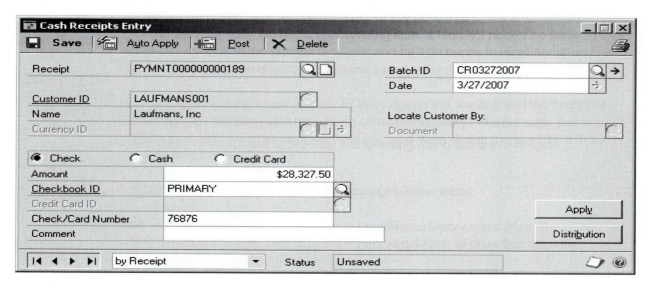

The payment is applied to the invoice by click the Apply button and entering the selections shown below.

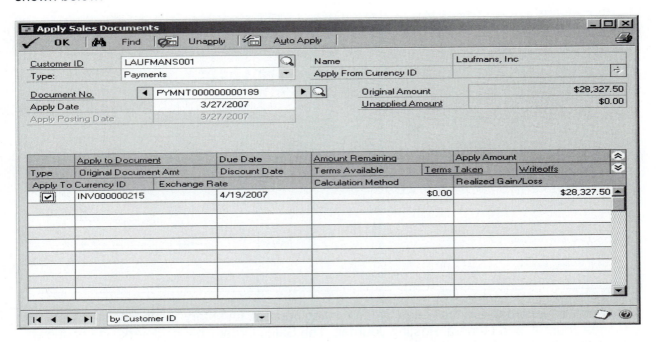

The transaction is then saved and the batch posted in the batch window. The posting reports that print are shown below, in order of appearance.

```
System:      5/16/2005   8:27:00 PM           S&S, Inc Project DB              Page:      1
User Date:   3/27/2007                     CASH RECEIPTS POSTING JOURNAL       User ID: sa
                                              Receivables Management

Batch ID:      CR03272007       Audit Trail Code:   RMCSH00000050   Batch Frequency:   Single Use
Batch Comment: March 27 2007 cash receipts
Trx Total Actual:       1                  Trx Total Control:       0
Batch Total Actual:       $28,327.50       Batch Total Control:          $0.00
Approved: NO                    Approved By:            Approval Date:


Receipt         Doc Date     Post Date    Customer ID     Name                    Check Number
---------------------------------------------------------------------------------------------------
   Transaction Description           Original Amount    Write Offs   Discounts Taken      Unapplied
---------------------------------------------------------------------------------------------------
PYMNT000000000189   3/27/2007   3/27/2007   LAUFMANS001    Laufmans, Inc           76876
                                 $28,327.50        $0.00        $0.00           $0.00




        General Ledger Distributions
        Account Number            Account Description      Account Type      Debit Amount     Credit Amount
        1100-00                   Cash                     CASH              28,327.50             0.00
        1200-00                   Accounts Receivable      RECV                   0.00        28,327.50
                                                                           -----------------   -----------------
                                                                              28,327.50        28,327.50

        Applied Distributions
        Type    Document Number              Apply Date         Discount       Write off      Amount Applied
        SLS     INV000000215                 3/27/2007              0.00            0.00           28,327.50
                                                                -----------------   -----------------   -----------------
                                                                   0.00            0.00           28,327.50


                                   -----------------   -----------------   -----------------   -----------------
                        Totals:      $28,327.50          $0.00           $0.00            $0.00
                                   =================   =================   =================   =================
```

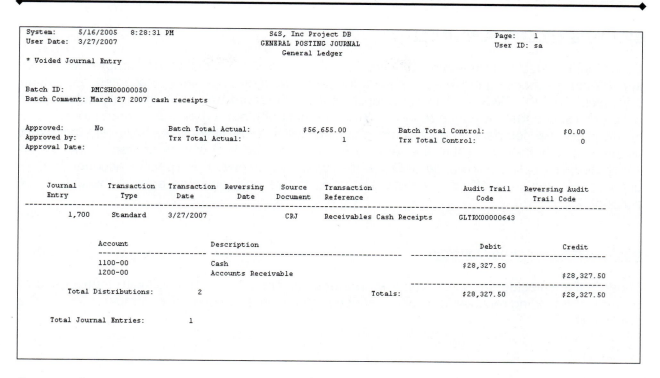

```
System:     5/16/2005    8:28:31 PM              S&S, Inc Project DB                    Page:      1
User Date:  3/27/2007                         GENERAL POSTING JOURNAL                   User ID: sa
                                                General Ledger
* Voided Journal Entry


Batch ID:       RMCSH00000050
Batch Comment:  March 27 2007 cash receipts


Approved:        No           Batch Total Actual:       $56,655.00     Batch Total Control:        $0.00
Approved by:                  Trx Total Actual:                  1     Trx Total Control:              0
Approval Date:



   Journal     Transaction  Transaction  Reversing   Source   Transaction                 Audit Trail   Reversing Audit
   Entry         Type         Date         Date     Document   Reference                      Code        Trail Code
-----------------------------------------------------------------------------------------------------------------------
    1,700       Standard     3/27/2007                 CRJ     Receivables Cash Receipts   GLTRX00000643


           Account              Description                                         Debit            Credit
         -----------------------------------------------------------         ----------------------------------------
           1100-00              Cash                                             $28,327.50
           1200-00              Accounts Receivable                                               $28,327.50
                                                                         -----------------------------------------
       Total Distributions:      2                              Totals:          $28,327.50       $28,327.50


       Total Journal Entries:    1
```

Once again, an edit list should be prepared prior to posting cash receipts. The total on the edit list should be compared to the mailroom's control total to verify data entry.

E5:7 Sales Series Reporting Practice

The report is created using the Posting Journal reports category. It must be clarified that the report is the Sales Posting Journal, not the Invoice Posting Journal. The invoice journal reports transactions posted through the Invoice Processing Tier. The Laufmans' invoice was generated through Sales Order processing, thus the posting report is found under sales journals.

This report is modified to enter the filtering criteria illustrated below and then printed.

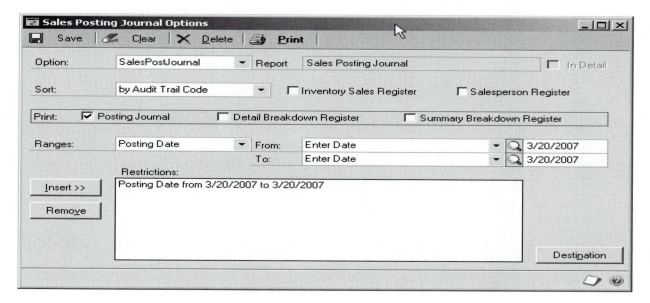

E5:8 Write-Off Posting Accounts

Great Plains selected these two accounts from Posting Setup, explained in Chapter 3. As for justification on choosing these accounts under setup, we look to generally accepted accounting principles (GAAP). S&S uses the allowance method to record bad debt, thus any subsequent write-offs reduce the allowance reserve. You can think of it as: When the estimate for reserve is prepared the company knows some accounts will not be collectible, however, the exact accounts are unknown. Thus, the reserve for uncollectible accounts is posted to the contra asset account called allowance. Once the company knows the specific account that is uncollectible, the write-off entry merely reclasses the reserve estimate against the actual AR account.

E5:9 Test Receivable Controls

Great Plains selected the credit limit from Barter's customer card. The software then looked at Barter's outstanding receivable balance, added the new order amount, and compared this to the credit limit.

CHAPTER 6 EXERCISES

E6:1 Practice With Vendor Cards

1. The vendor's card is created using the *Cards>>Purchasing>>Vendor* menu. The new card appears below. Notice the Vendor ID follows Ashton's primary key scheme.

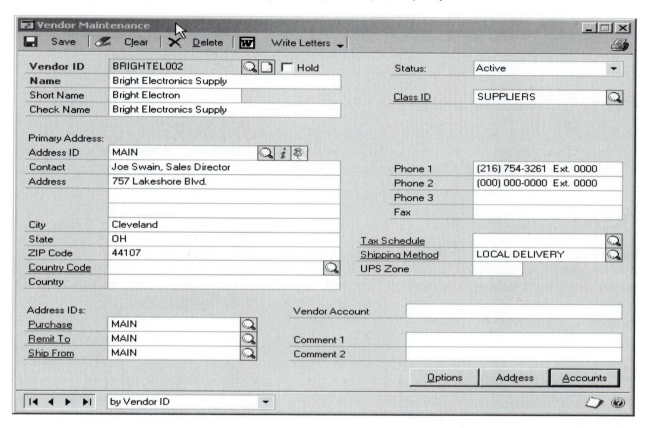

2. Unfortunately, after assigning a Vendor ID, this ID cannot be changed. Prior to assigning transactions, the vendor can be deleted and reentered; however, after transactions post the only choice is to place a hold on the existing vendor card and create a new card. Third party vendors offer utilities that change vendor and customer ID's. These utilities cost about $1,500. Unfortunately, many companies find out too late that their vendor and customer ID assignment schemes do not accommodate lookups, for instance, when assigning IDs with a numerical scheme. The numeric scheme does not let the user type the first few letters of a vendor's name prior to executing a look up. Moreover, upon launching the lookup, vendors do not appear alphabetically.

E6:2 Working with Purchase Orders

1. Within a PO, lookup an item and notice the New and Open icons. Both icons open the Item Maintenance window permitting the creation of "on-the-fly" inventory items. Remember, users recording transactions, such as POs, should not have authorization to create new master

records, such as inventory items. Advanced Security is the only way to control access to this window, thus illustrating the complexities of implementing internal controls in a software environment.

2. The New status lists POs that have not printed. Therefore, when monitoring release of orders to vendors, both Changed and New should be included.

3. First, advanced security restricts PO access to authorized employees. Next, the PO contains a field to identify the Buyer. Next, with purchase order enhancements, the approval status restricts printing. Finally, the PO must be signed to authorize release to the vendor. The PO should only be authorized by purchasing department employees.

E6:3 Control Reporting

The Received/Not Invoiced analysis report lists outstanding receipts awaiting vendor invoices. Accounts Payable should review this report before posting invoices. When controls over PO and receiving activities are effective, this report serves to authorize input of vendor invoices.

E6:4 Cashier Internal Controls

It is critical to have strong internal controls over the cashier department. First, Purchasing menus should be restricted to only Select Checks, Edit Checks, and Print Checks. You may permit Batches because the window will not open the Transaction Entry window without permission. Cashiers should keep check stock locked and attended when printing checks. Also, S&S' owners should prepare bank reconciliations.

E6:5 Practice a Return

The return transaction is shown below.

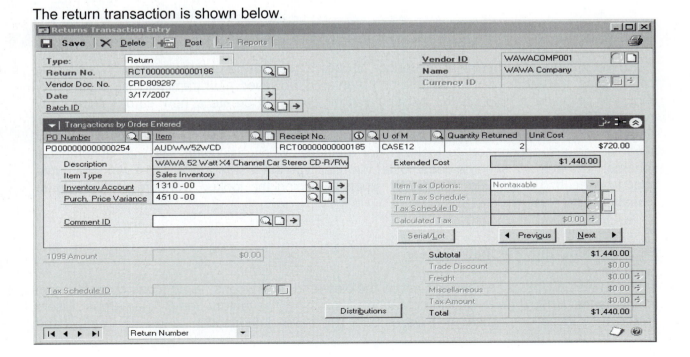

The distribution accounts for this transaction are as follows.

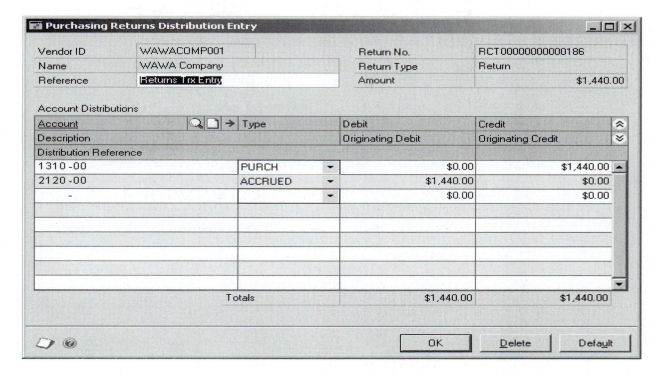

E6:6 Credit Memo Practice

The credit memo is entered using the *Transaction Entry* menu. Note the transaction's type.

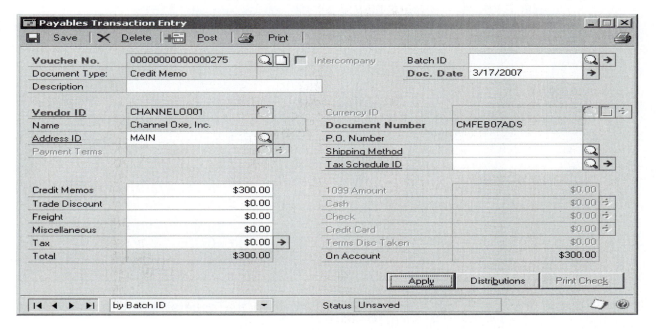

The next windows show the Distribution and Apply buttons. The memo is applied to S&S' outstanding invoice with the vendor. Credit memos remain suspended unless applied. If you posted the transaction and failed to apply, then use the *Apply Payables Documents* menu to apply.

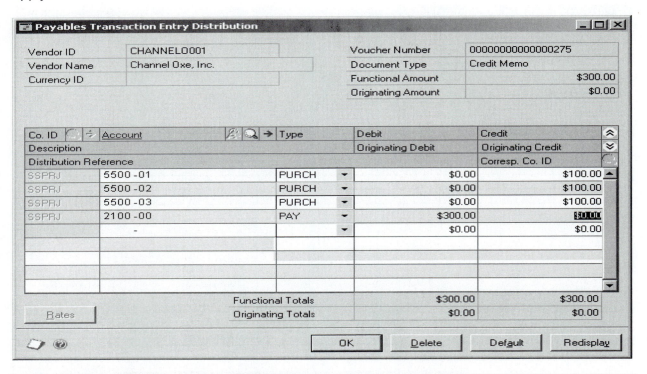

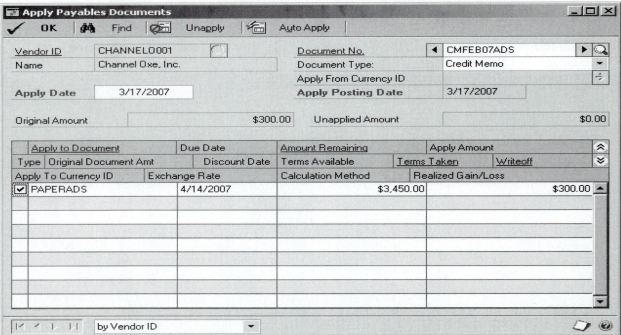

If you entered the memo as a single transaction, then the general ledger transaction is suspended. Posting can be finalized using the *Series Post* menu.

E6:7 Practice on Purchasing Series Reporting

1. Like the Sales Series, the ending balance for March on the Trial Balance report should reconcile to the March balances for accounts 2100-00 Accounts Payable and 2105-00 Purchase Discounts Available. If not, then you look for the discrepancy using the methodology discussed in Chapter 5.

2. For the check register, first create a report definition, and then enter the screening criteria. If you have been careful on dates, then the date range should suffice. The second figure shows the report.

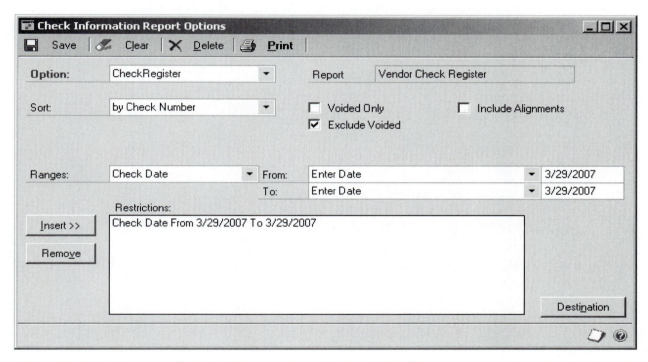

```
System:      5/20/2005   5:35:07 PM              S&S, Incorporated                    Page:    1
User Date:   3/17/2007                      VENDOR CHECK REGISTER REPORT              User ID: sa
                                               Payables Management

Ranges:         From:                     To:                              From:          To:
  Check Number  First                     Last          Check Date         3/29/2007      3/29/2007
  Vendor ID     First                     Last          Checkbook ID       First          Last
  Vendor Name   First                     Last

Sorted By:   Check Number

* Voided Checks

Check Number    Vendor ID       Vendor Check Name       Check Date  Checkbook ID   Audit Trail Code       Amount
----------------------------------------------------------------------------------------------------------------
358             JAVIXCAM001     Javix Cam, Inc.         3/29/2007   PRIMARY        PMCHK00000042       $11,564.00
359             OFFICERE001     Office Rex, Inc.        3/29/2007   PRIMARY        PMCHK00000042        $3,769.13
360             PBFUELC0001     PB Fuel Company         3/29/2007   PRIMARY        PMCHK00000042       $87,689.28
361             RIGHTMAR001     Right Marketing, Inc.   3/29/2007   PRIMARY        PMCHK00000042          $750.00
362             SONICPAN001     Sonic Pan, Inc.         3/29/2007   PRIMARY        PMCHK00000042       $70,800.00
363             SUBISHII001     Subishi, Inc.           3/29/2007   PRIMARY        PMCHK00000042      $150,000.00
364             SUNYUNGH001     Sunyung Home, Inc.      3/29/2007   PRIMARY        PMCHK00000042      $135,000.00
365             UNITEDHE001     United Health Insurance 3/29/2007   PRIMARY        PMCHK00000042        $6,185.85
                                                                                                  --------------------
Total Checks:        8                                                Total Amount of Checks:       $465,758.26
                                                                                                  ====================
```

E6:8 Payables Management Controls

1. A vendor hold controls purchases to poor performing vendors. Remember, master records with historical transactions cannot be deleted; therefore, placing holds on vendor cards denies future activities.

2. S&S only permits duplicate invoices for recurring transactions because often these invoices do not supply invoices such as monthly rent expense. Therefore, Great Plains will continue to deny the entry of duplicate invoice numbers for other transaction.

3. S&S allows receiving without a PO but provides a password for approval. This setting provides flexibility for purchasing activities while maintaining receipt authorization.

CHAPTER 7 EXERCISES

E7:1 Practice With Employee Cards

The HR department is authorized to make changes to employee master record. For S&S, this is the owners. The changes to Thomas' federal withholdings are shown below.

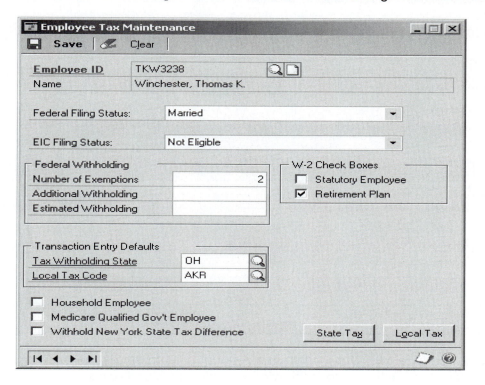

The changes to April's 401-K are shown below.

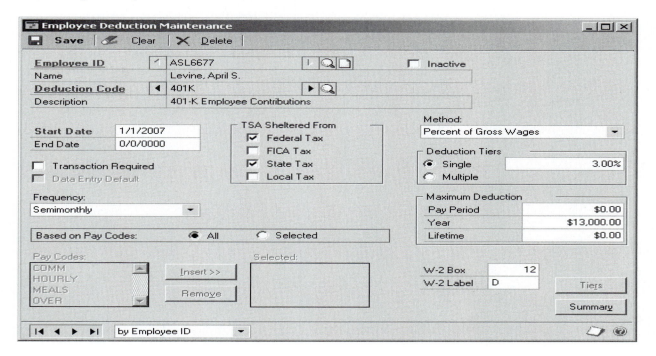

E7:2 Enter Commission and Expense Payments

The commission transaction appears below. The Amount column stores the commission payments.

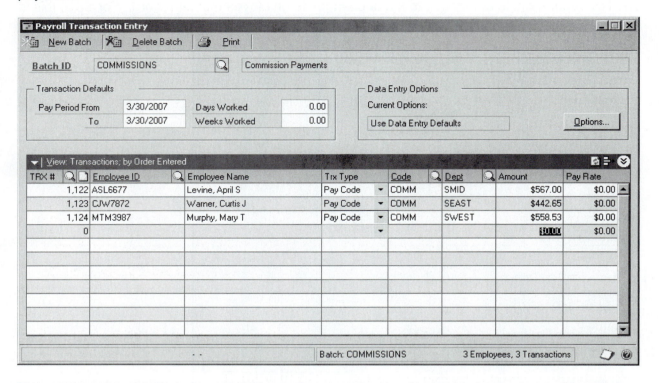

The expense transaction appears below. Once again, the Amount column stores the expense payments. After entering these transactions, close the window and audit report prints.

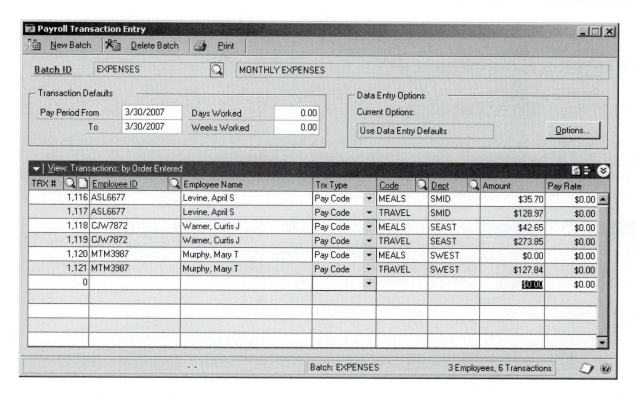

E7:3 Payroll Reporting

1. The Payroll Summary report does not include the state and local tax liabilities. Therefore, accounts payable also needs the State Tax Summary and Local Tax Summary reports.

2. The Pay Code Summary report shows total deposits for the payroll account. Along with wage information, the report lists the employee payments for commissions and expense reimbursements.

CHAPTER 8 EXERCISES

E8:1 Practice With Adjusting Entries

The recurring batch folder for depreciation appears below. The total recurring postings is set to 10 so the batch does not post past December. Normally companies adjust depreciation schedules at the end of the year, thus Ashton will create a new batch in January 2008. Click post to print the posting report illustrated.

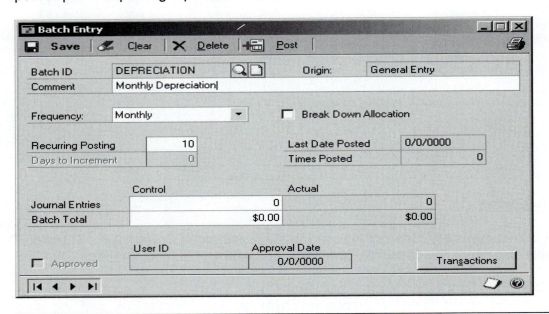

5/26/2005 2:19:06 PM	S&S, Incorporated			Page: 1
3/31/2007	GENERAL POSTING JOURNAL			User ID: sa
	General Ledger			

urnal Entry

   DEPRECIATION
nt: Monthly Depreciation

No	Batch Total Actual:	$29,368.10	Batch Total Control:	$0.00
:	Trx Total Actual:	1	Trx Total Control:	0
te:				

l	Transaction Type	Transaction Date	Reversing Date	Source Document	Transaction Reference	Audit Trail Code	Reversing Audit Trail Code
,699	Standard	3/31/2007		GJ	Monthly Depreciation	GLTRX00000644	

Account	Description	Debit	Credit
1515-00	Accum Depr - Buildings		$1,275.00
1525-00	Accum Depr - Office Furn/Fixtures		$1,979.17
1535-00	Accum Depr - Vehicles		$6,131.27
1545-00	Accum Depr - Computer Hardware		$3,437.50
1555-00	Amortization - Computer Software		$1,861.11
5810-00	Depreciation Expense	$12,822.94	
5820-00	Amortization Expense	$1,861.11	
otal Distributions: 7	Totals:	$14,684.05	$14,684.05